Eat
In Northern Ireland

Restaurants, Coffee Shops, Pubs & Hotels - *plus* **'A Taste of Ulster'**

Northern Ireland Tourist Board

Published by the Northern Ireland Tourist Board
59 North St, Belfast BT1 1NB. ☎ (01232) 231221

Copyright © Northern Ireland Tourist Board 1995

All rights reserved. No part of this publication may be reproduced or transmitted in any form or by any means, electronic or mechanical, including photocopy, recording or any information storage and retrieval system, without permission in writing from the publisher.

ISBN 0 946871 74 4

Fifteenth edition

Printed by The Universities Press (Belfast) Ltd.   6m/11/94

Contents

	Page
Acknowledgments	5
A Taste of Ulster	6
Special mentions	25
How to use the guide	28
Belfast districts - map	32
City Centre	33
Golden Mile	43
University and Malone	47
East of the River	57
North and West of the River	63
County Antrim	71
County Armagh	105
County Down	119
County Fermanagh	159
County Londonderry	171
County Tyrone	191
Index to towns and villages	208

Acknowledgments

The editors are grateful for all the help they have received in compiling the main listings for this, the fifteenth edition of *Where to Eat in Northern Ireland.*

Information provided by organisations and individuals outside the Tourist Board has enabled us to maintain the wide coverage which makes this small book uniquely useful.

The response from local authorities was most helpful, particularly with regard to cafés and unlicensed restaurants. All twenty-six councils supplied us with information on the eating-out scene in their area. This local knowledge ensures that we continue to provide a useful service to visitors and, we hope, give some welcome publicity to small and out-of-the-way places.

Thanks are also due to the Healthy Eating Circle for keeping us up to date with details of their members.

Some places that deserve to be included in the book may not have come to our attention. In this case we would be glad to hear of them for the next edition. Please write to *Where to Eat in Northern Ireland,* Northern Ireland Tourist Board, 59 North St, Belfast BT1 1NB.

A Taste of Ulster

A Taste of Ulster's distinctive symbol is your guarantee of a menu featuring the best of Ulster produce. You will find traditional and modern dishes created from the finest local ingredients wherever you see the special hexagonal plaque on display.

Listed in this special section are restaurants, pubs and coffee shops which have attained Taste of Ulster membership (applied for under a voluntary registration scheme). These are shown in green preceded by ★ in the main listings. Many have received special mentions in well known guide books and we have indicated these in the entry. Major credit cards are accepted unless indicated otherwise.

A Taste of Ulster

Belfast

Bewleys Oriental Café (p 33)
A branch of the famous traditional Irish café company, founded over 150 years ago. Wide range of blended and roasted coffees, speciality teas and splendid home-baked pastries and savouries.

Bittles Bar (p 33)
City centre bar offering classic Belfast pub grub with fresh soups, bread and stew. Champ – a dish of creamed potatoes and scallions – served with sausage is a local favourite. Fine collection of local art. No credit cards.

Bocoose (p 43)
This friendly restaurant on the lively Dublin Road offers traditional and modern Ulster food. Only the best local produce from land and sea is served. The wine list is extensive.

Clare Connery at Malone House (p 49)
Clare Connery places a particular emphasis on fish, game and vegetables. Vegetarian dishes are a speciality. The restaurant is in a lovely Georgian mansion three miles from the city centre.

The Clarence (p 35)
Steps lead down to this attractive basement wine bar and restaurant, beside City Hall. Popular with business people. Menus change daily and home-made desserts are a speciality.

Dundonald Old Mill, Dundonald (p 59)
A splendid coffee house at one of Northern Ireland's most popular visitor attractions. The 300-year-old mill has the largest waterwheel in Ireland. Large range of local crafts on sale.

A Taste of Ulster

Belfast (contd)

Duke of York (p 35)
In a bustling alleyway near St Anne's Cathedral, this is one of Belfast's oldest bars. Recently refurbished, the original fittings create an old style atmosphere. Food is fresh and varied and served in both bars. Live music in the evenings. No credit cards.

Dukes Hotel (p 50)
In a tree-lined avenue close to Queen's University and Botanic Gardens. Chef Gerard Manley's modern French style cooking is complemented by an extensive wine list. Special 'county' menus feature produce from Antrim and Down. Snacks in the bar. Ackerman.

The Eastender (p 59)
This luxurious lounge bar and restaurant has a striking decor of shipping memorabilia, antique mirrors and a hundred drawings of famous east Belfast characters. Baked ham with black velvet sauce is popular at lunch time.

The Elk, Dundonald (p 59)
The Elk was a 1993 Bushmills Bar of the Year regional winner. The Irish hot pot in the self-service restaurant is good, and good value.

Fillers Coffee Shop (p 59)
A bright, modern self-service restaurant featuring traditional home baking. The emphasis is on healthy eating and vegetarian alternatives are available. No credit cards.

Morning Star (p 38)
Historic pub in one of Belfast's 18th-century 'entries'. Ulster's best - seafood, home-reared meat, poultry and fresh vegetables - is served in the upstairs lounge restaurant and in the bar. Gourmet nights.

A Taste of Ulster

Belfast (contd)

Nick's Warehouse (p 39)
Nick's city centre restaurant and wine bar are on two floors of an atmospheric converted warehouse near St Anne's Cathedral. Fresh and interesting food is cooked with enthusiasm by chef/patron Nick Price. Ackerman, Bridgestone, Egon Ronay, Good Food Guide, Michelin.

Peppermill Coffee Shop (p 53)
In the university area, this welcoming coffee shop offers home-made scones, breads and pastries. Soups and salads are prepared with fresh local vegetables. No credit cards.

Roscoff (p 45)
Bright, uncluttered restaurant with a dynamic style. Paul Rankin complements classical French training with healthy Californian ideas. Creative use of organic vegetables and local seafood. Midway between City Hall and Queen's University. Ackerman clover, Bridgestone, Egon Ronay star, Good Food Guide, Michelin star.

Skandia (p 40)
This unlicensed restaurant is ideal for family dining with special menus for children. Extensive hours allow diners to enjoy any meal from breakfast to a late supper after the theatre. Close to the Grand Opera House, central for shopping.

Stormont Hotel (p 62)
The Stormont overlooks the landscaped grounds of the former Northern Ireland parliament. In McMaster's restaurant, head chef Billy McAteer offers fine local produce. Less formal fare is served in the brasserie.

White's Tavern (p 41)
This 17th-century tavern is in an old trading alley where the *Mercury* newspaper was founded in the 1850s. It enjoys an established reputation for fine home cooking with an interesting range of local dishes.

A Taste of Ulster
County Antrim

Brown Jug, Ballymoney (p 81)
Offering a good selection of home-cooked dishes, this pleasant coffee shop has convenient parking. No credit cards.

Bushmills Inn, Bushmills (p 82)
Close to the world's oldest licensed whiskey distillery, this hotel is a restored coaching inn. Specialities include salmon from the nearby Bush river with Bushmills whiskey. In summer and at weekends, the Victorian-style bar is open for simpler fare.

Galgorm Manor, Ballymena (p 77)
Local fish and game in season feature prominently on menus in this 4-star hotel, converted from a fine gentleman's estate. Head chef Clifford Caskey and his team use only top quality produce.
Egon Ronay.

Grouse Inn, Ballymena (p 77)
In Ballymena's bustling town centre, the Grouse Inn is renowned for friendly service and the relaxed atmosphere of its grill bar and wood panelled Bailiff's Parlour restaurant. Chef Archie Stewart bases his menu on the best seasonal ingredients.

Hillcrest Country House, Bushmills (p 89)
A stone's throw from the Giant's Causeway, this attractive licensed restaurant has panoramic coastal views. Fine sauces accompany many dishes and local seafood is well prepared.

Laurel Inn, Lisburn (p 96)
Presentation and taste are the hallmark of chef Chris Scott's innovative modern cuisine. The fish is notable, and fresh herbs are used extensively. Wide choice of fine wines.

A Taste of Ulster

Antrim *(contd)*

Londonderry Arms Hotel, Carnlough (p 83)
Charming coaching inn in a small fishing village on the Antrim coast road 14 miles north of Larne. A reputation for good food, cooked simply - wheaten bread, soups, pies, lamb and beef, and smoked Glenarm salmon.

Magherabuoy House Hotel, Portrush (p 101)
The hotel is set in a popular seaside resort on this splendid coast. A wide range of seafood is on offer and chef Kieran Laverty's quality dishes are served by friendly and efficient staff.

Marine Hotel, Ballycastle (p 74)
On the seafront at Ballycastle, the hotel offers good local produce in its restaurant and bar, and afternoon teas are a speciality.

National Trust Tea Room, Giant's Causeway (p 89)
Chef/manager Adrian Fletcher offers a daily choice of home-cooked fare, including a range of delicious soups and traditional breads, scones and cakes.

Sweeney's Wine Bar, Portballintrae (p 99)
There are fine views of the north Antrim coast from the conservatory. This converted 17th-century stable block retains much of its original character. Customers come from all over for the diverse menu. No credit cards.

Tea House, Ballymoney (p 82)
A haven for morning coffee or afternoon tea amid Victorian decor and pine furnishings. Home-baked pastries and savouries are complemented by a good selection of speciality teas. No credit cards.

A Taste of Ulster

Antrim (contd)

Templeton Hotel, Templepatrick (p 103)
A hotel with interesting architectural features near the international airport. All tastes are catered for and local produce is used in the preparation of a wide range of dishes. One mile from M2, Templepatrick exit. Ackerman.

Top of the Town, Antrim (p 73)
Friendly efficient staff and good home cooking by chef Christopher McDonald is the hallmark of this charming old pub. An award-winning beer garden is a bonus!

Wallace Restaurant, Lisburn (p 97)
This small, intimate restaurant has built up an appreciative following. The imaginative menu changes frequently and daily specials are determined by local produce in season.

Wysner's Ballycastle (p 74)
Carrick-a-rede salmon and Bushmills malt cheesecake are among dishes with a local resonance on this restaurant's sophisticated, good-value menus. A French-style café downstairs offers an extensive daytime menu. Bridgestone.

A Taste of Ulster
County Armagh

Archway, Armagh (p 105)
In an old Victorian archway near the historic Mall, this pretty coffee house reflects the owner's interest in local history and crafts. The apple pies are made with local Bramleys. No credit cards.

Famous Grouse Country Inn, Loughgall (p 111)
The atmosphere of this country inn, in the heart of the orchard county, is relaxed and friendly. Careful cooking combines admirably with quality local produce. An excellent snack menu is available until 9 pm each evening.

Hearty's Folk Cottage, Crossmaglen (p 110)
Thatched country kitchen, open Sunday only, famous for its hot scones, fresh apple pie and cakes. Even the butter is home made. Irish traditional music. Antiques and crafts on sale.

Navan Centre, Armagh (p 107)
Three well presented hot meals, one vegetarian, and a variety of snacks are served in the smoke-free coffee shop seven days a week. Another enjoyable memory to take away from this splendid interpretive centre at Ulster's most historic site.

Old Thatch, Markethill (p 114)
Modelled on a traditional thatched cottage, this unusual coffee shop in Alexander's busy department store has a fine range of home-made cakes and scones. Try the speciality jam!

Wheel and Lantern, Armagh (p 108)
A coffee shop in Lennox's department store. Brick, beams and oak furniture create an old-world atmosphere and freshly baked scones with Bewley's coffee is the morning speciality.

A Taste of Ulster

County Down

Adelboden Lodge, Groomsport (p 136)
The restaurant has splendid sea views and fine home cooking. The wholemeal wheaten bread is baked with a light hand by chef/owner Margaret Waterworth. Vegetarian dishes. Bridgestone.

Aylesforte House, Warrenpoint (p 156)
Easily located on the main road, the restaurant offers a buffet lunch daily, with extensive à la carte and fixed price evening menus. Head chef Peter Magill consistently emphasises local fresh produce. Adventurous bistro menu.

Back Street Café, Bangor (p 122)
Experience innovative modern cuisine in a relaxed atmosphere. Chef/proprietor Peter Barfoot likes at least half his starters and entrées to be fresh fish dishes. Local produce is a main feature. Bridgestone.

Bay Tree, Holywood (p 137)
This little coffee house is warm and welcoming. On summer days, doors open on to a pretty terrace. The soups and salads and Sue Farmer's cinnamon scones are all freshly prepared.
Craft shop. A smoke-free zone! Egon Ronay.

Brass Monkey, Newry (p 146)
Characterful bar with a country farmhouse atmosphere, stone floors and a spiral staircase. The fish comes from Kilkeel and meat and poultry is County Down-bred. Try the superb Ulster 'Monkey' Fry and fine steaks.

Buck's Head, Dundrum (p 133)
This is a characterful country pub on the main road from Belfast to the Mournes. Wood panelling, an open fire and a pretty view to the patio and garden gives the dining room a pleasant ambience.

A Taste of Ulster

County Down (contd)

Burrendale Hotel, Newcastle (p 144)
In a magnificent setting at the foot of the Mourne mountains, Denis Orr and his team create delicate flavours, with an insistence on fresh ingredients. Families love Denis's high tea menu.

Carmichael's, Holywood (p 138)
An interesting and popular pub near the Belfast-Bangor railway line. The railway theme creates a unique and fun atmosphere.

Castle Espie Coffee Room, Comber (p 129)
Set in a nature reserve with views of Strangford Lough, home of Ireland's largest collection of ducks, geese and swans. A splendid backdrop for the fine food. No credit cards.

Coffee Plus, Donaghadee (p 131)
This cheerful coffee shop in a pretty fishing village is ideal for morning coffee or a light lunch. The home-baked desserts are very good. Another non-smoking coffee shop. No credit cards.

Culloden Hotel, Cultra (p 130)
Chef Paul McKnight offers a wide range of dishes in the Mitre restaurant which looks on to landscaped gardens. This characterful gothic mansion hotel is 7 miles from Belfast on the A2 Bangor road. Ackerman, Egon Ronay.

Deane's on the Square, Helen's Bay (p 136)
Mossiman-trained chef/owner Michael Deane offers modern Irish and British cooking with the emphasis on presentation and taste. Deane's was built in 1863 by the Marquis of Dufferin. The atmosphere is quite distinctive. Bridgestone, Egon Ronay, Good Food Guide.

A Taste of Ulster

County Down *(contd)*

Dufferin Arms, Killyleagh (p 141)
A traditional Irish pub with a cellar bar/restaurant. The atmosphere is relaxed and the food delicious, with music Thursday through Saturday, Sunday brunch, the newspapers and piano.

The George, Bangor (p 124)
Chef Colin McCreedy offers an extensive menu in the refurbished 'Poacher's Arms', located in an original 1860 building. The emphasis is on healthy eating and vegetarians are particularly welcome.

Gilberry Fayre, Gilford (p 135)
This former schoolhouse has an agreeable pine interior. Even with its emphasis on healthy eating, the coffee shop has a mouth-watering array of sweets! Disabled visitors welcome. No credit cards.

Grace Neill's, Donaghadee (p 131)
Seafaring Donaghadee's oldest tavern, Grace Neill's is recognised as Ireland's oldest pub by the Guinness Book of Records. The pub grub is good and local fish features prominently.

Hampton's Coffee Shop, Hillsborough (p 136)
Tea and coffee is prepared from filtered water for a fuller flavour and the scones are always delicious. Another smoke-free zone. Self-service.

Heatherlea Tea Rooms, Bangor (p 124)
This pleasant coffee shop at the rear of Roulston's home bakery is popular with shoppers. Wide range of good home-baked breads. No credit cards.

A Taste of Ulster

County Down (contd)

Hillside, Hillsborough (p 136)
Imaginative dishes with a touch of nouvelle cuisine in this 18th-century restaurant/pub with a herb garden at the back. Off M1/A1 south of Belfast. Bridgestone, Michelin.

Ivanhoe Inn, Carryduff (p 128)
This family-run restaurant/pub is a well known landmark on the main Belfast-Newcastle road. The building dates back to the early 1900s. Specialities are Steak & Guinness pie and Ardglass prawns. The choice steaks come highly recommended.

Knott's Cake & Coffee Shop, Newtownards (p 151)
In a large Victorian building with high ceilings, this airy coffee shop offers a wide range of breads and cakes as well as hot pies, stews and casseroles. A popular lunchtime spot. No credit cards.

Lisbarnett House, Killinchy (p 141)
Cosy traditional atmosphere in this family-run former post house at Lisbane, on the main Comber-Killinchy road. Fresh local produce is well prepared and presented.

McLogans, Newry (p 147)
These lounge bars and restaurant are situated right beside the Buttercrane shopping centre. The daily carvery is very popular and the establishment is well known for its high quality service seven days a week.

No 1 Gallery, Moira (p 143)
A quaint coffee shop with stone walls and original wooden beams. The soups, salads, casseroles, and sweet and savoury pancakes are all prepared on the premises, fresh every day. Entrance through craft shop.

A Taste of Ulster

County Down (contd)

O'Hara's Royal Hotel, Bangor (p 125)
This family-owned hotel enjoys a reputation for good food and friendly atmosphere. Award-winning chef Alex Taylor offers French-style modern cuisine using the best county Down produce.

Old Inn, Crawfordsburn (p 130)
The hotel is one of Ireland's oldest hostelries, with records dating back to 1614. The hospitality is warm and genuine with excellent locally produced dishes from the kitchen of chef Brian McMillan. Ackerman.

Old School House, Comber (p 129)
Restaurant close to Strangford Lough. Avril Brown bases her cooking on traditional methods, but experiments with new combinations of seasonal produce. A regular and happy clientèle. On A22, 3 miles south-east of Comber.

Portaferry Hotel, Portaferry (p 153)
This country hotel, privately owned and managed, has an idyllic outlook across Strangford Lough. Chef Anne Truesdale's seafood dishes make the very best of the area's plentiful supplies of fish and shellfish. Ackerman, Bridgestone, Egon Ronay.

Primrose Bar, Ballynahinch (p 120)
A former blacksmith shop, the Primrose combines character and excellent cuisine. Discerning eaters come from a distance for Helen Gordon's open prawn sandwiches and wheaten bread.

Rayanne House, Holywood (p 138)
The pleasant dining room in this guesthouse, run by the McClelland family, is open to non-residents though you must book ahead. The McClellands are ex-restaurateurs and their culinary skills are much in evidence.

A Taste of Ulster

County Down (contd)

Red Fox Coffee Shop, Hillsborough (p 137)
Just off the main street, with views of the parish church and grounds. Owner Mo Mullan offers nutritious home-made food. (Craft shop across the courtyard.) No credit cards.

Rosemary Jane Tea Room, Crossgar (p 130)
An intimate atmosphere in a fine old building. Rosemary McKillen's menu includes vegetarian dishes using local organic vegetables and imaginative soups, salads and desserts - especially the banoffee! No credit cards.

The Stables, Groomsport (p 136)
Rustic brick, pitch pine and equestrian memorabilia provide the atmosphere in this pub/restaurant overlooking Belfast Lough. It won the 'Bushmills Bar of the Year' award in 1992. Snacks and grills are prepared with as much care as the extensive à la carte menu.

Wheatear Coffee Lounge, Bangor (p 127)
A bright and busy self-service coffee shop which offers a very wide range of high quality savouries and sweets. There is a gluten-free menu. No credit cards.

White Gables Hotel, Hillsborough (p 137)
Paul Cullen's inspiration comes from far and wide but he uses fresh Ulster produce – prime beef, free range poultry and organically grown vegetables. Bridgestone.

A Taste of Ulster
County Fermanagh

Le Bistro, Enniskillen (p 161)
Le Bistro coffee shop in the Erneside shopping centre is a friendly family-run place. The Johnstons use only the best local produce and all food is freshly prepared.

Drumshane Hotel, Lisnarick (p 168)
The lost art of cooking at table has been revived by Noel Smith, formerly of Dublin's Burlington Hotel. His accomplished flambé dishes and Irish Coffee are created with panache. His seven-course candlelit dinners are memorable experiences.

Hollander Restaurant, Irvinestown (p 165)
Interesting decor, with red brickwork, mahogany bar and souvenirs from Holland. Chef Stephen Holland produces some superb dishes – like salmon en croûte, beef Wellington and garlic chicken. On A32, 9 miles from Enniskillen. Bridgestone.

Tullyhona Guesthouse, Florencecourt (p 164)
The restaurant is open to non-residents for breakfast and lunch in summer. Rosemary Armstrong's menu features home produce and some wonderful desserts. Follow signs for Marble Arch caves. No credit cards.

A Taste of Ulster

County Londonderry

Badgers, Londonderry (p 179)
A lively bar with ambience. A trio of chefs - Bill, Bernadette and Paddy - prepare a wide range of dishes using the freshest best local ingredients.

Beech Hill Country House, Londonderry (p 179)
This hotel in an 18th-century mansion retains an old-world elegance. Chef Noel McMeel's adventurous menu has more than a touch of nouvelle cuisine, and his desserts are outstanding. Bridgestone, Egon Ronay, Good Food Guide.

Brown's Restaurant, Londonderry (p 179)
Set in a refurbished railway station, Brown's presents a range of the best in local produce – meat, fowl, fish and vegetarian dishes complemented by a varied wine list.

Ditty's Home Bakery & Coffee Shop, Magherafelt (p 186)
This small coffee shop is in a well known home bakery. The range of breads and confectionery is excellent and there is a choice of hot dishes. No credit cards.

Fioltas Bistro, Magherafelt (p 186)
Chef Paul Glass offers a wide range of dishes at this spacious bistro. The menu is based around the best available county Londonderry products. Lunch discounts for senior citizens.

The Little Tea Shop, Coleraine (p 174)
Decorated in a warm and cosy style, this non-smoking establishment has easy access for disabled visitors. Afternoon cream tea is a favourite and the lunch menu includes a good selection of simple well prepared family dishes.

MacDuff's Restaurant, Coleraine (p 174)
The best of country house cooking, with a modern touch, in cellar of Georgian rectory, now a guesthouse. Specialities include local game. Ackerman, Bridgestone, Egon Ronay, Good Food Guide, Michelin.

A Taste of Ulster

County Londonderry (contd)

Mary's Bar, Magherafelt (p 186)
Roast pheasant, wild Ulster salmon and home-made pies are among the dishes that attract customers from a wide area. There is an upstairs carvery and food is also served by friendly staff in a comfortable lounge downstairs.

Metro Bar, Londonderry (p 182)
Charming little pub in the shadow of the city walls. Lots of alcoves create a cosy atmosphere at lunchtime. Everything from soup and sandwiches to a hearty beef stew in Guinness. No credit cards.

Morelli's, Portstewart (p 188)
This bright and cheerful seafront café offers a clear view to the sea. As well as hot dishes, Morelli's is a long established and famous ice cream parlour with an amazing array of exotic ices. No credit cards.

Salmon Leap, Coleraine (p 175)
On a picturesque stretch of the Bann at Coleraine, the Salmon Leap restaurant is the place to go for superlative salmon. Service is friendly and efficient. Good wine list.

Schooner's, Londonderry (p 184)
Overlooking Lough Foyle and the historic city of Londonderry, the restaurant/wine bar offers a high standard of cuisine. Local fish figures prominently and vegetables are treated with respect.

Waterfoot Hotel, Londonderry (p 185)
The hotel has an interesting design and offers excellent views of the River Foyle and the Donegal mountains. Chef Kevin McGowan uses fish straight from the Foyle and local vegetables.

A Taste of Ulster

County Tyrone

The Courtyard, Cookstown (p 194)
Ploughs and cartwheels create a rustic feel in this attractive coffee shop. The wholesome, home-made food echoes the theme. No credit cards.

Grange Lodge Country House, Dungannon (p 197)
This ivy-covered Georgian retreat is open to non-residents at weekends for dinner. Norah Brown cooks many award-winning dishes. Exit M1 at junction 15, follow A29 south for 1.5 miles, left at signpost 'Grange', right, then first house on right. Bridgestone.

Greenmount Lodge, Omagh (p 202)
Open to non-residents at weekends for dinner. The Lodge, once part of an 18th-century estate, is renowned for its quality Ulster beef and lamb reared on its own farm, and Louie Reid is well known for her delicious desserts. No credit cards.

Greenvale Hotel, Cookstown (p 195)
Formerly a 19th-century gentleman's residence, the hotel provides a homely and cosy atmosphere in the Orchard Room, popular with families for Sunday lunch.

Inn on the Park, Dungannon (p 197)
A family hotel tucked away in wooded gardens. The extensive menu ranges from bar snacks to à la carte dining, and chefs Richard Torode and Andrew Rusk use the finest local produce.

Mellon Country Inn, Omagh (p 202)
Right opposite the Ulster-American Folk Park. Rustic brick and natural wood decor. The food is traditional with perceptible French influences. Extensive restaurant menu and a fast lunchtime buffet service in the bar.

A Taste of Ulster

County Tyrone (contd)

Rosamund's Coffee Shop, Augher (p 191)
In one of the old Clogher Valley Railway station houses. The cooking is simple and good and dishes feature Clogher Valley cheese. Local crafts and linen on sale. No credit cards.

Royal Arms Hotel, Omagh (p 203)
Long established town centre hotel restaurant. Local lamb, home-made soups and traditional desserts issue from the kitchens of head chef Cuan who believes in fresh Ulster produce above all else. Vegetarian dishes.

Suitor Gallery, Ballygawley (p 191)
Tea room/craftshop in a converted barn at the bottom of an orchard on the Ballygawley roundabout. The vegetable soup and wheaten bread is prepared by owner/cook/artist Beryl Suitor. Wide selection of cakes and pastries.

Special mentions

Although not members of A Taste of Ulster, these restaurants feature in the latest editions of well known guides to good eating. They too are shown in green in the main listings, preceded by ★

Belfast

Antica Roma – p 47. Bridgestone, Good Food Guide, Egon Ronay, Michelin.

Ashoka – p 47. Bridgestone.

Bananas – p 43. Bridgestone.

Belfast Castle – p 65. Ackerman, Bridgestone.

Bengal Brasserie – p 47. Bridgestone, Egon Ronay.

Bishops – p 47. Good Food Guide.

Chez Delbart – p 49. Bridgestone.

Crown Liquor Saloon – p 43. Ackerman, Bridgestone.

Europa Hotel – p 44. Egon Ronay.

French Village – p 51. Bridgestone.

Friar's Bush – p 51. Bridgestone.

La Belle Epoque – p 44. Ackerman, Bridgestone, Good Food Guide, Michelin.

La Bohème – p 44. Bridgestone, Good Food Guide.

Long's Fish Restaurant – p 67. Bridgestone.

Mr JD's – p 60. Bridgestone.

Manor House – p 53. Bridgestone, Egon Ronay, Michelin.

Restaurant 44 – p 45. Ackerman, Bridgestone, Michelin.

Saints and Scholars – p 55. Bridgestone, Michelin.

Special mentions contd

Speranza – p 45. Egon Ronay.

Spice of Life – p 40. Bridgestone.

Strand – p 55. Ackerman, Bridgestone, Egon Ronay, Good Food Guide, Michelin.

Truffles – p 41. Bridgestone.

Upper Crust – p 41. Bridgestone.

Villa Italia – p 56. Bridgestone, Egon Ronay.

Welcome – p 56. Ackerman, Bridgestone, Egon Ronay.

County Antrim

Auberge de Seneirl, Bushmills – p 82. Bridgestone, Good Food Guide.

Dunadry Inn, Dunadry – p 87. Ackerman.

Ginger Tree, Newtownabbey – p 98. Bridgestone, Good Food Guide, Michelin.

Manley, Ballymena – p 79. Bridgestone, Michelin.

Ramore, Portrush – p 101. Ackerman clover, Bridgestone, Egon Ronay star, Good Food Guide, Michelin red M.

Sleepy Hollow, Newtownabbey – p 98. Bridgestone, Michelin.

Water Margin, Ballymena – p 80. Bridgestone, Michelin.

Windrose, Carrickfergus – p 85. Egon Ronay, Michelin.

County Down

Barn, Saintfield – p 154. Bridgestone, Michelin.

Gaslamp, Newtownards – p 150. Bridgestone.

The Grange, Waringstown – p 156. Bridgestone, Michelin.

Iona, Holywood – p 138. Bridgestone.

Lobster Pot, Strangford – p 155. Ackerman.

Ming Court, Newtownards – p 151. Bridgestone.

Sullivans, Holywood – p 138. Egon Ronay.

Special mentions contd

County Fermanagh

Cedars, Irvinestown – p 165. Bridgestone.
Franco's, Enniskillen – p 161. Bridgestone.
Melvin House, Enniskillen – p 163. Bridgestone.
Rafters, Newtownbutler – p 168. Bridgestone.
The Sheelin, Bellanaleck – p 159. Ackerman, Bridgestone, Good Food Guide.

County Londonderry

Fiorentini's, Londonderry – p 181. Bridgestone.
Kitty's of Coleraine, Coleraine – p 174. Bridgestone.

County Tyrone

Top Bar, Dungannon – p 198. Good Food Guide.

How to use the guide

This handy paperback will fit neatly into a pocket or the glove compartment of your car, The 1,800 eating places listed here range from the smallest coffee shop and fish & chip café to the smart places that get into food guides.

Everyone is familiar with that uneasy feeling when, driving through some newly discovered countryside, enjoying the sights and sounds, you are wondering all the same where to stop for a bite to eat. Might there be a tea-room in the next village? Dare you press on?

To resolve this dilemma we have listed places by town and village within each county. Some villages have only one eating place - perhaps a hotel or maybe just a pub serving hot pies and pizzas. The important thing is to know what is available in the area and this book should help you find them.

The canny traveller will plan ahead, of course, and a telephone call before setting out is sensible, particularly at weekends when many restaurants are booked and some hotels may have arranged a dinner-dance, which may not suit you.

Entries are grouped by town and village in each county. There is a map at the back of the book and an index to towns and villages. The Belfast section is divided into five areas, shown on the sketch map on page 32.

City Centre — the BT1 postcode area.
Golden Mile — includes the many restaurants along Great Victoria St (BT2).
University and Malone - area around Queen's University and Lisburn Rd (BT7 & 9).
East of the River - from the Lagan to the eastern suburbs (mostly BT4-6, 8 & 16).
North and West of the River - from the Lagan to the city limits (BT10-15 & 17).

Restaurants are divided into three price bands which are based on the average cost of a three-course meal - a starter, main course of meat or fish, plus two vegetables and a sweet. We have included 10 per cent service and VAT, but not wine or coffee.

£	£5 to £10
££	£10 to £15
£££	over £15
M	followed by £, ££, or £££ refers to average cost of lunch
E	followed by £, ££, or £££ refers to average cost of evening meal

When no symbol is used, a three-course meal or equivalent will cost less than £5. In general, midday meals cost less than evening meals. E£ means that an evening meal is £5-£10 but you can still get lunch for under £5 in the same place. Some restaurants offer special early evening menus which are good value.

If you are dissatisfied in any way, tell the waiter or ask for the manager - always more effective than writing after you get home. Your comments will help them to improve the service.

Restaurants participating in the Healthy Eating Circle are indicated by ☻. They provide healthy food choices and set aside non-smoking areas. For further information contact the Health Promotion Agency.
☎ (01232) 311611.

You will find that hotels are good places for meals and snacks throughout the day. For many visitors afternoon tea offers a welcome break from sightseeing. Served from around three o'clock it consists of a pot of tea, sandwiches, and cakes or scones.

High tea starts at about five o'clock and is usually over by seven. Some overseas visitors are quite defeated by the notion of high tea. A typical high tea consists of sausages, or a lamb cutlet, with a plate of cakes and scones. Home-baked ham and salad may be served, and since Ulster is the country of good bread, it is not unusual to have several varieties of bread on the table.

Licensed restaurants in Northern Ireland are fortunate in that they can serve a complete range of drinks including wine, beer and all kinds of spirits. All licensed establishments are indicated by ♀ and those places which we know from experience welcome customers bringing in a bottle of wine are indicated by 🍾.

Pubs in Northern Ireland are open seven days a week. They are open all day from Monday to Saturday 1130am-11pm, with half-an-hour 'drinking up' time, so that you can savour that last pint. On Sunday most open at lunchtime and in the evening (12.30-2.30pm and 7-10pm) although some publicans continue to observe the traditional Sabbath and remain closed.

More pubs are now providing food all day and this is why we have given the full licensing hours in many cases. Even so, experience has shown that the widest choice is served around lunchtime and, in some pubs, in the early evening. Many pubs will make you a pot of tea at any time during the day.

Some telephone numbers listed here may change in the course of the year. If you cannot get through dial 100 and ask the operator for help.

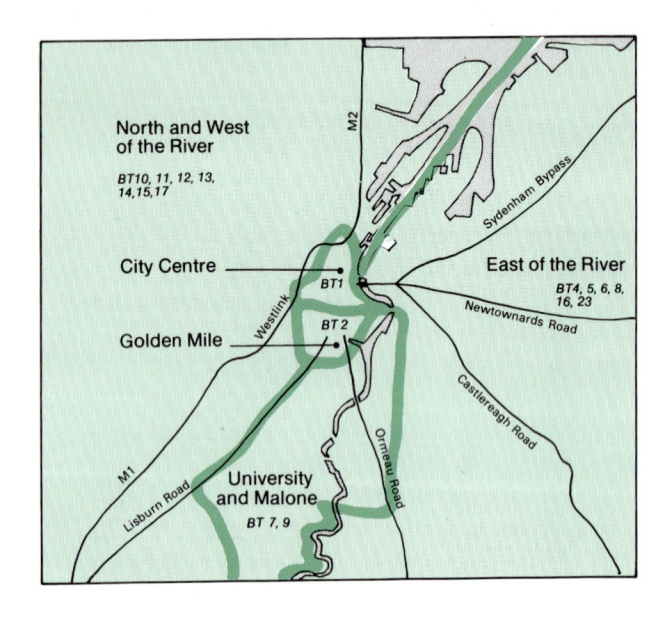

Belfast postal districts
Use this sketch map, based on postal districts, to locate restaurants in the Belfast area.

BELFAST

City Centre *(BT1)*
(STD 01232)

Alambra
114 North St, BT1. ☎ 240682.
0930-1730 Mon-Sat. Burgers, fries, chicken.

Arizona ♀
10 Gresham St, BT1.
☎ 323590. 1130-1500 Mon-Thur, until 1700 Fri & Sat. Pub grub.

Bambricks
58 Wellington Place, BT1.
☎ 234303. 0800-1530 Mon-Fri, 1100-1530 Sat. Sandwich bar & restaurant.

Bamford's Home Bakery
49A Upper Arthur St, BT1.
☎ 242284. 0800-1700 Mon-Sat. Rolls, pies, sandwiches.

Benny's
10 Short St, BT1. ☎ 743128.
0800-1600 Mon-Fri, 0800-1300 Sat. Ulster fry, sandwiches.

Bethel
3 Donegall Square East, BT1.
☎ 439525. 0930-1730 Mon-Sat. Chicken, salads, pizza. Coffee shop in book store.

★ **BEWLEY'S**
Donegall Arcade, BT1.
☎ 234955. 0800-1730 Mon-Sat, until 2030 Thur. Breakfast, lunch, pastries, afternoon tea, speciality coffees. Self-service. £.

★ **BITTLES** ♀
70 Upper Church Lane, BT1.
☎ 311088. 1130-1500 Mon-Sat. Irish stew, champ.

Blackthorn ♀
3 Skipper St, BT1. ☎ 331087.
1200-1430 Mon-Sat. Roast beef, fish, salads.

Blinkers
1 Bridge St, BT1. ☎ 243330.
1000-2245 Mon-Sat. Grills, burgers, set lunch.

Blooms
46 Upper Arthur St, BT1.
☎ 313500. 0730-1530 Mon-Fri. Sandwiches, sausage rolls.

Bodega ♀
4 Callender St, BT1.
☎ 243177. 1130-1800 Mon-Sat, until 2100 Thur. Cajun chicken, stir fry, pub grub. E£.

BELFAST *City Centre*

Bonne Bouche
19 Fountain St, BT1.
☎ 241454. 0730-1730
Mon-Sat, until 2100 Thur.
Ulster fry, set lunch.

Boots ⊖
35 Donegall Place, BT1.
☎ 242332. 0900-1730
Mon-Sat, until 2015 Thur.
Coffee, cakes, baked potatoes,
lasagne. Self-service restaurant
in department store.

Bradan Bar ♀
83 May St, BT1. ☎ 230295.
1200-1430 Mon-Sat. Pub
grub.

Brown's Fish Restaurant
30 Chichester St, BT1.
☎ 232100. 1130-1900 Mon-
Wed, until 2330 Thur-Sat,
1000-1800 Sat. ££.

Burger King
Cleaver House, Donegall
Place, BT1. ☎ 245314.
0800-2300 Mon-Thur, until
2400 Fri & Sat, 1000-2300
Sun. Burgers, breakfast, coffee.

C & A ⊖
46 Donegall Place, BT1.
☎ 232636. 0930-1700
Mon-Sat, until 2030 Thur.
Coffee shop in department
store.

New Yorker Deli & Diner
Fountain Centre, College St.
☎ 439295. 0800-1700 Mon-
Fri, 0900-1700 Sat. Breakfast,
lunches, crêpes.

Café Poirot
51 Fountain St, BT1.
☎ 323130. 0745-1715 Mon-
Sat & 2000 December. Bistro
style. French bread, jambons,
asparagus soup, kebabs.

Café Renoir
5 Queen St, BT1. ☎ 325592.
0945-1700 Mon-Sat. Club
triple sandwich, chicken &
prawn open sandwiches, hot
chocolate.

Campbell's
11 Donegall Square West,
BT1. ☎ 322658. 0730-1700
Mon-Sat. Self-service café in
cake shop.

Capstan Bar ♀
10 Ann St, BT1. ☎ 329148.
1200-1430 Mon-Sat.
Hamburgers, salads, pub grub.

Carlton ♀
11 Wellington Place, BT1.
☎ 326861. 1200-1900 Mon-
Sat. Steaks, haddock with
mustard & banana sauce,
Portavogie scampi. A la carte.
E£.

Castle Court Centre
12 Royal Avenue, BT1.
☎ 235122. Coffee shops &
restaurant. 0930-1730 Mon-
Sat, until 2100 Thur (coffee
shops). Danish pastries,
muffins, sandwiches.
Restaurant 1200-1500 Mon,
Tues, Wed, Fri & 1200-1800
Sat. Lasagne, chilli, scampi,
salad bar.

City Centre **BELFAST**

Castle Mews ♀
34 Bank St, BT1. ☎ 330443.
1200-1600 Mon-Sat. Pub grub.

Chalet d'Or
48 Fountain St, BT1.
☎ 324810. 0900-1800
Mon-Sat, until 2000 Thur. Set lunch, Ulster fry, grills.

Chalet d'Or
Castle St, BT1. ☎ 249820.
0930-1700 Mon-Sat. Soup, stew, set lunch.

Chaney's
23 High St, BT1. ☎ 245688.
1000-1800 Mon-Sat, until 2100 Thur. Grills, snacks, set lunch. £.

★ **CLARENCE** ♀
18 Donegall Square East, BT1.
☎ 238862. 1230-1430
Mon-Fri. A la carte: champagne sorbet, salmon & monkfish with ginger sauce. Bar lunch: pâté, salads, sandwiches. ££.

Crow's Nest ♀
26 Skipper St, BT1. ☎ 325491.
1200-1500 Mon-Sat. Pub grub.

Dr B's Kitchen ☺
9 Bridge St, BT1. ☎ 321213.
0930-1400 Mon-Fri. Baked Irish ham, pork in cider sauce, sirloin of beef in pepper sauce.

Deer's Head ♀
5 Garfield St. ☎ 239163.
1200-1900 Mon-Sat. Soup, baked potatoes, club sandwiches, lasagne.

Delaney's ♀
Lombard St, BT1. ☎ 231572.
0900-1700 Mon-Sat, until 2100 Thur. Breakfast, lasagne, home-baked pies, self-service. A la carte. £.

★ **DUKE OF YORK** ♀
3 Commercial Court, BT1.
☎ 241062. 1200-1400
Mon-Fri, 1200-1700 Sat. Steaks, vegetarian lasagne, filled rolls. Live music.

Eighteen Steps ♀
17 Ann St, BT1. ☎ 326247.
1130-1700 Mon-Wed, until 2000 Thur-Sat. Open sandwiches, home-made pies, steaks.

Fat Harry's ♀
93 Castle St, BT1. ☎ 232226.
1200-2100 Mon-Sat. Steaks, grills, scampi. £.

Forte's
92 Castle St, BT1. ☎ 327189.
0915-1745 Mon-Sat. Soup, burgers, sandwiches.

Fountain Tavern ♀
16 Fountain St, BT1.
☎ 242049. 1130-2230
Mon-Sat. Steak casserole, quiche, baked potatoes.

NICK'S
RESTAURANT & WINE BAR
35-39 Hill St. Belfast
Telephone: (01232) 439690

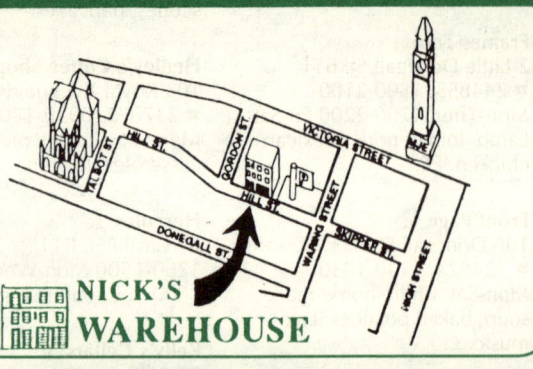

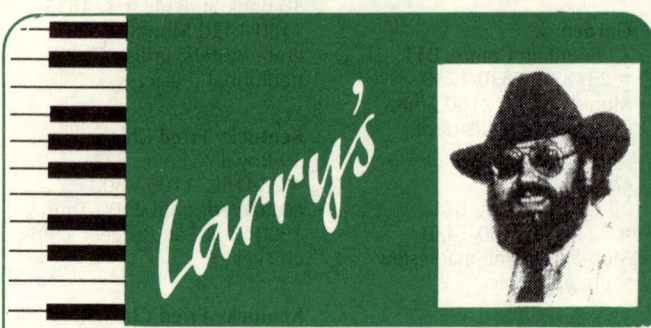

NICK'S WAREHOUSE

Larry's

WORLD RENOWNED PIANO BAR AND RESTAURANT
36 BEDFORD STREET, BELFAST
(next to Ulster Hall)

☎ **325061**

Eat, drink and be entertained by our singing waitresses and resident piano player

until 1.30 am
(last orders 1.15 am)

City Centre **BELFAST**

Frames ♀
2 Little Donegall St, BT1.
☎ 237214. 1200-1500
Mon-Fri. Moussaka, beef
casserole, plaice

Frames Too ♀
2 Little Donegall St, BT1.
☎ 244855. 1800-2100
Mon-Thur, 1700-2200 Fri-Sat.
Lamb, loin of pork, Mexican
chicken. E£.

Front Page ♀
106 Donegall St, BT1.
☎ 324924. 1130-1730
Mon-Sat. Chilli, home-made
soup, baked potatoes. Live
music. £.

Garden ♀
32 Fountain Centre, BT1.
☎ 231823. 0830-1730
Mon-Sat, until 2100 Thur.
Grills, fish. A la carte. £.

Garrick ♀
29 Chichester St, BT1.
☎ 321984. 1200-1430
Mon-Sat. Home-made stew,
soup, apple pie.

Globe Tavern ♀
Joy's Entry, BT1. ☎ 326711.
1130-2300 Mon-Sat. Grills,
salads.

Golden Bloom
9 Wellington St, BT1.
☎ 240281. 0745-1730
Mon-Sat. Ulster fry, pies,
sandwiches.

Hardy's
12 Fountain Lane, BT1.
☎ 236308. 0800-1700 Mon-
Sat, until 2100 Thur. Beef &
Guinness pie, home-baked
scones, pancakes.

Hedley's Coffee Shop ☕
103 Royal Avenue, BT1.
☎ 237077. 0930-1700
Mon-Sat. Cottage pie,
casseroles. In china shop.

Hercules ♀
61 Castle St, BT1. ☎ 324587.
1200-1500 Mon-Wed, 1200-
1800 Thur-Sat. Pub grub.

Kelly's Cellars ♀
30 Bank St, BT1. ☎ 324835.
1130-1430 Mon-Sat. Pub
grub, oysters, grills. Live
traditional music.

Kentucky Fried Chicken
39 Royal Avenue, BT1.
☎ 234188. 1100-1800
Mon-Wed, until 2100 Thur &
1900 Fri & Sat. Burgers, chips,
chicken.

Kentucky Fried Chicken
7 Wellington Place, BT1.
☎ 325146. 1100-2300
Mon-Thur, until 2330 Fri &
Sat. Burgers, chips, chicken.

Kitchen Bar ♀
16 Victoria Square, BT1.
☎ 324901. 1200-1400
Mon-Sat. Ulster fry, soup, Irish
stew, champ. Real ale.

BELFAST
City Centre

Krusty Korner
76 Lower North St, BT1.
☎ 232047. 0900-1700 Mon-Sat. Set lunch, sandwiches, coffee.

Le Café
38 Hill St, BT1. ☎ 311660. 0930-1430 Mon-Fri. Tagliatelli, chicken curry, vegetarian. Newspapers.

Le Petit Pain ⊙
Ross's Court, William St South, BT1. ☎ 332440. 0800-1730 Mon-Sat, until 2100 Thur. Croissants, bagels, baguettes, pastries.

Linen Hall Library ⊙
17 Donegall Square North, BT1. ☎ 321707. 1000-1600 Mon-Fri, until 1400 Sat. Soup, sandwiches, scones. Café in reading room.

Little Knife & Fork
29 North St, BT1. ☎ 439619. 0900-1800 Mon-Sat, until 2200 Thur. Fish & chips, sausages.

Littlewoods Green Room
Ann St, BT1. ☎ 241537. 0900-1715 Mon-Sat, until 2100 Thur. Grills, set lunch. Restaurant in chain store.

McDonald's
2 Donegall Place, BT1.
☎ 311600. 0700-2000 Mon-Sat, until 2200 Thur, 1100-1800 Sun. Breakfast, burgers, chicken.

Mr Sandwich
20 Church Lane, BT1.
☎ 326275. 0800-1600 Mon-Fri. Irish stew, sandwiches, snacks.

Maysfield Leisure Centre
East Bridge St, BT1. ☎ 241633. 1000-2200 Mon-Fri, until 1600 Sat, 1100-1700 Sun. Fish, chicken, lasagne.

Mermaid ♀
5 Wilson's Court, High St, BT1. ☎ 327829. 1230-1430 Mon-Sat. Pub grub.

Miss American Pie
Ross's Court, William St South, BT1. ☎ 311055. 0900-1730 Mon-Wed & Fri, until 2100 Thur. Chilli, club sandwiches, doughnuts.

Monico ♀
17 Lombard St, BT1.
☎ 323211. 1200-1500 Mon-Sat. Pub grub.

★ **MORNING STAR** ♀

17 Pottinger's Entry, BT1.
☎ 323976. 1130-2100 Mon-Sat. Seafood, pan fried lamb fillet with ginger & garlic, carrot & stilton soup. £. Gourmet night last Sat of the month.

The Mulberry
38 Upper Arthur St, BT1.
☎ 249009. 0730-1700 Mon-Sat. Salad bar, pizzas.

City Centre **BELFAST**

Muldoon's
13 Corporation Square, BT1.
☎ 232415. 1200-1500
Mon-Sat. Burgers, salads, fish, pies.

Next Café
20 Donegall Place, BT1.
☎ 249636. 0930-1700 Mon-Fri, 0930-1730 Sat. Coffee shop in department store.

★ **NICK'S WAREHOUSE**
35 Hill St, BT1. ☎ 439690.
Restaurant: 1200-1430 Mon-Fri, 1800-2100 Tues-Sat. Duck with apple, fillet of halibut with langoustine & sweet peppers. M££. Wine bar: 1200-1500 Mon-Fri, 1800-2330 Tues-Sat. Lettuce & cucumber soup, hot & sour beef with water chestnuts. Real ale.

Ormeau Bakery
27 Fountain St, BT1.
☎ 328340. 0800-1630
Mon-Sat. Baked potatoes, soup, pies.

Oxford
Oxford St Bus Depot, BT1.
☎ 331289. 0830-1730
Mon-Sat. Burgers, sandwiches, coffee.

Paddy's Bar
96 Ann St, BT1. ☎ 327162.
1200-1500 Mon-Thur, 2210 Fri & Sat. 1230-1430 Sun. Wine bar. Theme days. Mexican dishes, fish.

Pancake House
Haymarket, Royal Avenue, BT1. ☎ 240141. 0800-1730 Mon-Sat, until 2100 Thur. Savoury & sweet pancakes, fish, chips.

The Parliament
2 Dunbar St, BT1. ☎ 314515.
1130-1500 Mon-Sat. Home-made soups, champagne paté, baked gammon, and honey-eyed pineapple. Vegetarian.

Patio Restaurant
BHS, 24 Castle Place, BT1.
☎ 243068. 0930-1645
Mon-Wed, 0900-1645 Thur-Sat. Coffee shop and restaurant in department store.

Pat's Bar
19 Prince's Dock St, BT1.
☎ 744524. 1200-1430 Mon-Fri. Lasagne, pizza, set lunch. Live traditional music.

Penny Farthing
94 Donegall St, BT1.
☎ 249423. 1200-1530
Mon-Sat, 1230-1430 Sun.
Set meals, grills.

Poachers
Unit 10, Victoria Centre, BT1.
☎ 332162. 0900-1600
Mon-Fri. Home baking, sandwiches.

Queen's Bar
4 Queen's Arcade, BT1.
☎ 321347. 1200-1800
Mon-Sat, until 2000 Thur. Club sandwich, steak pie black velvet, vegetable lasagne.

BELFAST
City Centre

Romano's
12 Queen St, BT1. ☎ 249484. 0830-1730 Mon-Sat. Set lunch, grills.

Roost ♀
Church Lane, BT1. ☎ 233282. 1130-2300 Mon-Sat. Irish stew, chicken in basket.

Ross's Court
☎ 236634. 0900-1730 Mon-Sat, 0900-2100 Thur. Six different styles of food in shopping mall. Chinese, Italian, baked potato, French bakery, salad - burger bar, coffee shop.

Rotterdam Bar ♀
54 Pilot St, BT1. ☎ 746021. 1200-1400 Mon-Sat. Sandwiches, Irish stew. Live music. Beer garden.

Rumpole's ♀
81 Chichester St, BT1. ☎ 232840. 1200-1500 Mon-Sat, 1600-2200 Tues & Thur-Sat. Crab pâté, seafood pancake, chicken & ham pie.

Sarah's
Arthur Square, BT1. ☎ 326517. 0730-1700 Mon-Sat, until 2100 Thur. Breakfast, sandwiches, coffee.

Shakespeare ♀
103 Victoria St, BT1. ☎ 328788. 1130-2300 Mon-Sat. Pub grub.

Skandia ♦ ☺
12 Callender St, BT1. ☎ 245385. 0930-1800 Mon-Sat, until 2100 Thur. Salads, open sandwiches, charcoal grill. £.

★ **SKANDIA** ♦ ☺
50 Howard St, BT1. ☎ 240239. 0930-2300 Mon-Sat. Grills, salads, open sandwiches, gateaux. E£.

Snakkers
63a Prince's Dock St, BT1. ☎ 352387. 0800-1600 Mon-Fri, until 1400 Sat. Home-made savoury pies, casseroles, Ulster fry, roasts.

★ **SPICE OF LIFE** ♦ ☺
62 Lower Donegall St, BT1. ☎ 332744. 0900-1700 Mon-Sat. Soup, lasagne, salads. Wholefood & vegetarian.

Strikes
19 Bridge St, BT1. ☎ 320945. 0900-1800 Mon-Sat, until 1900 Thur. Set lunch, soup, grills, toasties.

Thompson's Garage
6 Patterson's Place, Donegall Sq East, BT1. ☎ 323762. 1130-1800 Mon-Sat. Sandwiches, soup.

Tiffins
4 Montgomery St, BT1. ☎ 320906. 0800-1930 Mon-Fri. Coffee, scones, sandwiches.

City Centre **BELFAST**

★ **TRUFFLES**
4A Donegall Square West, BT1. ☎ 247153. 0830-1800 Mon-Sat. Coffee shop: Ulster fry, curries. Restaurant: minute steak, stuffed pork fillet, spring chicken in barbecue sauce.

★ **UPPER CRUST**
15 Lombard St, BT1. ☎ 323132. 0930-1630 Mon-Sat. Home-made pies, chicken & broccoli bake, gateaux.

Washington
15 Howard St, BT1. ☎ 241891. 1230-2300 Mon-Sat. Mexican, barbecue ribs, steaks, pancakes. Music. E££.

Whistle Stop
Central Station, East Bridge St, BT1. ☎ 238637. 0800-1900 Mon-Sat. Soup, stew, fish & chips. Self-service.

★ **WHITE'S TAVERN**
Winecellar Entry, High St, BT1. ☎ 243080. 1200-1430 Mon-Sat. Chicken and broccoli bake, savoury crepes, filled baked potatoes. Traditional music on Thur.

Windsor Dairy
4 College St, BT1. ☎ 327157. 0830-1730 Mon-Sat, until 2100 Thur. Home baking, Irish stew, coffee.

Woolworth's
11 High St, BT1. ☎ 322888. 0900-1730 Mon-Sat, until 2100 Thur. Snacks, grills, salads. Restaurant in department store.

The PORT SIDE Inn

for an
Excellent choice of beers, wines & spirits in a friendly, welcoming atmosphere
Superb food at reasonable prices
Lunch served 12 noon - 6 pm
Monday to Friday
12 noon - 3 pm Saturday
Try our special of the day
Private parties catered for
Portside Pubs Ltd,
Dargan Road, Belfast
☎ (01232) 370746

ARTHUR'S
LICENSED RESTAURANT

Situated just off Great Victoria Street and 2 minutes walk from the Opera House, this small but smart restaurant has a regular clientele who appreciate excellent cuisine and service. Fully licensed, Arthur's is a perfect place to relax and meet friends or entertain business clients.

Arthur's - Belfast's best kept secret.
Open for lunch: Mon - Fri noon - 4.30 pm
Evening Meals: Mon - Sat 6 pm - 11 pm

7 Hope Street
Belfast ☎ 333311

Bocoose

Licensed Restaurant

Wide variety of steak,
fish & chicken dishes
with vegetarian options
complemented by an extensive
wine list.

85 Dublin Road, Belfast.
☎ **(01232) 238787**

BELFAST

Golden Mile *(BT2)*
(STD 01232)

Arthur's
7 Hope St, BT2. ☎ 333311. 1200-1430 Mon-Fri, a la carte, 1800-2300 Mon-Sat. Ginger chicken strips, lemon sole with prawns, profiteroles with peach ice cream. E£££.

★ **BANANAS**
4 Clarence St, BT2. ☎ 244844. 1200-1500 Mon-Fri, 1700-2300 Mon-Sat. Warm mussel & potato salad, chicken with pineapple, coconut & rum sauce, bitter chocolate truffle torte. E£££.

Beaten Docket
48 Great Victoria St, BT2. 242986. 1200-1500 Mon-Sat. Pub grub, champ. A la carte. E£.

★ **BOCOOSE**
85 Dublin Rd, BT2. ☎ 238787. 1200-1430 Mon-Fri, 1700-2330 Mon-Sat, 1700-2200 Sun. Mexican style chilli bean soup, grilled fish, chicken & steak with spice herb butter. E£££.

Boyne Bridge
2 Sandy Row, BT2. ☎ 327938. 1130-1700 Mon-Sat. Ulster fry, lasagne.

Britannic
Amelia St (above Crown Liquor Saloon), BT2. ☎ 249476. 1130-1430 Mon-Fri. Beef & Guinness pie, ploughman's platter, pickled beef.

Café India
60 Great Victoria St, BT2. ☎ 243727. 1200-1400 & 1730-2330 Mon-Sat, 1730-2230 Sun. European & Indian. E£££.

Crescent
197 Sandy Row, BT2. ☎ 320911. 2100-0130 Mon-Sat. Pub grub.

★ **CROWN LIQUOR SALOON**
46 Great Victoria St, BT2. ☎ 249476. 1130-1500 Mon-Sat. Bar lunches, champ, oysters, stew. Victorian pub in National Trust care.

BELFAST   *Golden Mile*

Dempsey's Terrace ♀
43 Dublin Rd, BT2.
☎ 234000. 1200-1500 &
1700-2130 Mon-Sat. Mussels
in garlic, white wine & cream
sauce, duck stuffed with lime,
peach & nuts. E££.

Dome & Limelight ♀
17 Ormeau Avenue, BT2.
☎ 325942. 1900-2200
Mon-Sat. Sandwiches, grills,
salads. Live music. E£.

Drury Lane ♀
2 Amelia St, BT2. ☎ 238008.
1230-1500 & 1800-2130
Mon-Sat. Chicken, steaks. £.

Emerald City ♀
59 Dublin Rd. ☎ 235072.
1200-1400 & 1700-2330
Mon-Thur, until 2430 Fri &
Sat, 1630-2300 Sun. Chinese
& European. ££.

Equinox
32 Howard St, BT2.
☎ 230089. 0930-1730
Mon-Sat. Home-made soup,
filled croissants, tagliatelli with
smoked ham & cream sauce. £.

★ **EUROPA HOTEL** ♀

Great Victoria St, BT2.
☎ 327000. Last orders 2330.
A la carte. M£, E£££.

Explorers 🍸
89 Dublin Rd. ☎ 245550.
1700-2330 Mon-Sat, until
2300 Sun. Chicken sphinx,
lamb with redcurrant & mint
sauce, calypso banana.

Graffiti Italiano ♀
50 Dublin Rd, BT2. ☎ 249269.
1800-2300 Mon-Sat. Italian
££.Tuscan tomato soup,
steamed mussels, Italian
bread, sea-food spaghetti.

Harvey's ♀
95 Great Victoria St, BT2.
☎ 233433. 1700-2300
Mon-Thur & Sun, until 2400
Fri & Sat. Tacos, barbecue
ribs, deep-pan pizza. E£.

Hungry Jack's
10 Bedford St, BT2.
☎ 326601. 0800-1600
Mon-Fri. Sandwiches made to
order.

Jenny's
81 Dublin Rd, BT2.
☎ 249282. 0900-1700
Mon-Sat. Lasagne, quiche,
salads.

★ **LA BELLE EPOQUE** ♀

61 Dublin Rd, BT2. ☎ 323244.
1200-2330 Mon-Fri,
1800-2330 Sat. Fillet of beef
with seed mustard cream
sauce, roast breast of Barbary
duck with grape sauce.

★ **LA BOHÈME** ♀

103 Great Victoria St, BT2.
☎ 240666. 1200-2400 Mon-
Fri & 1800-2400 Sat. £££.
Chicken pieces with prune
stuffing & red wine sauce, wild
salmon with fresh basil sauce.

Golden Mile

BELFAST

Larry's Piano Bar ☐
36 Bedford St, BT2.
☎ 325061. 1700-0115
Tues-Sat. A la carte. Pasta,
steaks, fish. Live music. E££.

Morrison's ☐
21 Bedford St, BT2.
☎ 248458. 1200-1430
Mon-Sat. Oriental spiced
chicken, salmon in orange
sauce, salads. E£.

Oriental International ☐
25 Dublin Rd, BT2.
☎ 232485. 1200-1400 &
1700-2400 Mon-Thur, until
0030 Fri & Sat, 1630-2330
Sun. Peking, Cantonese &
European. E££.

Pizza Hut ☐
44 Dublin Rd, BT2.
☎ 311222. 1200-2400
Mon-Sat, 1200-2300 Sun.
Pizzas, salad bar. £

Pizza Hut
Belfast Superbowl, 4 Clarence
St West, BT2. ☎ 331466.
1000-0030 Mon-Sat, 1200-
0030 Sun. Pizza, garlic bread.

Plaza Hotel ☐
15 Brunswick St, BT2.
☎ 333555. Last orders
2130. A la carte. Smoked
salmon, steak, Belvoir pork,
chocolate mousse. E£££.

Ponte Vecchio ♦
73 Great Victoria St, BT2.
☎ 242402. 1700-2330
Mon-Sat, until 2200 Sun.
Pizzas, pasta. E££.

★ **RESTAURANT 44** ☐ ⊙
44 Bedford St, BT2.
☎ 244844. 1200-1500 &
1800-2300 Mon-Sat. Casserole
of shellfish, char-grilled fillet
of beef with gamba prawns &
orange butter sauce, garden
berry pudding. E£££.

Robinson's ☐
38 Great Victoria St, BT2.
☎ 247447. 1230-1430 &
1700-1930 Mon-Sat. Four
themed bars.

★ **ROSCOFF** ☐
Lesley House, Shaftesbury
Square, BT2. ☎ 331532.
1215-1415 Mon-Fri,
1830-2230 Mon-Sat. Sliced
duck breast with crispy confit,
sauté turbot & prawns,
chocolate soufflé with Black
Bush anglaise. M££. E£££.

Salvo's
117 Great Victoria St, BT2.
☎ 247891. 1700-2330
Mon-Sat. Pizza, pasta, fish,
chicken.

★ **SPERANZA** ☐
16 Shaftesbury Square, BT2.
☎ 230213. 1730-2330
Mon-Sat. Italian. Pizzas,
pasta.

Spires
Church House, Fisherwick
Place, Brunswick St, BT2.
☎ 312881. 0900-1730
Mon-Sat, until 2000 Thur.
Ulster fry, chicken, scampi.

BELFAST *Golden Mile*

Springfellows & Joxers
12 Brunswick St, BT2.
☎ 248398. 1130-2100
Mon-Sat. A la carte. E£.

Starlite Café
60 Great Victoria St, BT2.
1100-2400 Sun-Wed,
1100-1400 Thur-Sat. Fast
food.

Summer Palace
126 Great Victoria St, BT2.
☎ 439353. 1800-0100
Mon-Sat, until 2200 Sun.
Chinese. E££.

Tokyo Joe's Warehouse
9 Bruce St, BT2. ☎ 1800-2300
Wed-Sat. Pizzas, pasta,
desserts.

Vico's Refettorio
10 Brunswick St, BT2.
☎ 321447. 1230-1430
Mon-Sat & 1900-2200 Sun.
Italian. Pasta, veal, salads. ££.

BISHOPS
traditional
FISH & CHIPS
restaurant

Belfast's most popular
restaurant for tourists

A fare of fresh fish and
chips served in a
traditional atmosphere

Situated in the heart of
Belfast's nightlife, on the
Golden Mile
Opening Hours
11 am - 3 am
Mon - Sun
Takeaway service available
Bishops
Experience a taste of the past
34 Bradbury Place, Belfast
(opposite the Manhattan pub)

CUTTERS WHARF

Modern European Cuisine

Late bar Mon. - Sat.

All major credit cards accepted

Last meal orders
Mon. - Fri. noon - 10.30 pm
Sat. 6 pm - 10.30 pm
Sun. noon - 1.15 am

*Cutters Wharf, Lockview Road,
Stranmillis, Belfast.*
☎ *663388*

BELFAST

University and Malone *(BT7 & 9)* *(STD 01232)*

★ ANTICA ROMA ♀
67 Botanic Avenue, BT7.
☎ 311121. 1830-2300 Mon-Sat. Salad of mussels, squid, clams & garlic, escalope of veal with cheese & ham filling. E££.

★ ASHOKA ♀
363 Lisburn Rd, BT9.
☎ 660362. 1200-1400 Mon-Fri & 1730-2330 Mon-Thur, 2400 Fri-Sat, 1730-2230 Sun. Indian & European. E££.

Attic ♦
54 Stranmillis Rd, BT9.
☎ 661074. 1100-1500 & 1700-2230 Mon-Sat, 1100-1500 & 1630-2100 Sun. Steaks, chicken, fish.

Aubergines & Blue Jeans ♀
1 University St, BT7.
☎ 233700. 1930-2300 Mon-Sat & 1000-2200 Sun. Beggar's banquet, hot and spicy baguettes, speciality coffees. Bistro. No booking.

Balmoral Inn ♀
703 Lisburn Rd, BT9.
☎ 666109. 1200-2200 Mon-Sat. Pub grub.

Bamford's
353 Ormeau Rd, BT7.
☎ 491110. 0830-1730 Mon-Sat. Sandwiches, soup, stew.

★ BENGAL BRASSERIE ♀
339 Ormeau Rd, BT7.
☎ 647516. 1200-1400 Mon-Fri, 1730-2315 Mon-Sat, until 2215 Sun. European, Indian. A la carte. E££.

Bishops
7 Bradbury Place, BT7.
☎ 313547. 1700-0300 Mon-Sun. Roast chicken, burgers, baked potatoes.

★ BISHOPS RESTAURANT
34 Bradbury Place, BT7.
☎ 311827. 1100--0300 Mon-Sun. Kilkeel fish, chips, Ulster fry, salads.

BELFAST — *University and Malone*

Bleeckers ♆
42 Malone Rd, BT9.
☎ 663114. 1700-2330
Mon-Fri, 1200-2300 Sun.
American. Burgers, pasta. E£.

Bluebells
50 Botanic Avenue, BT7.
☎ 322662. 0800-2230
Mon-Sat, 1000-1800 Sun.
Ice cream desserts, quiche,
cappuccino coffee.

Bob Cratchit's ♆
Russell Court, 38 Lisburn Rd,
BT9. ☎ 332526. 1200-1900
Mon-Sat, 1230-1500 Sun.
Lasagne, club sandwich,
burgers. £.

Bonnie's Museum Café
11A Stranmillis Rd (opp. Ulster
Museum). ☎ 664914. 0900-
1730 Mon-Sun. Brunch,
fisherman's pie, paté, home-
made soup, homebaked
baguettes, herbal teas.

Bookfinders
47 University Rd, BT7.
☎ 328269. 1000-1730
Mon-Sat. Soup, toasties, pasta
with courgette chicken sauce.

Botanic Inn ♆
23 Malone Rd, BT9.
☎ 660460. 1200-1500
Mon-Sat, 1230-1430 Sun.
Pizzas, grills, pub grub.

ANTICA ROMA

RESTAURANT

NOW OPEN FOR LUNCH

67/69 Botanic Avenue, Belfast BT7 1JL
☎ 311121 Fax: 310787

University and Malone — **BELFAST**

Café Montmartre
102 Stranmillis Rd, BT9.
☎ 668032. 1100-2300
Mon-Sat. Fish & chips, grills.

Capers ☒
44 Bradbury Place, BT7.
☎ 247643. 1130-1430 &
1700-2330 Mon-Sat. Italian.
Pizzas, pasta, vegetarian
lasagne, curry. £.

Cargoes
613 Lisburn Rd, BT9.
☎ 665451. 0900-1700 Mon-
Sat. Mediterranean salads,
prawn paté, home-made
cinnamon scones, own salad
dressing. Café in delicatessen.

Chelsea ☒
346 Lisburn Rd, BT9.
☎ 665136. 1200-1800
Mon-Wed, until 2000
Thur-Sat, 1200-1430 Sun.
Pizza, salads, open
sandwiches.

★ CHEZ DELBART ☒
10 Bradbury Place, BT7.
☎ 238020. 1700-2400
Mon-Sat, until 2130 Sun.
French-owned bistro. Escalope
of pork with creamy mustard
sauce, mixed kebabs, savoury
& sweet pancakes. E££.

Chicago Pizza Pie Factory ☒
1 Bankmore Square,
Dublin Rd, BT7. ☎ 233555.
1200-2300 Mon-Thur, until
0100 Fri & Sat, 1200-2230
Sun. Pizza, burgers, salads.

Cincinnati Cooler Company
Botanic Avenue, BT7.
☎ 320570. 0800-2230
Mon-Sat, 1130-2130 Sun.
Home-made frozen yoghurts,
American apple pie.

Claire's
35 Botanic Avenue, BT7.
☎ 245321. 0745-1700
Mon-Sat. Quiche, lasagne.

★ CLARE CONNERY AT MALONE HOUSE ☺
Barnett Demesne, BT9.
☎ 681246. 1000-1630 Mon-
Sat. Coffee, lunch, afternoon
teas. Restored 19th-century
house overlooking Lagan
Valley.

Cloisters
Queen's University,
1 Elmwood Avenue, BT9.
☎ 245133. 0900-2100
Mon-Sat. Refectory in
student's union building.
Advance booking essential.

Conversations ☺
141 Stranmillis Rd, BT9.
☎ 664212. 0900-1700
Mon-Sat. Prawn salad, chilli,
banoffi, coffee.

Cutter's Wharf ☒
Lockview Rd, Stranmillis, BT9.
☎ 663388. Bar: 1200-1430
Mon-Sun. Irish stew, Ulster fry.
Restaurant: 1200-2230 Mon-
Fri, 1800-2230 Sat. Apple &
cheese flan, monkfish, mussels
& scampi. E££.

BELFAST

University and Malone

Dragon City
82 Botanic Avenue, BT7.
☎ 439590. 1200-2400
Mon-Sun, closed Wed.
Cantonese. £££.

Dragon Palace
16 Botanic Avenue, BT7.
☎ 323869. 1200-1400 &
1700-2400 Mon-Thur, until
0100 Fri & Sat, 2400 Sun.
Peking & European. £££.

★ **DUKES HOTEL**

65 University St, BT7.
☎ 236666. Last orders 2130.
Glenarm salmon, mushrooms
with guinness, beef sirloin
with Bushmills whiskey.
A la carte. £££.

Eglantine Inn
32 Malone Rd, BT9.
☎ 381994. 1200-2000
Mon-Sat. Pub grub, daily
special. £.

Elms
36 University Rd, BT7.
☎ 322106. 1100-1900
Mon-Sat. Champ, stew, ribs,
chilli. Live music.

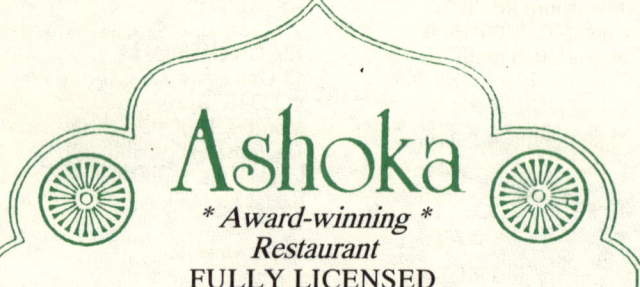

Ashoka
* Award-winning *
Restaurant
FULLY LICENSED

Meals served every day from 5.30 pm - 7 pm
Sunday all evening

Business Lunch £4.50 - Maharaja Lunch £6.95

à la carte menus also available • booking recommended
Opening hours: Mon-Fri 12 noon to 2 pm;
Mon-Sat 5.30 pm - 11.30 pm; Sun 5.30 pm - 10.30 pm

363/365 Lisburn Road, Belfast
☎ **(01232) 660362 - Fax: (01232) 660228**

University and Malone **BELFAST**

Empire ♀
42 Botanic Avenue, BT7.
☎ 328110. 1200-2000
Mon-Sat. Pizza, pasta. Bar in former variety theatre.

Errigle Inn ♀
320 Ormeau Rd, BT7.
☎ 641410. 1130-1500 & 1700-2330 Mon-Fri, 1130-2300 Sat, 1200-2200 Sun. Pub lunch, daily special. A la carte. Roof garden. Live music. E£.

The Fly ♀
5 Lower Crescent, BT7.
☎ 246878. 1200-1430 Mon-Sat. Soup, pub grub.

Four in Hand ♀
116 Lisburn Rd, BT9.
☎ 665440. 1200-1500 Mon-Fri. Pub grub.

★ FRENCH VILLAGE

70 Stranmillis Rd, BT9.
0915-1715 Mon-Sat.
Ploughman's lunch, gateaux.

★ FRIAR'S BUSH ♣

159 Stranmillis Rd, BT9.
☎ 669824. 1200-1430 Tues-Fri, 1830-2300 Thur-Sat. Terrine of wild venison, pork in cider, turbot.

Gigolo's Restaurant
23 Donegall Pass, BT7.
☎ 246900. 1230-1430, 1700-2330 Tues-Sat. Italian cuisine. ££.

Giovanni's ♀
27 University Rd, BT7.
☎ 439300. 1700-2300 Mon-Thur, until 2400 Fri & Sat, 1630-2100 Sun. Tagliatelli with tomato, chilli & garlic sauce, pizzas, steaks. E££.

Good World
627 Lisburn Rd, BT9.
☎ 666821. 1200-1400 Mon-Sat, 1700-2400 Mon-Thur & Sun, until 0100 Fri & Sat. Chinese & European. E£.

Graffiti
258 Ormeau Rd, BT7.
☎ 693300. 1000-2200 Mon-Sat, 1100-1500 Sun. Breakfast, pasta, steak, vegetarian.

The Greek Shop ♣
43 University Rd, BT7.
☎ 333135. 1200-1500 Mon-Fri, 1800-2200 Tues-Sat. Taramosalata, pikilia, sword fish kebabs, moussaka, baklava, Greek coffee. E£££

Hong Kong ♀
361 Ormeau Rd, BT7.
☎ 491621. 1200-1400 Mon-Sat, 1700-2400 Mon-Thur & Sun, 1700-0100 Fri. Peking, Cantonese & European. E£.

Isibeal's
699 Lisburn Rd, BT9.
☎ 682726. 1200-2400 Mon-Sat. Chicken, chips, sausages.

BELFAST
University and Malone

Jharna Tandoori ♀
133 Lisburn Rd, BT9.
☎ 381299. 1200-1400 &
1730-2330 Mon-Sat, 1700-
2330 Sun. Indian. E££.

Just Cooking
332 Lisburn Rd, BT7.
☎ 682810. 0900-1645 Mon-
Sat. Casseroles, home-made
soup, home-made wheaten
bread and scones.

Kentucky Fried Chicken
Bradbury Place, BT7.
☎ 325129. 1000-0230 Mon &
Tues, until 0400 Wed-Sat,
0300 Sun. Hamburgers, chips,
chicken, muffins.

King's Head ♀
Lisburn Rd, BT7. ☎ 660455.
1200-1430 Mon-Sat. Chilli,
lasagne, open sandwiches.
Opposite King's Hall. E££.

Lavery's ♀
12 Bradbury Place, BT7.
☎ 327159. 1200-1700
Mon-Fri, until 1400 Sat. Pub
grub.

Dempseys Terrace

RESTAURANT AND BAR

Enjoy the delightful surroundings of
Dempseys theme bars while sampling the
delicious menu - either for lunch or
evening meals.

A HOUSE OF PUBS

TASTY LUNCHES 12 NOON - 3 PM
EXCELLENT EVENING CUISINE FROM 5 PM
CATERING FOR EVERYONE'S TASTE

45 Dublin Road • Belfast • ☎ 234000

University and Malone **BELFAST**

Legends ♊
133 Lisburn Rd, BT9.
☎ 661652. 1730-2400
Mon-Sat, 1700-2300 Sun.
Pizza, pasta, steaks.

McDonald's
24 Bradbury Place, BT7.
☎ 332400. 1000-0200
Sun-Wed, 1000-0300
Thur-Sat. Hamburgers, french fries, milk shakes.

Mad Hatter
2 Eglantine Avenue, BT9.
☎ 681005. 0900-1715 Mon-Sat. Quiche, lasagne, gateaux.

Maharaja ♊
62 Botanic Avenue, BT7.
☎ 234200. 1200-1400
Mon-Sat, 1700-2345
Mon-Sat, until 2300 Sun.
Indian & European. E££.

Malone Lodge Hotel ♊ ☺
60 Eglantine Avenue, BT9.
☎ 382409. 1200-1400
Mon-Sat. Lunch, coffee.

Maloney's ♊
33 Malone Rd, BT9.
☎ 682929. 1230-1430 &
1730-2300 Mon-Sat,
1730-2200 Sun. Chicken breast stuffed with tiger prawns in a lobster & Cognac sauce, seafood tagliatelli. ££.

Mandarin Palace ♊
157 Upper Lisburn Rd, BT9.
☎ 622142. 1700-2300
Mon-Fri, until 0100 Sat & Sun.
Cantonese & European. E£.

The Manhattan ♊
23 Bradbury Place, BT7.
☎ 233131. 1200-2200
Mon-Sat. Clam chowder, cajun chicken. E£.

★ **MANOR HOUSE** ♊
47 Donegall Pass, BT7.
☎ 238755. 1200-1430, 1700-2400 Mon-Sat, until 1300-2400 Sun. Exotic Chinese, Cantonese. E£££.

Mortar Board ☺
3 Fitzwilliam St, BT9.
☎ 310313. 0900-1700
Mon-Sat, until 2300 Thur.
Salads, quiche, coffee.

New Jade Palace ♊
717 Lisburn Rd, BT9.
☎ 381116. 1200-1400 &
1700-2400 Tues-Fri, 1700-0030 Sat, 1600-2300 Sun.
Chinese, Cantonese & European. Set lunch Mon-Fri.
E££.

O'Hara's
3 Botanic Avenue, BT7.
☎ 326567. 0830-1730
Mon-Sat. Coffee shop in home bakery. Sandwiches, stew, pies.

Pavilion ♊
296 Ormeau Rd, BT9.
☎ 641545. 1200-1430 &
1700-2200 Mon-Sun. Grills, salads, set lunch. E£.

★ **PEPPERMILL**
112 Lisburn Rd, BT9.
☎ 666537. 0900-1700
Mon-Sat. Coffee, home-made pies, salads.

THE STRAND
12 STRANMILLIS ROAD
☎ *(01232) 682266*

The Original And Still The Best
OPEN 7 DAYS PER WEEK
We serve food from
12 Noon - 11.30 pm

LUNCH & TEA-TIME COMPLETE MEAL ONLY £4.25
Served Mon. - Fri. 12 noon to 7 pm
Sat. 12 noon to 7 pm

BOTTLE OF HOUSE WINE
(Moreau Select) Only £6.25

SUNDAY BRUNCH £5.95
• To Start •
Glass of Bucks Fizz
• To Follow •
Smoked Salmon with Scrambled Eggs
or
Ulster Fry
or
Eggs Benedict on Toasted Muffins with Bacon
• To accompany the above •
Tea or Coffee with Toast, Butter and Preserves

Full à la Carte menu also available
** Egon Ronay Recommended 1985-1994 **

THE BRITANNIC

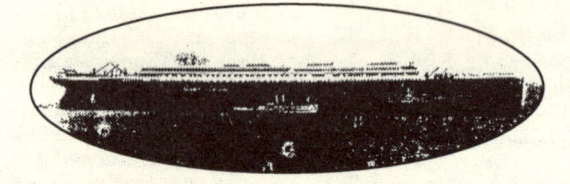

The White Star Liners renowned for passenger comfort

Only the very wealthy could avail themselves of the luxury which today's Britannic Lounge recreates using furnishing and superb woodwork restored when the ship was stripped in 1915. Enjoy a meal and a drink in the splendour of the Golden Age of Ship Building.

You won't sail into New York Harbour but then neither did the Britannic

University and Malone **BELFAST**

Pierre Victoire
30 University Rd, BT7.
☎ 315151. 1200-1500, 1800-2300 Mon-Sat. ££.

Queen's Espresso
17 Botanic Avenue, BT7.
☎ 325327. 0900-1730 Mon-Sat. Grills, salads, toasties, coffee.

Queen's University
Great Hall, University Rd, BT7. ☎ 245133. 1015-1130 & 1200-1400 Mon-Fri. Lunch, coffee, afternoon tea.

Rajput Indian Cuisine
461 Lisburn Rd, BT9.
☎ 662168. 1200-1400 & 1700-2400 Mon-Sat, 1700-2300 Sun. Indian. Set meals, à la carte. £££.

Regency Hotel
13 Lower Crescent, BT7.
☎ 323349. Last orders 2400. Set lunch, high tea. £££.

Renshaws Hotel
75 University St. ☎ 333366. Last orders 2230. A la carte. ££.

Ruby Tuesday's
629A Lisburn Rd, BT9.
☎ 661220. 0815-1915 Mon-Fri, until 1715 Sat & Sun. Breakfast, Ulster fry, chicken, pasta, salads.

★ **SAINTS & SCHOLARS**
3 University St, BT7.
☎ 325137. 1200-2300 Mon-Sat, 1200-1430 & 1730-2130 Sun. Alsace onion flan, wok-roasted monkfish, chicken bourride. £££.

Spuds
37 Bradbury Place, BT7.
☎ 331541. 1000-0100 Mon-Sun. Baked potatoes, lasagne, chips with bolognese sauce & cheese, burgers.

Stables Restaurant
Upper Malone Rd (beside Lady Dixon Park). ☎ 601087. 1000-1730 Mon-Sun. Light lunches, peppered pork, stew, home-made soup.

★ **STRAND**
12 Stranmillis Rd, BT9.
☎ 682266. 1200-2330 Mon-Sat, 1200-1500 & 1900-2200 Sun. Irish lamb noisettes, baked aubergine stuffed with minced steak, apple, nuts & raisins. ££.

Taj Mahal
96 Botanic Avenue, BT7.
☎ 313999. 1730-2230 Mon-Sat, 1730-2300 Sun. Indian food, garlic chilli chicken, chicken in orange sauce, spinach leaves and cheese. ££.

BELFAST — *University and Malone*

Tea House
245 Lisburn Rd, BT9.
☎ 382211. 1000-1615 Mon-Sat. Coffee, speciality teas, lasagne, open sandwiches, muffins. Café below bookshop.

Terrace ♀
255 Lisburn Rd, BT9.
☎ 381655. Wine bar bistro: 1900-2130 Mon-Sat. Restaurant: 1200-1500 & 1800-2300 Mon-Sun. Smoked salmon, brill with prawns & dill butter, stuffed duck. £££.

Three Bears
455 Ormeau Rd, BT7.
☎ 491636. 0900-1630 Mon-Sat. Shepherd's pie, quiche, open sandwiches, banoffi pie. Café above fashion shop. £.

TL2 Restaurant
157 Stranmillis Rd, BT9.
☎ 667749. 1200-1530, 1700-2330 Mon-Sat, 1700-2100 Sun. Steaks, beef, salad with raspberry dressing, pastrami salad, seafood dishes. ££.

Ulster Museum ☺
11A Stranmillis Rd, BT9.
☎ 381251. 1000-1630 Mon-Sat, 1430-1630 Sun. Lasagne, chicken tikka, pies, curries.

★ **VILLA ITALIA** ♀
39 University Rd, BT7.
☎ 328356. 1730-2330 Mon-Fri, 1600-2330 Sat, 1600-2230 Sun. Italian. Pizzas, pasta, steaks. ££.

★ **WELCOME** ♀
22 Stranmillis Rd, BT9.
☎ 381359. 1200-1400 & 1700-2330 Mon-Fri, 1730-2300 Sat & Sun. Cantonese, Hong Kong & European. £££.

Wellington Park Hotel ♀
21 Malone Rd, BT9.
☎ 381111. Last orders 2145. Dressed crab, prawns, steaks. £££.

York Hotel ♀
59 Botanic Avenue, BT7.
☎ 329304. Last orders 2030. A la carte. ££.

BELFAST

East of the River
(BT4-6, 8, 16 & 23)
(STD 01232)

Avenue One ♀
175 Newtownards Rd, BT4.
☎ 455608. 1130-1500, 1700-2200 Mon-Sat. Pub grub.

Avoniel Leisure Centre
Avoniel Rd, BT5. ☎ 451564.
1030-2200 Mon-Fri, 1000-1600 Sat & Sun. Chilli, sandwiches, home baking.

Barclay ♀
Milltown Hill, Shaws Bridge, BT8. ☎ 491203. 1200-1445, 1700-2200 Mon-Thur, 1700-2345 Fri-Sat, 1200-2030 Sun. A la carte, Carvery. E££.

Beechill Inn ♀
Cedarhurst Rd, BT8.
☎ 693193. 1130-2300 Mon-Sat, until 2130 Thur-Sat, 1230-1430 & 1900-2200 Sun. A la carte, set meals. E££.

Belfast City Airport ♀
Airport Rd, BT3.
☎ 457745. 0515-1900 7 days. All day breakfast, lunch, snacks.

Belmont ♀
295 Upper Newtownards Rd, BT4. ☎ 652295. 1230-1430 Mon-Sat. Pub grub.

Bethany
246 Newtownards Rd, BT4.
☎ 54498. 1130-2245 Mon-Fri, until 1945 Sat. Fish & chips.

Castle
152 Castlereagh Rd, BT5.
☎ 731461. 1200-1400 & 1600-2245 Mon-Thur, 1200-2245 Fri & Sat. Grills.

Cedars Coffee House
334 Beersbridge Rd, BT5.
☎ 457201. 0900-1730 Mon-Sat. Quiche, lasagne, shepherd's pie.

Chatters Coffee House
64 Bloomfield Avenue, BT5.
☎ 731654. 0930-1645 Mon-Sat. Coffee, scones, lunch.

Coffee Corner
2 Castlereagh Rd, BT5.
☎ 732522. 0930-1600 Mon-Sat, closed Wed. Coffee, cake, lunch.

Coffee Pot
340 Newtownards Rd, BT4.
☎ 655415. 0830-1600 Mon-Sat, until 1330 Wed, 1630 Sat. Soup, stew, desserts.

Maloney's
Est. 1991

33/35 Malone Road, Belfast BT9 6RU
Open for lunch and evening meal
FULLY LICENSED
*

The in-place in town to eat out
*

Phone NOW for reservations
*

Live entertainment Friday & Saturday Night

TELEPHONE (01232) 682929

MAXWELLS

Fully licensed restaurant offering

Fantastic food

Fine wines

Friendly service

ALL AT REASONABLE PRICES
- PRIVATE FUNCTION ROOM - FOR ALL OCCASIONS
- PRIVATE CAR PARK • CHILDREN WELCOME

Restaurant opening hours:-

Business lunch   12.00 pm - 2.30 pm
Dinner   6.30 pm - 10 pm
Bar snacks available during these hours

60 Eglantine Avenue, Belfast
☎ **(01232) 382409**

Cosy Bar 🍷
44 Omeath St, BT6.
☎ 458178. 1930-2430 Thur-Sat. Pub grub. Set lunches.

Desano's
344 Newtownards Rd, BT4.
☎ 451608. 1200-2000 Tues, Thur & Fri-Sun in summer, Fri-Sun only in winter. Ice cream parlour.

Dundonald Ice Bowl
Dundonald, BT16.
☎ 482611. Burgers, chips. Café: 1400-2200 Mon-Thur, 1000-2200 Fri-Sun.

★ DUNDONALD OLD MILL

231 Belfast Rd, Dundonald, BT16. ☎ 480117.
1000-1715 Mon-Sat, 1100-1715 Sun. Home baking, quiche, lasagne, pastries. Waterwheel & craft shop.

★ THE EASTENDER 🍷

237 Woodstock Rd, BT6.
☎ 732443. 1130-2330 Mon-Sat. Baked ham with black velvet sauce, champ, home-made soup.

Eda Inn 🍷
41 Belmont Rd, BT4.
☎ 658810. 1700-2330 Mon-Sun. Chinese & European. E££.

★ ELK INN 🍷

793 Upper Newtownards Rd, Dundonald, BT16.
☎ 480004. 1130-2200 Mon-Sat. Irish hot pot, baked gammon, roast duck, banoffi. E££.

★ FILLERS COFFEE SHOP

233 Saintfield Rd, BT8.
☎ 701409. 1000-1730 Mon-Sat, until 1900 Thur & Fri. Lasagne, salads, apple pie, coffee.

Four Winds Inn 🍷
111 Newton Park, Saintfield Rd, BT8. ☎ 401957.
1200-1430 & 1900-2200 Mon-Sat, closed Xmas & Easter. Hot & cold lunch buffet, evening à la carte. Open fires. M£, E£££.

Fusco's
369 Woodstock Rd, BT6.
☎ 458736. 1030-2130 Mon-Sun. Italian. Ice cream.

Gardener's Rest
Hillmount Nursery Centre, Upper Braniel Rd, BT5.
☎ 448213. 0900-1645 Mon-Sat, 1400-1700 Sun. Coffee, lunch.

Golden Bloom
47 Comber Rd, BT16.
☎ 798661. 0830-1730 Mon-Sat. Stew, curry, soup, pies. Café in cake shop.

BELFAST

East of the River

Hillmount Nursery Centre
56 Upper Braniel Rd, BT5.
☎ 448213. 0900-1700 Mon-Sat, 1400-1700 Sun. Pies, pasties, soup, sandwiches.

Holly's
74 Holywood Rd, BT4.
☎ 653345. 0830-1630 Mon-Sat, until 2200 Thur-Sat. Chicken & ham pie, steaks, chicken maryland.

Hong Kong ♃
9 King's Square, BT5.
☎ 792560. 1700-2400 Mon-Sun, until 0100 Fri & Sat. Chinese & European. Set lunch, dinner Mon-Thur. E£.

La Mon House Hotel ♃
41 Gransha Rd, BT23.
☎ 448631. Last orders 2200 Mon-Sat, 2100 Sun. Buffet lunch, carvery Sun. A la carte. M£, E£££.

Leaf & Berry
516 Upper Newtownards Rd, BT4. ☎ 471774. 0930-1630 Mon-Fri, 1000-1600 Sat. Speciality coffees, lunch. Self-service.

★ **Mr J.D.'S**
222 Newtownards Rd, BT4.
☎ 458383. 1130-1900 Mon-Sat. Fish & chips.

Mr Pickwick's Kitchen
Connswater Shopping Centre, BT5. ☎ 459965. 0900-1730 Mon-Sat, until 2100 Wed-Fri. Baked potatoes, Irish stew, doughnuts.

Melting Pot ♃
38 Mountpottinger Rd, BT5.
☎ 454080. 1200-1430 Mon-Sat. Pub grub.

Morton & Simpson ☻
Breda Shopping Centre, BT8.
☎ 491795. 0900-1630 Mon-Sat. Sandwiches, soup, champ.

Neighbours Coffee Shop
10 Cregagh Rd, BT6.
1030-1630 Mon-Sat. Lasagne, home-made pies, curries.

Nuts in May
24 Belmont Rd, BT4.
☎ 471109. 0930-1730 Mon-Sat. Coffee, scones, home-made biscuits in health food store.

Old Moat Inn ♃
993 Upper Newtownards Rd, BT4. ☎ 480753. 1200-1500 & 1800-2130 Mon-Sat. Lasagne, quiche, set lunch. Bistro menu. £.

Park Avenue Hotel ♃
Holywood Rd, BT4.
☎ 656520. Last orders 2030, Sun 1930. Closed Xmas. Smoked salmon, grilled halibut. A la carte. E££.

East of the River **BELFAST**

Peking House
374 Upper Newtownards Rd, BT4. ☎ 671033. 1200-1400 & 1700-2400 Mon-Sat, 1630-2400 Sun. Cantonese & European. E££.

Piggly Wigglys
Library Court, 3 Eastleigh Drive, Upper Newtownards Rd, BT4. ☎ 672114. 0930-1700 Mon-Sat. Feuilleté of lentils, marinated rabbit, guinea fowl with lemon grass.

Pizza House
991 Upper Newtownards Rd, BT16. ☎ 482533. 1200-1400 & 1700-2300 Mon-Sun. Indian & European.

Poppins Restaurant
241 Upper Newtownards Rd, BT4. ☎ 671893. 0900-1630 Mon-Sat. Pies, quiche, pizza.

Quarry Inn
Quarry Corner, Upper Newtownards Rd, BT4. ☎ 480492. 1200-1500 Mon-Sun, 1800-2130 Mon-Sat, 1230-1930 Sun. Carvery, bistro. E££.

Queen's Inn
King's Square, King's Rd, BT5. ☎ 792395. 1200-1430 Mon-Sat, 1700-1900 Fri & Sat. Set lunch, pub grub.

Rendezvous
443 Newtownards Rd, BT4. ☎ 451100. 0900-1600 Mon-Sat. Set lunch, home-baked pies, salads.

Ritchie's
142 Castlereagh Rd, BT5. ☎ 457318. 1200-1400 & 1630-1900 Mon-Sat. Fish & chips.

Robinson Centre
Montgomery Rd, BT6. ☎ 703948. 1000-2200 Mon-Fri, 1000-1800 Sat, 1400-1800 Sun. Pasta, chicken kiev, potato skins, salads.

Rose Bowl
59 Belmont Rd, BT4. ☎ 652895. 0930-1630 Mon-Sat. Soup, sandwiches, quiche.

Rosetta
75 Rosetta Rd, BT6. ☎ 649297. 1230-1430 Mon-Sat, 1900-2100 Thur-Sat. Pub grub.

Scoffs Coffee House
52 Bloomfield Avenue, BT5. ☎ 450183. 0800-1730 Mon-Sat. Honey-glazed Ulster ham, champ, variety of home-made scones.

Shanghai
18 Holywood Rd, BT4. ☎ 650400. 1200-1400 Mon-Sat, 1700-2400 Mon-Sun. Chinese & European. Set lunch.

Silver Leaf
15 Belmont Rd, BT4. ☎ 471164. 1200-1400 & 1600-2230 Mon-Fri, 1600-2000 Sat. Fish & chips, charcoal grills.

BELFAST

East of the River

★ STORMONT HOTEL ♀
587 Upper Newtownards Rd, BT4. ☎ 658621. Last orders 2130. Brasserie: salads, open sandwiches. A la carte. £££token£.

Stormont Inn ♀
165 Holywood Rd, BT4. ☎ 654509. 1230-1500 Mon-Sat. Pub grub.

Trafalgar
139 Bloomfield Avenue, BT4. ☎ 451130. 1600-2300 Mon-Sat, until 1830 Wed. Pies, fish & chips.

Wellworths
1009 Upper Newtownards Rd, BT16. ☎ 481118. 0900-1700 Mon-Sat, until 2100 Wed-Fri. Daily specials, hamburgers, sausage & bacon. Restaurant in chainstore.

Willows
273 Woodstock Rd, BT6. ☎ 458210. 0900-1645 Mon-Sat. Toasties, salad, chips, coffee.

BELFAST

North and West of the River
(BT10-15 & 17)
(STD 01232)

Alexandra ☷
1 York Rd, BT15. ☏ 742838. 1230-1430 Thurs-Sat, 1900-2200 Sat. Pub grub.

American Bar ☷
65 Dock St, BT15.
☏ 747494. 1130-2300 Mon-Sat, 1230-1430 Sun. Pub grub.

Anchor
150 Sandy Row, BT12.
☏ 231415. 0830-1700 Mon-Sat. Soup, stew, home-made ice cream.

Andersonstown Leisure Centre
Andersonstown Rd, BT11.
☏ 625211. 1100-2200 Mon-Fri, until 1600 Sat & Sun. Chilli, sandwiches, home baking.

Arnie's
Balmoral Fruit Market, Boucher Rd, BT12. ☏ 663282. 0600-1500 Mon-Sat. Champ, roasted ham shank, home-made broth, Arnie's fry, Chinese chicken.

Balmoral Hotel ☷
Blacks Rd, BT10. ☏ 301234.
Grill bar: 1130-2300 Mon-Sat. Steak, chicken, fish.
Restaurant: last orders 2200. A la carte. E£.

Bay Leaf
Park Centre, Donegall Rd, BT12. ☏ 235773.
0900-1800 Mon, Tues & Sat, 0900-2100 Wed-Fri. Set lunch, grills, snacks.

Beattie's Supper Saloon
220 Shankill Rd, BT13.
☏ 240273. 0930-1830 Mon-Sat. Ulster fry, fish & chips.

Beechmount Leisure Centre
281 Falls Rd, BT11. ☏ 328631.
1200-1500 & 1800-2100 Mon-Fri, 1000-1500 Sat & Sun. Chips, burgers.

Stage Coach Inn

Enjoy the Olde Worlde experience in our Fully Licensed Restaurant and Bars.

Come along and sample the fine cuisine of our à la carte and table d'hote menus.

Private parties and business meetings catered for.

52 Queensway, Derriaghy, Dunmurry.
☎ (01232) 625141

BELFAST PARKS

Cave Hill
Heritage Centre

The centre highlights various aspects of the Cave Hill area with static, moving and interactive displays which include:

* A Walk in the Country Park
* The View from the Hill
* Wish You were Here

ARCHAEOLOGY - INDUSTRY
FOLKLORE - WILDLIFE
HISTORY - RECREATION

Open Daily
Apr - Sep 9 am - 9 pm
Oct - Mar 9 am - 6 pm
   Sundays 9 am - 6 pm

All at Belfast Castle
Antrim Road
BELFAST
☎ 776925

CAVE HILL COUNTRY PARK

Belfast City Council, Parks and Amenities Section

North and West of the River **BELFAST**

★ BELFAST CASTLE ♀

Antrim Rd, BT15. ☎ 776925. On slopes of Cave Hill. Ben Madigan restaurant: 1230-1430 Sun. Lunch. Afternoon tea 1100-1700 Sun. Cellar restaurant: 1100-2300 Mon-Sat. Carrot & orange soup with croutons, grilled salmon with cajun spices & lime & sour cream dip. E£££.

Belfast Zoo

Antrim Rd, BT15.
☎ 776277. Ark Restaurant: 1000-1730 Mon-Sun summer, 1000-1600 winter. Plaice, chicken nuggets, sandwiches. Mountain Tea House: 1030-1700 Mon-Sun Easter-Aug, weekends only Sept, closed winter. Sandwiches, ice cream, gateaux.

Bellybusters

50 Park Shopping Centre, BT12. ☎ 243534.
0900-1730 Mon-Sat. Burgers, fish, chips, chicken.

Ben Madigan ♀

192 Cavehill Rd, BT15.
☎ 391071. 1230-1500 Mon-Sat. Lunch. £. Pub grub.

Big Boppers Inn

118 Antrim Rd, BT15.
☎ 752022. 1900-2300 Fri & Sat, 1200-1500 & 2100-0130 Sun. Rest. Beef stroganoff, roast chicken, fish. E£.

Blackstaff Bar ♀

149 Springfield Rd, BT12.
☎ 324355. 1200-1500 & 1700-2000 Mon-Sat. Pub grub. £.

Broadway Bar ♀

196 Falls Rd, BT12. ☎ 247651. 1200-1430 & 1700-2000 Mon-Sat. Scampi, chicken, lasagne.

The Burger Bar

119 Andersonstown Rd, BT11.
☎ 611465. 1200-2400 Mon-Wed & Sun, until 0100 Thur-Sat. Burgers, fish, chicken, sausages.

Burger King

Yorkgate, York St, BT15.
☎ 746060. 0900-2400 Mon-Thurs, 0900-0100 Fri-Sat, 1400-2300 Sun. Hamburgers, fries, fishburgers, vegetarian burgers.

Cagney's Bar ♀

39 Falls Rd, BT12. ☎438196. 1200-1500 Mon-Sat. Pub grub.

Chester Park ♀

466 Antrim Rd, BT15.
☎ 770811. 1200-1430 Mon-Fri, 1800-2200 Mon-Sat, 1230-1430 & 1900-2100 Sun. Set lunch, home-made soup, steaks. £.

BELFAST
North and West of the River

China City ♀
5 Glen Rd, BT11. ☎ 600115.
1700-2400 Thur-Sun, 0100
Fri-Sat. Peking & Cantonese
food. £.

Circus Bar ♀
10 Antrim Rd, BT15.
1200-1500 Mon-Sat. Salads,
lasagne.

Coffee House
132 Andersonstown Rd, BT11.
☎ 617155. 0830-1730 Mon-
Sat. Quiche, lasagne, pies.

Concepts ◯
100 York St, BT15.
☎ 743873. 1000-1800 Mon &
Tues, until 2100 Wed-Fri,
0900-1800 Sat. Baked
potatoes, quiche.

Cosy Grill
81 Upper Lisburn Rd, Finaghy,
BT10. ☎ 613555. 0930-2000
Mon-Sat. Coffee, grills. E£.

Country Fayre
294 Limestone Rd, BT15.
☎ 740919. 0900-1630 Mon-
Sat. Ulster fry, grills, coffee.

Devenish Arms ♀
37 Finaghy Rd North, BT10.
☎ 301479. 1900-2200 Fri-Sun,
1230-1430 Sun.
A la carte. E£.

Devine's
297 Antrim Rd, BT15.
☎ 747604. 0900-1800
Mon-Sat. Sandwiches, Irish
stew.

Diamond Jubilee ♀
150 Peters Hill, BT13.
☎ 325352. 1200-1500 Sat,
1900-2200 evenings. Pub
grub.

Dicey Reilly's ♀
123 New Lodge Rd, BT15.
☎ 323631. 1300-1530 Wed-
Sat, 1200-1630 Sun. Light
meals, pub grub, champ, stew.

Ed's Bread
6 Shaw's Rd, BT11.
☎ 612077. 0900-1700
Mon-Sat. Irish stew, pasties,
sandwiches.

Fortwilliam Lodge ♀
2 Fortwilliam Park, BT15.
☎ 370537. 1030-1800
Mon-Sat. Quiche, coffee,
home-baked bread, cakes.

Francie's ♀
12 Ardoyne Ave, BT14.
☎ 742325. 1200-1500 Mon-
Sat, 1800-2330 Wed-Sat,
1230-1400, 1900-2100 Sun.
Pub grub.

Gallery
333 Crumlin Rd, BT14.
☎ 745408. 0900-1500
Mon-Thur, until 1400 Fri.
Toasties, soup, burgers.

Glenowen Inn ♀
108 Glen Rd, BT11.
☎ 613224. 1130-2230
Mon-Sat, 1230-1500 &
1900-2200 Sun. Set meals.
E££.

BELFAST
North and West of the River

Glenview Arms ♀
167 Oldpark Rd, BT14.
☎ 745455. 1200-1400 Wed, Sat, Sun. Pub grub.

Golden Bloom
124 Upper Lisburn Rd, BT10.
☎ 798661. 0800-1730 Mon-Sat. Pizzas, quiche, pies.

Goodman's Ice Cream Parlour
129 Andersonstown Rd, BT11.
☎ 603303. 1200-2200 Mon-Fri, 1000-2200 Sat & Sun. Fudge cake, ice cream, hot scones, coffee.

Gourmet Foods
648 Antrim Rd, BT15.
☎ 778263. 0800-1900 Mon-Fri. Moussaka, roast beef, lamb.

Grove Leisure Centre
Grove Cafeteria, North Queen St, BT15. ☎ 351599. 0900-2100 Mon-Fri, 1000-1600 Sat-Sun. Salads, lasagnes, chips, fries, grills.

Grove Tavern ♀
203 York Rd, BT15.
☎774295. 1230-1430 Mon-Sat. Pub grub.

Hawthorne House
Fulton's Fine Furnishings, Boucher Crescent, BT12.
☎ 382168. 0930-1730 Mon-Sat, until 2100 Thur. Salmon, chicken & broccoli bake, home-baked scones.

Jamaica Inn ♀
69 Jamaica St, BT14.
☎ 747112. 1900-2100 Mon-Fri, 1200-1400 Mon-Sat. Pub grub.

Laurel Glen Road House ♀
Dairy Farm Lane,
208 Stewartstown Rd, BT11.
☎ 601737. 1200-1500 Mon-Sat, 1230-1400 Sun. Pub grub, Ulster fry, soup.

★ **LONG'S FISH RESTAURANT**

39 Athol St, BT12.
☎ 321848. 1145-1830 Mon-Fri. Traditional fish & chips.

McErlean's
456 Antrim Rd, BT15.
☎ 370759. 0830-1730 Mon-Fri, 0900-1700 Sat. Cornish pasties, curries, Ulster fry.

Mile Cafeteria
351 Shankill Rd, BT13.
☎ 322439. 1000-2200 Mon-Fri, 1000-1800 Sat. Salads, pizzas, Ulster fry.

Moby Dick
Dargan Rd, BT3. ☎ 776208. 0800-1630 Mon-Fri. Sausage, eggs, daily special.

Mount Inn ♀
156 North Queen St, BT15.
☎ 741769. 1200-1500 Mon-Sat. Set lunch.

BELFAST
North and West of the River

Muldoon's ♀
13 Corporation Square.
☎ 232415. 1200-1500
Mon-Sat. Burgers, salads, fish, pies.

NG's
Ballysillan Leisure Centre, 71 Ballysillan Rd, BT14.
☎ 391040. 1000-2200 Mon-Fri, until 1600 Sat, 1100-1700 Sun. Pies, stew, sandwiches.

Olympia Leisure Centre
Boucher Rd, BT12.
☎ 233369. 1000-1400 & 1600-2200 Mon-Fri, 1000-1600 Sat. 1200-1800 Sun. Ulster fry, coffee.

Opels Recreation Centre
41 Suffolk Rd, BT11.
☎ 601386. 0900-2100 Mon-Fri. Pizza, soup, desserts.

Orpheus ♀
59 York St, BT15. ☎ 238967.
1200-1430 & 1600-1800 Mon-Sat. Pub grub.

Patio
Kennedy Centre, 564 Falls Rd, BT12. ☎ 628118. 0900-2000 Mon-Fri, 0900-1730 Sat, 1100-1730 Sun. Home-made pies, lasagne, burgers.

Piper
17 York Rd, BT15.
☎ 749545. 0830-2230 Mon-Fri, until 1900 Sat. Bacon rolls, egg soda, spicy pork, fish & chips.

Portside Inn ♀
Dargan Rd, BT3. ☎ 370746.
1200-1800 Mon-Fri, 1200-1500 Sat. Grills, salads. £.

Red Barn Barbeque
127 Andersonstown Rd, BT11.
☎ 625558. 1200-0030 Mon-Sun. Fish & chips, pasties.

Robert Stewart's Spirit Grocers ♀
149 Ballyskeagh Rd, BT17.
☎ 629779. 1200-1430, 1700-2000 Mon-Sat. 1230-1430 Sun. Pub grub. £.

Rock Bar ♀
491 Falls Rd, BT12. ☎ 323741.
1200-2200 Mon-Sat. Pub grub. £.

Rocktown Bar ♀
120 Great Georges St, BT15.
☎ 242414. 1200-1430 Mon-Sat. Pub grub.

Rosebank Tavern ♀
Rosebank Enterprise Park, Flax St, BT14. ☎ 753329.
1200-1430, 1700-2100 Fri & Sat. Soup, Irish stew, toasties, grills.

Saltshaker Centre
174 Antrim Rd, BT15.
☎ 747114. 1000-1700 Mon-Sat. Grills, burgers, chilli.

Sandwich Choice
Unit 9A, Hillview Trade Centre, Crumlin Rd, BT14.
☎ 740759. 0900-1630 Mon-Fri. Salads, filled rolls, bacon sodas.

North and West of the River **BELFAST**

Shaftesbury Inn
739 Antrim Rd, BT15.
☎ 370015. 1200-1600 Mon-Sat, 1700-2100 Mon-Thur, until 2200, Fri & Sat. Beef stroganoff, carvery, salads. E£.

Shankill Leisure Centre
Shankill Rd, BT13.
☎ 241434. 1000-2200 Mon-Fri, 1000-1600 Sat & Sun. Burgers, salads, stew.

Sliabh Dubh
179 Whiterock Rd, BT11.
☎ 311916. 1200-2130 Mon-Sat, 1230-1400 & 1900-2100 Sun. Pub grub.

Somerton Inn
1 Somerton Rd, BT15.
☎ 778016. 1200-1500 Mon-Sat. Chicken, scampi.

Three Kegs Inn
Boucher Rd, BT12. ☎ 664018. 1130-1430 Mon-Sat. Pizzas, grills.

Traversa
151 Upper Lisburn Rd, Finaghy, BT10. ☎ 603322. 1200-1400 & 1700-0100 Mon-Thur, until 0200 Fri, 1700-0200 Sat, until 0100 Sun. Pizzas, burgers, pasta.

Trinity Lodge
2 Monagh Grove, BT11.
☎ 603733. 1230-2130 Mon-Sat. Pub grub.

Tudor Coffee House
123 Falls Rd, BT12. ☎ 231035. 0800-1700 Mon-Sat. Home-made vegetable soup, Ulster fry, gammon, shepherd's pie, Danish pastries.

Tudor Lodge
778 Shore Rd, BT15.
☎ 777017. 1200-2100 Mon-Sat, 1200-1400 Sun. Chicken kiev, scampi, home-made pies. £

Village Tavern
165 Ligoniel Rd, BT14.
☎ 715328. 1200-1430 Mon-Sat, 1900-2130 Fri-Sat. Pub grub.

Whitefort Inn
67 Andersonstown Rd, BT11.
☎ 600243. 1200-1700 Mon-Wed, 1200-1900 Thur-Sat. Pub grub.

Whiterock Leisure Centre
195 Whiterock Rd, BT12.
☎ 233239. 1000-2100 Mon-Fri, 1000-1700 Sat & Sun. Soup, sandwiches, pies.

THE OLD SCHOOLHOUSE

DINE IN INTIMATE SURROUNDINGS & ENJOY FIRST CLASS FRENCH CUISINE IN OUR CHARMING CENTURY-OLD SCHOOLHOUSE WITH THE ATMOSPHERE ENHANCED BY A TRADITIONAL OPEN TURF FIRE

106 BALLYROBIN ROAD, MUCKAMORE, CO ANTRIM BT41 4TF
(NEAR AIRPORT)

ANTRIM

☎ **(01849) 428209**

Knockagh Lodge

RESTAURANT LOUNGE
CONSERVATORY
FUNCTION SUITE

OPEN 7 DAYS A WEEK

LUNCHES • BAR SNACKS
EVENING MEALS
WEDDINGS and FUNCTIONS
CATERED FOR

Panoramic views from our new conservatory are among the most breathtaking in the area

236 UPPER ROAD,
CARRICKFERGUS

☎ (01232) 861444/852930
Fax: (01232) 869911

FURAMA

Cantonese Restaurant

NO.1 FOR CANTONESE CUISINE

Why not treat yourself to a delicious meal in our luxury restaurant
Our proprietor Mr Chan selects our food daily to ensure maximum freshness

DISHES MADE TO ORDER

Sit-in or take-away service available

**ENJOY SUNDAY LUNCH
THREE-COURSE MEAL £5.30
FROM 1 pm - 3 pm**

Opening hours:
Mon - Thur 12 noon - 2 pm and 5 pm - 11.30 pm
Friday 12 noon - 2 pm and 5 pm - 12.30 am
Saturday 5 pm - 12.30 am
Sun 1 pm - 3 pm and 5 pm - midnight

**68 CHURCH STREET,
ANTRIM**
☎ **(01849) 465585**

MADDENS BAR
and restaurant

**Meals served daily
11.30 am - 3.30 pm**

Entertainment & late bars

Wednesday - Disco
and Late Bars

Thursday - Disco
and Late Bars

Friday - Live Band

Saturday - Disco
and Late Bars

**51 High Street,
Antrim, Co Antrim**

COUNTY ANTRIM

AHOGHILL
(STD 01266)

Diamond Bar ♀
17 The Diamond.
☎ 871251. 1200-1400
Mon-Sat. Pub grub.

Fair Hill Tavern ♀
29 Church St. ☎ 871223.
1130-1530 Mon-Sat, 1230-1430 Sun. Pub grub.

ALDERGROVE

Food Court ♀
Belfast International Airport.
☎ (01849) 453630.
0630-2200 Mon-Sun.
Hot & cold buffet, burger bar, salad bar, snacks, pastries. Self-service.

Aldergrove Airport Hotel ♀
☎ (018494) 22033. 1800-2400
Mon-Sun. French. E££.

White Horse Inn ♀
20 Dungonnell Rd.
☎ (018494) 28341.
1930-2230 Fri & Sat,
1230-1430 Sun. Steaks, chicken, duck. E£.

ANTRIM
(STD 01849)

Bailiwick Inn ♀
Market Square. ☎ 428807.
1200-1800 Mon-Wed, until 2000 Thur-Sat. Pub grub.

Castle Grill
Castle Centre. ☎ 468151.
0930-1700 Mon-Wed & Sat,
0930-2030 Thur & Fri. Snacks.

Deerpark Hotel ♀
71 Dublin Rd. ☎ 462480.
Last orders 2100 Mon-Sat,
2015 Sun. Sunday high tea.
A la carte. E£££.

Dunsilly Arms ♀
20 Dunsilly Rd. ☎ 466129.
1200-1400 Mon-Fri,
1700-2330 Mon-Thur, 0030
Fri-Sat.

Furama ♀
66 Church St. ☎ 465585.
1200-1400 Mon-Fri, 1700-2330 Mon-Thur, 0030 Fri-Sat,
1300-1500 & 1700-2400 Sun.

Galley
Antrim Arcade, High St.
0900-1730 Mon-Wed & Sat.
Fish, chicken.

Co. ANTRIM

Griddle
Castle Shopping Centre.
☎ 461193. 0900-1730
Mon-Wed & Sat, until 2130
Thur & Fri. Grills, pastries.

Hong Kong ☒
69 Church St. ☎ 428513.
1200-1400 & 1700-0030
Mon-Wed, 1200-0030 Thur,
until 0130 Fri & Sat, 1300-
2400 Sun. Chinese &
European. E££.

Lough Shore Café
Lough Shore, Sixmilewater.
1200-sunset Mon-Sun.
Grills, snacks, coffee.

McCartney's Bar ☒
10 Castle St. ☎ 428122.
1200-1430 Mon-Sat. Pub
grub.

Mrs Mac's
Castle Shopping Centre.
☎ 468151. 0930-1700
Mon-Wed & Sat, 0900-2030
Thur & Fri. Set lunch, curries,
chicken.

Madden's ☒
51 High St. ☎ 462177.
1130-1600 Mon-Wed,
1130-1800 Thur-Sat.
A la carte. Pub grub. Live
music.

Market Bar ☒
19 Market St. ☎ 467447.
1230-1430 Mon-Sat. Grills.

Morton & Simpson
Castle Centre. ☎ 461193.
0900-1730 Mon-Wed & Sat,
0900-2100 Thur & Fri.
Breakfast, snacks, fish,
chicken, lasagne.

Morwood's ☕
47 High St. ☎ 463575. 0800-
1730 Mon-Sat. Sandwiches,
home-baked bread, pastries.

Mullin's
30b Fountain St.
☎ 461478. 1400-2200
Mon-Sun. Ice cream,
sandwiches, coffee.

Old Rogue Bar ☒
19 Market Square. ☎ 466966.
1200-1430 Mon-Sat. Pub grub.

Old School House ☒
106 Ballyrobin Rd,
Muckamore. ☎ (01849)
428209. 1200-1500 & 1700-
2200 Mon-Sun. Set meals.
Consommé, supreme of
chicken, cheesecake, Sunday
lunch. E££.

Pepper Pot
Castle Shopping Centre.
☎ 460955. 0900-1700
Mon-Wed & Sat, 0900-2100
Thur & Fri. Set lunch, lasagne,
quiche, soups, stews.

Pogues Tavern ☒
88 Church St. ☎ 428098.
1200-1400 Mon-Sat.
Live music at weekends.

Antrim-Ballycastle — **Co. ANTRIM**

Railway Bar ♆
24 Railway St. ☎ 428261.
1230-1430 Mon-Sat.
Pub grub.

Ramble Inn ♆
236 Lisnavenagh Rd.
☎ 428888. 1200-2115 Mon-Sat, 1230-1430 Sun. Sunday lunches, grills. A la carte. E£.

Riverbank Café
Antrim Forum, Lough Rd.
☎ 464131. 1000-2200 Mon-Fri, until 1800 Sat, 1400-1800 Sun. Burgers, plaice, lasagne, salads. £.

Shane's Castle ♆
Carriage Room. ☎ 462216.
1230-1830 Tues-Thur, Sat & Sun July-Aug & bank hols. Sandwiches, burgers.

Shanogue House ♆
51 Sevenmile Straight.
☎ 428510. 1200-1430 Mon-Sat. Lunches, grills.

Skeffington
88 Church St. ☎ 428098.
1230-1500 Mon-Sat. Grills.

Sodas & Subs
30 Fountain St. ☎ 466469.
1200-2200 Mon-Sun. Soda sandwiches, subs (American style filled, toasted rolls).

Steeple Inn ♆
11 High St. ☎ 428527.
1200-1500 Mon-Sat. Burgers, fish & chips, daily specials.

★ **TOP OF THE TOWN** ♆
77 Fountain St. ☎ 428146.
1200-1500 Mon-Sat. Fish, chicken, salads.

Upper Deck ♆
18 High St. ☎ 460744.
1230-1400 Mon-Sat.
Grills, set lunch.

BALLINTOY

Carrick-a-Rede ♆
21 Main St. ☎ (012657) 62241. 1200-2100 Mon-Sat, 1230-1430 Sun in summer. Weekends in winter. Grills, carvery.

Roark's Kitchen
Ballintoy Harbour.
☎ (01267) 62225.
1100-1900 Mon-Sun June-Aug, Sat & Sun only May & Sept. Snacks.

BALLYCASTLE
(STD 012657)

Antrim Arms ♆
Castle St. ☎ 62284.
Last orders 2030. Closed 2nd & 3rd weeks in Oct. A la carte. E££.

Beach House
Bayview Rd. ☎ 62262.
0900-2200 Mon-Sun Mar-Oct. Lasagne, pizza, home-made pies.

Co. ANTRIM   *Ballycastle-Ballyclare*

Cellar Pizzeria
The Diamond. ☎ 63037.
1730-2300 Sun-Thur, 1730-2330 Fri & Sat. Pizza, kebab, salads.

Checkers Bistro
43 Castle St. 1130-2400 Mon-Thur, until 0200 Fri & Sat, 1430-2400 Sun. Burgers.

Donnelly's Coffee Shop
28 Ann St. ☎ 63236.
0900-1800 Mon-Sat, until 1700 Sun. Soup, pizza, quiche, pies.

Drumawillan House
1 Whitepark Rd. ☎ 62539. Evening meals. Booking essential.

Gawn Inn ♀
Silvercliffs, Clare Rd.
☎ 63202. 1200-1500 Mon-Sat, 1230-1430 Sun. Pub grub.

Good Season
39 Ann St. ☎ 63124.
1700-2330 Tues-Sun. Chinese and European.

Hillsea
28 Quay Hill. ☎ 62385.
1700-1930 Mon-Sun June-Aug. Home cooking. Booking essential.

Lakeside Tea Room
Watertop Farm. ☎ 62576.
1030-1730 Mon-Sun July & Aug. Coffee, salads, pastries.

McCarroll's ♀
7 Ann St. ☎ 62123.
1130-2300 Mon-Sat,
1200-1400 & 1900-2200 Sun.
Lasagne, sandwiches, curries.

★ MARINE HOTEL ♀ ☻
1 North St. ☎ 62222.
Last orders 2045. A la carte.
££.

Open Door
74 Castle St. ☎ 62251.
0900-1730 Mon-Sat, until 1430 Wed, 0900-1900 Mon-Sat July & Aug. Quiche, curry, teas.

The Strand ♀
9 North St. ☎ 62349.
1100-2130 Mon-Sun.
Pub grub.

★ WYSNER'S ♀ ☻
16 Ann St. ☎ 62372.
0800-1730 Mon-Thur, until 2200 Fri & Sat. 0800-2200 Mon-Sat in summer. Steak, gammon, Ulster fry. A la carte.
££££.

BALLYCLARE
(STD 01960)

The Ballyboe ♀
2 North End. ☎ 352997.
1130-1430 Mon-Sat.
Breakfast. Pub grub.

Ballyclare-Ballygalley — Co. ANTRIM

Beck's
33 Main St. ☎ 342414.
0900-1700 Mon-Sat.
Sandwiches, pastries, pies.

Chimes
4a The Square. ☎ 352166.
0900-1700 Mon-Sat.
Pizza, salads, curries.

The Coffee Pot
63 Main St. ☎ 323731.
0900-1730 Mon-Sat.
Steaks, chicken, fish, snacks, salads.

Gathering Inn ♀
42 The Square. ☎ 352636.
1700-2400 Sun-Thur, until 0100 Fri & Sat. Chinese & European. E££.

Golden Dragon ♀
15 Rashee Rd. ☎ 340013.
1200-1400 Fri & 1700-2400 Tues-Sat, 1730-2330 Sun. Chinese & European. E£.

The Grange ♀
22 The Square. ☎ 323393.
1200-1430 & 1730-2130 Mon-Sat. Set lunch, rolls, salads.

Henry's ♀
22 The Square. ☎ 322239.
1200-1430 & 1700-2100 Mon-Sat. Pub grub.

Loafers
66 Main St. ☎ 352336.
0900-1600 Mon-Sat.
Sandwiches, pies, stews.

Red Hand Bar ♀
20 The Square. ☎ 323724.
1130-2300 Mon-Sat.
Sandwiches, soup.

Sportsman's Inn ♀
17 Main St. ☎ 322475.
1200-1500 Mon-Sat.
1230-1430 Sun.

Square Bar ♀
16 Main St. ☎ 323789.
1130-2300 Mon-Sat,
1230-1430 & 1900-2200 Sun. Soup, hamburgers, pies.

BALLYGALLEY
(STD 01574)

Ballygally Castle Hotel ♀
274 Coast Rd. ☎ 583212.
Last orders 2130. Set lunch. A la carte. E££.

Halfway House Hotel ♀
Coast Rd. ☎ 583265
Last orders 2045 Mon-Fri, 2100 Sat, 2000 Sun. Bar lunch, set lunch weekend. A la carte. E£££.

Lough's Restaurant ♀
260 Coast Rd. ☎ 583294.
1130-2030 Mon-Sun. Fish, salads. ££.

Lynden Heights ♀
97 Drumnagreagh Rd.
☎ 583560. 1700-1930 Wed-Sat, 1230-2000 Sun. Daily through summer. A la carte. Baked trout. Salmon, scampi. ££.

Co. ANTRIM — Ballygalley-Ballymena

Meeting House ♒
120 Brustonbrae Rd.
☎ 583252. 1200-1745 &
1900-2100 Mon-Fri, 0700-
2100 Sat, 1230-1400 Sun. Bar
lunches. Pub grub.

BALLYMENA
(STD 01266)

Adair Arms Hotel ♒
Ballymoney Rd. ☎ 653674.
Last orders 2130, Sun 1945.
Grill bar, set lunch. A la carte.
E££.

Bay Leaf Restaurant
23 Wellington St. ☎ 45148.
0900-1730 Mon-Wed & Sat,
0900-2000 Thur & Fri. Steak,
chicken, scampi, plaice.

Camerons
Broughshane St. ☎ 48821.
0900-1700 Mon-Wed, until
1900 Thur & Fri, until 1700
Sat. Soup, sandwiches,
desserts.

Caspers
19 Mill St. ☎ 49303.
0900-1800 Mon-Thur & Sat,
until 2100 Fri. Grills, set
lunch, desserts.

Central Bar ♒
36 Linenhall St. ☎ 49282.
1230-1400 Mon-Sat. Pub
grub.

Confucius ♒
45 Springwell St. ☎ 651638.
1200-1400 Mon-Sat,
1700-2400 Mon-Sun. Chinese
& European. E££.

Countryman Inn ♒
Grove Rd. ☎ 44814.
1200-1430 & 1700-2145
Mon-Sat. A la carte. Wine
bar, buffet.

Crusty Kitchen
Fairhill Shopping Centre,
Thomas St. ☎ 651436. 0900-
1730 Mon-Tues, until 2100
Wed-Fri, until 1800 Sat.
Sandwiches, baked potatoes,
pies.

Daisy May Café
25 William St. ☎ 41543.
1000-1600 Mon-Tues, 1000-
1700 Thur-Sat. Fish & chips,
sandwiches.

Desperate Dan's
12 Ballymoney St. ☎ 49677.
0900-1700 Mon-Sat.
Sandwiches, snacks.

Dillingers ♒
1 Wakehurst Rd. ☎ 44144.
1200-2230 Mon-Sat.
1130-1430 Sun.

Double Happiness ♒
83 Broughshane St. ☎ 45101.
1200-1400 & 1700-2400
Mon-Sat, until 2300 Sun.
Chinese and European E££.

Ballymena — **Co. ANTRIM**

Dunvale Arms
Dunclug Shopping Centre.
☎ 45159. 1130-2300
Mon-Sat, 1230-1430 &
1900-2200 Sun. Pub grub.

Fern Room
80 Church St. ☎ 656169.
0900-1700 Mon-Sat. Home-made soup, salads, vegetarian. Self-service in department store.

Food Web
Fairhill Shopping Centre, Thomas St. ☎ 655838. 0900-1730 Mon-Tues, until 2000 Wed, until 2100 Thur & Fri, 1800 Sat. Soup, sandwiches.

Fort Royal
4 Loughmagarry Rd, Crankill.
☎ 685588. 1200-2100
Mon-Sat, 1230-1430 & 1900-2200 Sun. A la carte, grills. E££.

★ GALGORM MANOR
☎ 881001. 1230-1430 & 1900-2130 Mon-Sat, 1800-2030 Sun. Dundrum oysters with smoked halibut, Donegal salmon with granary mustard, steamed chocolate pudding. E£££.

Gateway Café
52 Henry St. ☎ 47794.
0900-1700 Mon, Tues, Thur & Fri, until 1600 Wed & Sat.
1000-1300 Wed. Pizzas, sandwiches, desserts.

George Buttery
54 Mill St. ☎ 656170.
1130-1500 Mon-Sat,
1730-2100 Thur-Sat.
Grills, salads.

Go Sun
43 Bridge St. ☎ 656774.
1200-1400 Mon-Sat,
1700-2300 Mon-Thur,
until 2330 Sun, 1700-2430 Fri & Sun. Chinese & European. ££.

Greenhills
166 Glenravel Rd.
☎ (012673) 743.
1700-2100 Mon-Sat,
1900-2100 Sun. A la carte, steak, gammon.

Griddle Room
Morton & Simpson, Tower Centre. ☎ 48106.
0900-1730 Mon-Wed & Sat,
0900-2130 Thur & Fri.
Soup, bacon rolls, open sandwiches, Ulster fry.

★ GROUSE INN
2 Springwell St. ☎ 45234.
1100-2130 Mon-Thur, until 2200 Fri & Sat. Grill bar. A la carte 1800-2130 Wed-Sat, until 2200 Fri & Sat. E££.

Huckleberry's Too
78 Broughshane St. ☎ 631333.
1200-2200 Mon-Thur & 2300 Fri-Sat. 1600-2100 Sun.
American bistro style. Steaks, barbecued ribs, buff wings. Cajun a speciality. E££

The George Buttery

54 MILL STREET,
BALLYMENA
☎ (01266) 656170

Lunches served daily from
11.30 am - 3 pm
Monday - Saturday

THE GEORGE BISTRO

Serving evening meals
Thursday to Saturday
5 pm - 9 pm

THE INN

**36 WILLIAM STREET,
BALLYMENA
☎ (01266) 652319**

MEALS SERVED DAILY
12 - 2.30 pm

* Bar snacks, sandwiches toasties, baked potatoes and burgers
* Kiddies corner
* Irish stew served in bar all day - £1.50
* Take away meals available on request

GALGORM MANOR

It's a Pleasure

Galgorm, a luxury 4 star Country House Hotel
set in the midst of beautiful grounds enhanced
by the River Maine flowing beside the hotel.
The dining room hosts a superb **a la carte**
lunch & dinner 7 days a week

Gillies Bar – a traditional Irish pub
Serves tasty pub lunches every day (except Sunday)
Entertainment – Thursday, Friday, Saturday

The Great Hall with its eloquence & grandeur
ideal for weddings/conferences/banqueting
23 luxury ensuite bedrooms available

Ballymena (01266) 881001 Fax: (01266) 880080

Ballymena — **Co. ANTRIM**

The Inn ♀
36 William St. ☎ 652319.
1200-1430 Mon-Sat. Pub grub.

Jane's Kitchen ▮
4 Pats Brae. ☎ 656481.
0930-1630 Mon-Wed, until 2130 Thur-Sat. Soup, sandwiches, stew.

Jaunty's ♀
9 Larne St. ☎ 45978.
1200-2400 Tues-Sat, 1700-2330 Sun.
Fish & chips, chicken.

Kentucky Fried Chicken
27 Queens St. ☎ 46355.
1100-2400 Sun-Wed, 1300-0200 Thur-Sat. Chicken, barbecued ribs, coleslaw, apple pie.

Knockeden Lodge ♀
15 Crebilly Rd. ☎ 43334.
1130-1500 Mon-Fri, 1800-2000 Thur, 1730-2030 Fri & Sat, 1230-1430 Sun. Pub grub.

Leighinmohr House Hotel ♀
Leighinmohr Avenue.
☎ 652313. Last orders 2130 Mon-Sat, 2100 Sun. M£, E£££. Trout in white wine, flambé steaks. A la carte. Oyster bar and grill. ££. Buffet lunch Sun.

Lug o' th' Tub ♀
133 Ballycregagh Rd, Clough.
☎ 685423. 1230-1430 & 1800-2100 Mon-Sat. Pies, hamburgers.

McKendry's Bar ♀
19 Broughshane St. ☎ 47849.
1200-1500 Mon-Sat. Grills, Ulster fry.

★ **MANLEY** ♀

State Cinema Arcade, 70a Ballymoney Rd. ☎ 48967.
1200-1400 & 1730-2330 Mon-Thur, until 0030 Fri & Sat, 1600-2400 Sun.
Cantonese, Peking & European. E££.

Mr Pickwick's Baked Potato
Tower Shopping Centre.
☎ 42801. 0900-1730 Mon-Sat, 0900-2100 Thur & Fri. Baked potatoes with various fillings.

No. 77 ⌒
77 Church St. ☎ 653699.
0900-1730 Mon-Sat. Set lunch, soup, salads, desserts.

Old Oak ♀
26 Broughshane St.
☎ 49029. 0900-1730 Mon-Sat. Set lunch.

Peddlers Restaurant ▮
State Cinema Complex, Ballymoney Rd. ☎ 45177.
1100-2230 Mon-Sat, 1300-2000 Sun. Steaks, seafood, home-made specials.

Pizza Parlour ▮
Springwell St. ☎ 49245.
1700-2300 Mon, Tues & Sun, 1200-1400 & 1700-2300 Wed & Thur, 1200-2400 Fri & Sat. Pizzas, pasta.

Co. ANTRIM *Ballymena*

Pound Bar ♗
18 Corkey Rd. ☎ (0126564) 41287. 1530-2200 Mon-Sat, 1230-1430 & 1900-2200 Sun. Pub grub.

Raglan Bar ♗
20 Queen St. ☎ 652203. 1130-2300 Mon-Sat. Pub grub.

Red Peaches ♗
88 Lower Mill St. ☎ 651170. 1200-1400 & 1700-2400 Tues-Sat, 1600-2300 Sun. Cantonese & European. E££.

Rendezvous ♗
48 Ballymoney St. ☎ 44092. 0900-1730 Mon-Sat. Grills, toasties, curries.

Skandia ☺
Tower Shopping Centre. ☎ 46781. 0930-1730 Mon-Wed, until 2100 Thur & Fri, 1800 Sat. A la carte. £.

Solomon Grundy's ☺
64 Wellington St. ☎ 659602. 0900-1730 Mon-Wed, 0900-2200 Thur-Sat. Pizza, chilli, vegetarian. Kids' specials.

Sugar 'n' Spice
7 Church St. ☎ 46010. 0900-1730 Mon-Sat. Soup, salads, pies.

Terry's Burger Bar
Ballymoney St. ☎ 630831. 1000-2400 Mon-Wed, 1000-0200 Thur-Sat, 1500-2300 Sun. Burgers, fish, chips.

Tower Shopping Centre ☺
Morton & Simpson. ☎ 48106. 0900-1730 Mon, Tues, Wed, Sat, 0900-2100 Thur, Fri. Scones, pastries, savouries, salads.

Towers Tavern ♗
Unit 9, Ballee Centre. ☎ 48969. 1200-1500 Mon-Sat. Pub grub.

Tullyglass House Hotel ♗
178 Galgorm Rd. ☎ 652639. Last orders 2145, Sun 2045. A la carte. E££.

Village Restaurant
7 Fenaghy Rd, Galgorm. ☎ 491515. 0900-2200 Mon & Tues, until 2300 Wed-Sat. Chicken, fish, Ulster fry.

Vintage Bar ♗
9 Galgorm St. ☎ 651255. 1200-1430 Mon-Sat. Grills, steaks, salads.

★ WATER MARGIN ♗

8 Cullybackey Rd. ☎ 48368. 1200-1400 Mon-Sat, 1700-2400 Mon-Thur & Sun, until 0030 Fri & Sat. Cantonese & European. E£££.

Ballymena-Ballymoney — Co. ANTRIM

YMCA Café
44 Church St. ☎ 49335.
0900-1400 Mon-Thur. Stew, lasagne, pizza.

BALLYMONEY
(STD 012656)

Angler's Rest ♀
139 Vow Rd. ☎ Kilrea (012665) 40280. 1230-1430 Mon-Sun, 1730-2130, Mon-Sat, 1900-2030 Sun. A la carte. Sunday carvery. ££.

Anne's Hot Bread Shop
Main St. ☎ 62979.
0830-1800 Mon-Sat.
Snacks, soup.

Arches
29 Church St. ☎ 66088.
0900-1730 Mon-Sat.
Lasagne, steak, à la carte. £.

★ BROWN JUG
23 Main St. ☎ 62351.
0830-1730 Tues-Sat, until 1700 Mon. Salads, quiche, vegetarian, home baking.

Bush Tavern ♀
15 Market St. ☎ 63167.
1200-1500 Mon-Sat.
Lasagne, scampi.

Century Arms ♀
9 Church St. ☎ 63924.
1230-1800 Mon-Sat.
Pub grub.

Herald's ⊙
7 High St. ☎ 65400.
0800-1730 Mon-Sat.
Chicken, fish, lasagne, salads.

Hoi Yun ♀
Charles St. ☎ 63419.
1200-1400 Mon-Sat,
1700-2400 Mon-Fri,
1200-0030 Sat, 1700-2330 Sun. Chinese & European. E£.

Hot Food Bar
53 Main St. ☎ 63475.
0930-1730 Mon-Sat.
Fish & chips, burgers.

Leslie Hill Farm
Leslie Hill. ☎ 63109.
1400-1800 Wed-Sun Easter & summer. Teas, scones, cakes.

Manor Hotel ♀
69 Main St. ☎ 63208.
Last orders 2030 Mon-Fri, 2230 Sat. A la carte. Set lunch. E£.

Megabites
9 Charles St. ☎ 66514.
1130-2330 Mon-Thur, 1130-1430 Fri & Sat, 1630-2330 Sun. Chicken, fish, kebabs.

Parklight Restaurant ♀
57 Main St. ☎ 67111.
1200-1430 Mon-Sun, 1700-2130 Mon-Sat, until 2000 Sun. Fish, chicken, steaks, salads, à la carte. E££.

Co. ANTRIM — Ballymoney-Bushmills

Raymond's
2 Market St. ☎ 65834.
0900-1830 Mon-Sat,
1000-1830 Sun.
Set lunch, grills.

Riada Centre Cafeteria
33 Garryduff Rd. ☎ 65792.
1145-1400 & 1715-2045
Mon-Fri winter, 1145-2045
Mon-Fri summer. 1145-1715
Sat all year. Fish, chicken,
burgers.

★ **TEA HOUSE**
24 Church St. ☎ 67000.
0900-1700 Mon-Sat. Soup,
baked potatoes, sandwiches,
home baking. £.

BROUGHSHANE
(STD 01266)

Thatch Inn
57 Main St. ☎ 861223.
1200-1430 Mon-Fri.
Steaks, salads, grills.

Tullymore House
2 Carnlough Rd. ☎ 861233.
1200-1500 Mon-Sat. Carvery.
1700-2130 Wed-Sun. Bistro.
£££.

BUSHMILLS
(STD 012657)

Ahimsa
243 Whitepark Rd. ☎ 31383.
Vegetarian food a speciality. £.

★ **AUBERGE DE SENEIRL**
28 Ballyclough Rd. ☎ 41536.
1930-2200 Mon, Wed, Fri &
Sat. French. £££.

★ **BUSHMILLS INN**
25 Main St. ☎ 32339.
Last orders 2130. Restaurant:
salmon, strips of beef fillet in
cream & Bushmills whiskey.
££££. Brasserie: Ballyblue brie
& beef tomatoes. Weekends &
summer only. £.

Coffee Shop
65 Main St, The Diamond.
☎ 31706. 0900-1730
Mon-Sat, until 1900 in
summer. Sandwiches, grills,
cakes.

Dunluce Tea Room
Dunluce Rd. ☎ 31145.
1100-1830 Mon-Sun
Easter-Sept. Home baking,
tea, coffee.

Sportsman
150 Main St. ☎ 32334.
1130-2300 Mon-Sat,
1230-1400 & 1900-2200
Sun. Pub grub.

Valerie's Pantry
125 Main St. ☎ 31145.
0930-1730 Mon-Sat. Ulster
fry, Irish stew, pies.

CARNLOUGH
(STD 01574)

Black's Bar 🍺
Harbour Rd. ☎ 885226.
1130-2300 Mon-Sat, 1230-1430 & 1900-2200 Sun. Pub grub. Sandwiches, hamburgers.

Bridge Inn 🍺
2 Bridge St. ☎ 885669.
1200-2000 Mon-Sun.
Set lunch.

Glencloy Inn 🍺
2 Harbour Rd. ☎ 885226.
1200-1500 Mon-Sat. Lunches. All day snacks. Pub grub.

★ **LONDONDERRY ARMS** 🍺
20 Harbour Rd. ☎ 885255.
Last orders: 2100 Mon-Thur, 2130 Fri & Sat, 2015 Sun. Fresh lobster, scallops, home-made wheaten bread. M£, E££.

Marine Café
9 Marine Rd. ☎ 885509.
1100-2030 Mon-Sun.
Fish & chips.

Waterfall Bar 🍺
1 High St. ☎ 885606.
1230-1730 Mon-Sat summer, until 1500 winter, 1230-1430 Sun. Pub grub.

CARRICKFERGUS
(STD 01960)

Bamboo
Market Place. ☎ 3364314.
0830-1630 Mon-Sat.
Coffee bar in cake shop.

Bentra Roadhouse 🍺
1 Slaughterford Rd. ☎ 353666.
1700-2045 Mon-Sat. Pub grub, grills on Sunday. A la carte Fri, Sat evenings.

Brown Cow 🍺
9 Woodburn Rd. ☎ 364815.
1130-2300 Mon-Sat, 1230-1430 & 1900-2200. Sun. Pies, hamburgers.

Café No 10
10 West St. ☎ 360306.
0900-1600 Mon-Sat.
Snacks, grills.

Carrickfergus Castle
☎ 351881.
1000-1800 Mon-Sat & 1400-1800 Sun. Muffins, tray bakes, sausage rolls. Coffee shop in castle.

Castle Fast Food
10 Castle St. ☎ 368859.
1030-2400 Mon-Wed, 1030-0100 Thur, 1030-0200 Fri & Sat, 1400-2330 Sun. Fish & chips, chicken, hamburgers.

Central Bar 🍺
15 High St. ☎ 362282.
1130-2300 Mon-Sat.
Pub grub.

Co. ANTRIM — Carrickfergus

Coast Road Hotel ♀
28 Scotch Quarter. ☎ 351021.
Last orders 2045. Closed
25-26 December. Steak,
scampi, chicken. E££.

Courtyard Coffee House
Scotch Quarter. ☎ 351881.
1000-1630 Mon-Sat.
Pies, lasagne, salads.

Dobbins Inn Hotel ♀
6 High St. ☎ 351905.
Last orders 2115. Closed
25-26 December. Flambé
steak, sweets. Set lunch, bar
meals. Bistro Thur & Sat 8.30
pm. A la carte. E££.

Fergus Inn ♀
75 Belfast Rd. ☎ 364556.
1230-1430 & 1730-2200
Mon-Sat, 1230-1430 & 1730-
2030 Sun. Pub grub, à la carte.
E££.

Galley Café
Knight Ride Heritage Plaza,
Antrim St. ☎ 365853. 0900-
1700 Mon-Fri, 1000-1700 Sat,
1200-1700 Sun. Chicken, fish,
Ulster fry.

Gate & Northgate ♀
59 North St. ☎ 364136.
1200-1445 & 1700-2200
Mon-Sat, 1230-1430 & 1700-
2045 Sun. Steaks, chicken. A
la carte. E££.

Leisure Centre
Prince William Way.
☎ 351711. 1030-2200 Mon-
Fri, 1030-1530 Sat. Snacks.

Margaret's
10 West St. ☎ 360306. 0900-
1600 Mon-Sat. Snacks, grills.

Mermaid ♀
2 Governor's Place.
☎ 364257. 1130-2300
Mon-Sat. Soup, hamburgers.

New Four Seas ♀
9 Governor's Place.
☎ 351226. 1200-1400 &
1700-2400 Mon-Thur,
1700-0100 Fri & Sat,
1700-2400 Sun. Chinese &
European. A la carte. E£.

Old Tech Griddle
20 High St. ☎ 351904.
0900-1730 Mon-Sat. Stew,
curries, home-baked bread.
Bakery & restaurant.

Park Coffee Shop
Kilroot Industrial Estate.
☎ 369941. 0930-1630
Mon-Sat. Set lunch.

Pheasant Inn ♀
Woodburn Rd. ☎ 361094.
1130-2300 Mon-Sat,
1230-1430 & 1900-2200
Sun. Grills, chicken, salads,
snacks.

Prospect House ♀
Woodburn Rd. ☎ 365577.
1730-2115 Mon-Sat,
1230-1430 & 1700-2030
Sun. Set lunch, high tea.
A la carte. E££.

Carrickfergus-Crumlin **Co. ANTRIM**

The Sandwich Centre
6 North St. ☎ 367369. 1000-1630 Mon-Sat. Sandwiches, scones, tray bakes.

Smugglers' Restaurant 🍴
Albert Edward Pier, The Harbour. ☎ 366538. 1830-2130 Mon-Thur & Sun, until 2200 Fri & Sat. Skewered prawns, swordfish, steak Hornblower. Bistro Sun-Thur. E££.

Tourist Inn ♀
149 Larne Rd. ☎ 351708. 1130-2300 Mon-Sat, 1230-1430 Sun. Irish stew, filled rolls.

★ **WINDROSE** ♀
Rodgers Quay. ☎ 364192. 1200-1430 & 1730-2130 Mon-Sat, 1230-1400 bistro Sun, 1800-2130 Tues, Sat restaurant. A la carte. E£££.

YMCA
Lancastrian St. ☎ 363223. 1030-1400 Mon-Wed & Fri, 0800-1400 Thur.
Soup, stew, hamburgers.

CLOUGHMILLS
(STD 012656)

Roadside Restaurant
Logan's Fashion Store, 232 Frosses Rd. ☎ 38080. 1000-1800 Mon, Tues & Sat, 1000-2100 Wed-Fri. Stuffed chicken, haddock, curries, pastries. Set lunch May-Sept.

CRUMLIN
(STD 01849)

Airport Road Café
11 Tully Rd, Nutts Corner. 0730-1730 Mon-Fri, 0730-1400 Sat. Grills, set meals.

Breadbasket
78 Main St. ☎ 423073. 0900-1730 Mon-Sat. Home baking, toasties, pies, stew.

Bushe ♀
47 Main St. ☎ 452411. 1230-1430 Mon-Sat. Pub grub.

Caldhame Lodge
102 Moira Rd. ☎ 423099. Dinners, home cooking. Booking essential.

Camlin ♀
67 Main St. ☎ 453624. 1230-1430 & 1900-2200 Fri-Sat. 2130 Sun. A la carte.

Chestnut Inn ♀
126 Lurgan Rd. ☎ 453165. 1130-2300 Mon-Sat, 1230-1430 & 1900-2200 Sun. Pub grub.

Fiddlers Inn ♀
36 Main St. ☎ 452221. 1200-1430 Mon-Sun, 1800-2100 Mon-Thur. 2200 Fri-Sat. Grills, salads.

Co. ANTRIM — Cullybackey-Dervock

CULLYBACKEY
(STD 01266)

Village Inn ♀
Main St. ☎ 881290.
1230-1500 Mon-Sat,
1700-2030 Fri & Sat.
Set lunch, grills.

Wylie's ♀
93 Main St. ☎ 880200.
1800-2230 daily. Pub grub.

CUSHENDALL
(STD 012667)

Central Bar ♀
7 Bridge St. ☎ 71730.
1200-1500 as required. Roast beef, plaice, chicken, lamb. £.

Gillan's
6 Mill St. ☎ 71404.
0900-1800 Mon-Sat,
1300-1800 Sun in summer.
Salads, sandwiches, hot dogs.

Half Door Restaurant ♀
6 Bridge St. ☎ 71300.
1700-2100 Mon-Sun summer.
More limited hours in winter.
French ££.

Lurig Inn ♀
Bridge St. ☎ 71527.
1130-2300 Mon-Sat,
1230-1430 & 1900-2200
Sun. Chicken, curries, steak.

Thornlea Hotel ♀
6 Coast Rd. ☎ 71223.
Last orders 2115. Set lunch, high tea, carvery. A la carte. M£, E££.

CUSHENDUN
(STD 012667)

Bay Hotel ♀
20 Strandview Park. ☎ 61267.
Last orders 2045. Garlic mushrooms, steak in whiskey sauce. A la carte. E££.

National Trust Tea Room
☎ 61506. 1100-1900 Mon-Sat, until 2000 Sun summer, weekends only rest of year. Soup, quiche, salads, home baking. Teas in garden at rear.

Villa
185 Torr Rd. ☎ 61252.
1300-1930 Mon-Sun. Booking essential. Salmon in season, home baking.

DERVOCK
(STD 012657)

North Irish Horse ♀
15 Carncullagh Rd. ☎ 41205.
1130-2200 Mon-Sat. 1230-1430 & 1900-2200 Sun. Own smoked trout & eel, dressed crab & lobster, porterhouse steaks. A la carte. E£££.

Dervock-Dunmurry   **Co. ANTRIM**

Safari Wonderland
☎ 41474. 1030-1830
Mon-Sun Easter & June-Aug,
Sat & Sun in May, Sun only
Sept. Fish, snacks, salads. In
wildlife park.

DOAGH

McConnell's ♀
4 Main St. ☎ (01960) 352352.
1200-1400 Mon-Sat. Scampi,
soups, burgers.

DUNADRY

★ **DUNADRY INN** ♀

2 Islandreagh Drive.
☎ (01849) 432474.
Last orders 2145, Sun 2045.
Closed 24-25 Dec. Smoked
eel, veal, partridge, salmon.
E£££.

DUNMURRY

Beechlawn Hotel ♀ ☉
4 Dunmurry Lane. ☎ (01232)
612974. Last orders 2130
Mon-Sat. Seafood, steaks.
A la carte. E££.

Cobblestone Coffee Shop
236 Kingsway. ☎ (01232)
612324. 0900-1700 Mon-Sat.
Coffee, quiche, lasagne, apple
pie.

Colin Mill Lodge ♀
Good Shepherd Rd, Poleglass.
☎ (01232) 601238.
1230-1430 Tues-Sun, 1900-
2100 Sun. Chicken, curry,
steak.

Derby Bar ♀
Stewartstown Rd.
☎ (01232) 625253.
1200-2130 Mon-Sat, 1230-
1430 & 1900-2130 Sun. Pub
grub.

Dunmurry Inn ♀
195 Kingsway. ☎ (01232)
611653. 1130-1430 Mon-Sat.
Sandwiches, stew, salads.

Farmer's Inn ♀
91 Colinglen Rd. ☎ 600135.
1200-1430 & 1700-1900
Mon-Sun. A la carte.

Forte Crest Hotel ☉
300 Kingsway, BT17.
☎ 612101.
1230-1430 Sun-Fri, 1900-
2200 Sun-Sat. Irish salmon,
duckling, vegetable soup. Sun
carvery lunch.

Jeffer's
174 Kingsway. ☎ (01232)
617938. 0830-1700 Mon-Sat.
Coffee shop in home bakery.

Kentucky Fried Chicken
181 Kingsway. 1100-0100
Sun-Thur, 1100-0200 Fri &
Sat. Chicken, barbecued ribs,
apple pie.

Tullymore House

2 Carnlough Road, Broughshane, Ballymena

☎ (01266) 861233   Fax: (01266) 862238

*Situated in 16 acres of gardens in the heart
of the Braid Valley below Slemish mountain*

Pheasantry Carvery open 7 Days lunch & dinner
Draymans Rest - Enjoy a quiet relaxing drink
Chez Maud Bistro open Mon - Sun 5 pm - 9.30 pm
Three Trees Suite - ideal for weddings, dinners, conferences
11 ensuite bedrooms - all facilities

☎ (01266) 861233

BELLEVUE ARMS

129 Antrim Road, Glengormley

☎ (01232) 777138 Restaurant - (01232) 773041 Bar

Restaurant & Grill Bar
Open all day Mon-Sat 12 noon-10 pm
Menu ranging from bar snacks to à la carte.
Sunday opening hours -
12.30 pm - 2.30 pm 7 pm - 9.30 pm

Try our traditional Sunday lunch

*Choice of several main courses
Evening meals:- Choice of à la carte menu
pleasant staff and comfortable surroundings*

Dunmurry-Glenariff — Co. ANTRIM

Little Mermaid
Kingsway Shopping Centre.
☎ (01232) 612268. 0930-1730 Mon-Wed, until 2100 Thur & Fri, until 1900 Sat. Omelettes, baked potatoes, chilli.

Pizza Bellezza
232 Kingsway. ☎ (01232) 600202. 1600-2400 Sun-Thur, 1100-0100 Fri & Sat, 1300-2400 Sun. Pizzas.

The Pyramids
180 Kingsway. ☎ 624972. 1200-1400 Mon-Sat, 1700-2300 Mon-Thur, until 2400 Fri & Sat. Kebabs, pizza, lasagne.

Sportsman Inn ♀
101 Queensway. ☎ (01846) 663994. 1200-1500 Mon-Sat, 1730-2100 Fri & Sat, 1730-2100 Sun. Steaks, chicken, scampi. E£.

Stagecoach Inn ♀
52 Queensway, Derriaghy. ☎ (01232) 625141. 1230-1800 Mon, 1230-2000 Tues-Sat, 1230-1430 Sun. Carvery, set lunch. A la carte. E£.

Swillybrin Inn ♀
Suffolk Rd. ☎ (01232) 614754. 1230-1430 Mon-Sat, 1900-2130 Sun. Pub grub.

GIANT'S CAUSEWAY

Causeway Hotel ♀
40 Causeway Rd. ☎ (012657) 31226. Last orders 2130. A la carte, carvery. E££.

★ **HILLCREST COUNTRY HOUSE** ♀

306 Whitepark Rd. ☎ (012657) 31577. 1930-2130 weekends in winter, 1200-1430 & 1700-2130 7 days in summer. A la carte, high tea. ££.

★ **NATIONAL TRUST TEA ROOM**

Giant's Causeway Centre. ☎ (012657) 31582. 1045-1715 Mon-Sun Mar-June & Sept, until 1845 July & Aug. Soup, snacks, home baking.

GLARRYFORD
(STD 01266)

Crankhill Stores Café
133 Crankhill Rd. ☎ 85507. 0800-1930 Mon-Sat. Hot dogs, sandwiches, pastries.

GLENARIFF

Glen Tea House
99a Glen Rd. ☎ (012667) 71402. 1400-1800 Mon-Sun in summer, Sat & Sun only rest of year. Home baking, pastries, biscuits.

Co. ANTRIM — Glenariff-Glengormley

Manor Lodge
Glenariff Glen.
☎ (0126673) 221. 1100-2330 Mon-Sat, 1200-2130 Sun. Grills, high tea. £.

Mariners Bar
7 Main St. ☎ (012667) 71330. 1200-1500 Mon-Sat, 1230-1430 Sun. Salads, burgers.

Waterfall Restaurant
Glenariff Forest Park.
☎ (012667) 58769. 1100-2000 Mon-Sun Mar-Oct. Set meals, quiche, salads, high tea.

GLENARM
(STD 01574)

Coast Road Inn
3 Toberwine St. ☎ 841207. 1200-1500 Mon-Thur, 1200-1500 & 1700-2130 Mon-Sat. Grills, salads. Pub grub.

Drumnagreagh Hotel
Coast Rd. ☎ 841651.
Last orders 2100. A la carte. E££.

Heather Dew Tavern
1 New Row. ☎ 841221. 1200-1500 & 1700-2130 Mon-Sat. Grills, salads.

GLENGORMLEY
(STD 01232)

Beck's
329 Antrim Rd. ☎ 833854. 0900-1700 Mon-Sat. Coffee, snacks.

Bellevue Arms
129 Antrim Rd. ☎ (01232) 773041. 1200-2200 Mon-Sat, 1230-1430 & 1900-2130 Sun. Pub grub. Set meals. A la carte. E££.

Cavalier
8 Portland Avenue. ☎ 836759. 1000-2300 Mon-Thur, until 0100 Fri & Sat. Grills, fish & chips, coffee.

Chimney Corner Hotel
630 Antrim Rd. ☎ 844925. Last orders 2130. A la carte. E££.

Coffee Corner
14 Farmley Shopping Centre.
☎ 833031. 0900-1630 Mon-Sat, closed Wed. Coffee, cakes, snacks.

Huckleberry's
Unit 8, Farmley Shopping Centre. ☎ 838282. 1200-1430 & 1700-2200 Mon-Fri, 1200-2300 Sat, 1400-2130 Sun. Modern American. ££.

Glengormley-Larne **Co. ANTRIM**

Jasmin House 🍷
17a Ballyclare Rd. ☎ 841705.
1200-1400 & 1700-2400
Mon-Thur, until 0100 Fri &
Sat, 1300-2400 Sun. Chinese
& English.

Kentucky Fried Chicken
376 Antrim Rd. ☎ 843040.
1100-0100 Sun-Wed, until
0200 Thur, 0230 Fri & Sat.
Chicken, barbecued ribs,
coleslaw, apple pie.

Royal Thai 🍷
377 Antrim Rd. ☎ 848189.
1200-1400 & 1700-2400
Mon-Thur, until 0100
Fri & Sat, 1230-2400 Sun.
Chinese & Thai cuisine. £££.

Swiss Chalet 🍷
81 Ballyclare Rd. ☎ 848630.
1230-1430 Mon-Sat.
A la carte. £.

Village Inn 🍷
350 Antrim Rd. ☎ 836077.
1215-1445 Mon-Sat.
A la carte.

ISLANDMAGEE
(STD 01960)

Millbay Inn
77 Millbay Rd. ☎ 382436.
1200-1500 Mon-Sat, 1700-
2100 Wed-Sat, 1230-1400
Sun.

KELLS
(STD 01266)

Country House Hotel 🍷
20 Doagh Rd. ☎ 891663.
Last orders 2115. Buffet lunch,
Sunday high tea, à la carte.
Lobster, zabaglione. ££££.
(From Ballymena A36 (Larne
road) 2m, B59 to Doagh,
3.5m).

LARNE
(STD 01574)

Ann's Pantry
64 Main St. ☎ 260474.
0900-1700 Mon-Sat. Quiche,
baked potatoes.

Antoinette's Sandwich Bar
1 Quay St. ☎ 279905.
0900-1730 Mon-Sat.
Sandwiches, pastries, baked
potatoes.

Apsley's Scullery
11 Main St. ☎ 260510.
0900-2100 Mon-Sat, 0900-
1900 Sun. Stew, sandwiches,
pastries.

Ardella
3 Upper Cross St. ☎ 270908.
0930-1730 Mon-Thur & Sat,
0900-1900 Fri. Chicken, fish,
grills, desserts.

Co. ANTRIM — Larne

The Bailie ♗
111 Main St. ☎ 273947.
1130-1500 & 1700-2100
Mon-Sat, 1230-1430 & 1900-2100 Sun. Pub grub, high tea, Slemish herb chicken.

Bric-a-brac
4 Riverdale. ☎ 275657.
0900-1730 Mon, Wed-Sat.
Closed all day Tues. Home-made broth, coffee. In antique shop.

Butter Churn
61 Main St. ☎ 260575.
0800-1700 Mon-Sat. Quiche, baked potatoes.

The Cabin
6 Upper Main St. ☎ 270070.
0900-1730 Mon-Sat. Quiche, pies, lasagne, pavlova.

Captain's Kitchen
Harbour Terminal. ☎ 270284.
0630-2230 Mon-Sun. Burgers, pies, fish, salads.

Carnfunnock Country Park
☎ 270541. 1200-1800
Mon-Sun in summer,
1400-1700 weekends
Easter-June. Coffee, biscuits.

Carriages ♗
105 Main St. ☎ 275132.
1200-2300 Mon-Sat,
1700-2230 Sun. Grills, pizza.
E£.

**Central Bakery
 & Cottage Restaurant**
21 Lower Cross St. ☎ 260293.
0900-1730 Mon-Sat. Grills, snacks.

Chekkers Wine Bar ♗
33 Lower Cross St. ☎ 275305.
1200-1430 & 1700-2100
Mon-Sat, 1200-1400 &
1900-2100 Sun. Steaks, lasagne.

Connor's Kitchen
38 Main St. ☎ 274701.
0900-1630 Mon-Sat. Set lunch, baked potatoes.

Country Kitchen
Murrayfield Shopping Centre.
☎ 278306. 0900-1730 Mon &
Wed-Sat, 0900-1700 Tues.
Soups, stews, home-made broth, burgers.

Country Kitchen
968 Main St. ☎ 275811. 0815-1730 Mon-Sat. Stew, home-made broth, sandwiches.

Curran Court Hotel ♗
84 Curran Rd. ☎ 275505.
Last orders 2115 Mon-Sat, Sun 2015. Set lunch, Sunday high tea. A la carte. E££.

Dan Campbell's ♗
2 Bridge St. ☎ 277222. 1200-2130 Mon-Sat, 1230-1400 &
1700-2130 Sun. High tea.
A la carte. £££.

Larne | **Co. ANTRIM**

Die Windmolen
68 Main St. ☎ 275370.
0845-1800 Mon-Thur, 0900-2100 Fri, 0900-1800 Sat.
Chicken Kiev, lasagne, stew.

Eagle Bar ♀
1 Station Rd. ☎ 273817.
1130-2300 Mon-Sat. Pub grub.

Food For Thought
83 Main St. ☎ 279666.
0900-1730 Mon-Sat. Lasagne, sandwiches, coffee.

Harbour Diner
25 Olderfleet Rd. ☎ 272386.
0700-2300 Mon-Sun. Stews, grills.

Highways Hotel ♀
Ballyloran. ☎ 272272.
Last orders 2100, Sun 2130.
Roast ham, mixed grill.
A la carte. £££.

Kiln ♀
Old Glenarm Rd. ☎ 260924.
1200-1430 & 1700-2100 Mon-Sat, 1230-1430 & 1700-2000 Sun. Home-made chicken & ham pie, steak & kidney pie, rainbow trout.
A la carte. £££.

Kilwaughter House Hotel ♀
61 Shanes Hill Rd. ☎ 272591.
Last orders 2115 Mon-Sat, Sun 2030. Grills, scampi, steaks.
££.

Loafers ☺
8 Penny Lane, Point St.
☎ 273322. 0900-1700 Mon-Sat. Sandwiches, salads, lasagne, pastries.

Lotus Flower
117 Main St. ☎ 272102.
1200-1400 Mon-Sat,
1700-0030 Mon-Thur,
1600-0200 Sat, 1700-2400 Sun. Chinese & European.

Magheramorne House Hotel ♀
59 Shore Rd. ☎ 279444. Last orders 2100. A la carte. £££.

Maud's Ice Cream Parlour & Coffee Shop
79 Main St. ☎ 278065.
1100-2100 Mon-Sat, 1100-2000 Sun.

Rafters ♀
13 Point St. ☎ 274368.
1200-1430 Mon-Sat. Pub grub. Home-made soup, Irish stew.

Silver Lounge
124 Main St. ☎ 260040.
Winter 0930-1800 Mon-Sat, until 1400 Tues. Summer 0900-1800 Mon-Sat. Fish & chips. Set lunch.

Co. ANTRIM — Lisburn

LISBURN
(STD 01846)

Aldo Raffo
25 Market St. ☎ 662960. 1000-1800 Mon-Sat. Baked potatoes, salads, fish.

Al Pacino's
4 Smithfield Square. ☎ 661177. 1000-2400 Mon, Wed & Thur, until 0100 Fri, 0900-2400 Tues, 0930-0200 Sat, 1430-2330 Sun. Ulster fry, kebabs, fish.

Andrews
23a Market Square. ☎ 673189. 0900-1830 Mon-Sat. Ulster fry, silverside of beef, coffee.

Angelo's Ristorante
3A Market Lane. ☎ 672554. 1700-2200 Tues-Sat, 1400-2130 Sun. Pizza, pasta, fish, vegetarian dishes.

Bow Street Brasserie ☗
Bow Street Mall. ☎ 661650. 0900-1700 Mon & Tues, until 2100 Wed-Fri, 1730 Sat. Devon teas, grills, salads, pastries.

Burger King
1 Bow St. ☎ 660663. 1000-1900 Mon-Wed, until 2200 Thur-Sun. Burgers, chips, coffee.

Carnmore Antiques
39 Lambeg Rd. ☎ 673115. 1400-1700 Mon-Fri, 1100-1700 Sat. Scones, home-baked pastries. Tea shop in antique shop.

Chico's
158 Longstone St. ☎ 662182. 0900-2130 Mon-Sat, 1200-2130 Sun. Ice cream, baked potatoes, burgers.

Cooke Pot
134 Longstone St. ☎ 671204. 0900-1630 Mon-Sat. Irish stew, broth, chicken pie, shepherd's pie. Set lunch Tues & Fri.

Down Royal ♀
62 Ballinderry Rd. ☎ 602870. 1200-2130 Mon-Sat. Buffet lunch, à la carte 1900-2130 Wed-Sat. Chilli, open sandwiches, baked potatoes. E££.

Eats
25 Market Square. ☎ 662960. 1000-1800 Mon-Sat. Hamburgers, fries.

Family's Restaurant ☗
46 Market Square. ☎ 603033. 0800-1730 Mon-Sat, until 2100 Thur. Lasagne, sweet & sour pork, vegetarian, snacks.

Fonzie's
158 Longstone St. ☎ 662182. 0900-2130 Mon-Sun. Home-made ice cream, coffees, salads, baked potatoes.

Lisburn **Co. ANTRIM**

Gaffe Cutter ♎
25 Market Place. ☎ 666950.
1200-1430 Mon-Fri, 1700-2200 Mon-Sat. Burgers, open sandwiches. A la carte Sat. E£.

Golden Garden ♎
140 Longstone St.
☎ 671311. 1200-1400 Thur-Sat, 1700-2400 Mon-Sat. Chinese & European. E£.

Golden Pheasant ♎
Aughnaleck, Baillies Mills.
☎ 638056. 1200-2200 Mon-Sat, 1230-1430 & 1900-2200 Sun. Lunch, high tea. A la carte. E£.

Green Hall ♎
4 Airport Rd. ☎ 651617.
1230-1430 & 1730-2130 Mon-Sat, until 2015 Sun.
A la carte, high tea, set lunch. 18th-century manor house. E££.

Grooms ♎
Down Royal Park,
6 Dunygarton Rd, Maze.
☎ 621668. 1230-1430 & 1800-2200 Tues-Sat. Steaks, chicken, salads. A la carte. E££.

Hagues Bar ♎ ☺
32 Chapel Hill. ☎ 663224.
1230-1430 Mon-Sat. Chicken, plaice, home-made bread, teas.

Hedley's ☺
43 Bow St. ☎ 681337.
0900-1700 Mon-Sat. Home baking, savoury pies, curries.

Holmstead Inn ♎
314 Hillhall Rd. ☎ (01232) 826763. 1700-2100 Mon-Thur, until 1900 Fri & Sat, 1230-1430 Sun. Steak, chicken, fish. £.

Horseshoe Inn ♎
24 Crumlin Rd, Upper Ballinderry. ☎ 651087.
1130-2300 Mon-Sat,
1230-1430 & 1900-2200 Sun. Soup, hamburgers, grills, ste

Inglenook ☺
17 Market St. ☎ 665401.
0930-1700 Mon-Wed, until 2145 Thur-Sat. Lemon chicken, casseroles, chocolate cake. E££.
ak, basket meals. E£.

Irish Linen Centre
Café Crommelin,
Market Square. ☎ 663377.
0930-1700 Mon-Sat. 0930-2100 Thur. Speciality coffees, croissants, pastries in newly opened centre.

Jeffers ☺
20 Market Square.
☎ 663210. 0845-1700 Mon-Sat. Snacks, salads, beef, fish, home-made sweets.

La Piazza ♦
13a Market Square.
☎ 673158. 1130-1430 & 1730-2200 Mon-Sat. Tortellini alla panna, cannelloni, seafood, steaks. E££.

Co. ANTRIM — Lisburn

★ LAUREL INN
99 Carryduff Rd. ☎ 638422. 1730-2130 Mon-Sat, 1230-1430 & 1730-2130 Sun. Set menu. A la carte. ££.

Lisnoe Nursery
Duneight. ☎ 663565. 1400-1800 Sat & Sun in summer except July. Scones, coffee, cakes, home-made jams.

Lotus House
58 Bow St. ☎ 678669. 1200-1415 Mon-Sat, 1700-2400 Mon-Thur & Sun, 1700-0100 Fri & Sat. Chinese & European. E££.

Manor Inn
29 Longstone St. ☎ 662386. 1200-1445 Mon-Sat. Scampi, roasts.

Maze Station
228 Moira Rd, Maze. ☎ 621538. 1130-2300 Mon-Sat, 1230-1430 & 1900-2200 Sun. Scampi, chicken, salads.

Montgomery's
28 Castle St. ☎ 662656. 0800-1600 Tues-Thur, 0800-1800 Fri-Sat. Fish & chips, hot dogs, home-made ice cream.

Peking Palace
58 Chapel Hill. ☎ 670445. 1200-1400 & 1700-2400 Mon-Thur, until 0030 Fri & Sat, 1700-2400 Sun. Chinese & European. E£.

Penny Farthing
5 Antrim St. ☎ 663392. 0900-1700 Mon-Sat. Home baking.

Pizzarelly's
10 Bachelor's Walk. ☎ 671980. 1000-2200 Mon-Sat. Pizzas, soup, pasta, grills.

Racecourse Inn
60 Gravel Hill Rd. ☎ (01846) 621685. 1230-1430 & 1730-2130 Mon-Sat. High tea, à la carte, Sunday carvery.

Restbite
Lisburn Leisure Centre. ☎ 679564. 1030-2130 Mon-Fri, until 1700 Sat. Fish & chips, salads.

Roadside Café & Restaurant
1 Glenavy Rd. ☎ 651379. 0900-1700 Mon-Sat. Toasties, burgers, pastries.

Robin's Nest
41 Railway St. ☎ 678065. 1130-2300 Mon-Sat. Pub grub, pies, scampi.

Rumbles
42 Longstone St. ☎ 676292. 1100-0100 Mon-Sun. Burgers, fish, chicken.

Lisburn-Newtownabbey **Co. ANTRIM**

Sprucefield Shopping Centre ◔
Mount Charles Catering.
☎ 661244. 1000-2000
Mon & Tues, 0930-2100
Wed-Fri, until 1900 Sat.
Lasagne, beef stroganoff, chicken à la king.

Super Fry
19 Antrim St. ☎ 675857.
1100-1800 Mon-Sat, closed Wed. Fish & chips, grills.

Temple Golf & Country Club ♀
60 Church Rd, Boardmills.
☎ 639213.
1200-1430 & 1800-2100
Mon-Sat. 1200-1430 & 1730-2030 Sun.

Tidy Doffer ♀
133 Ravarnet Rd. ☎ 689188.
1200-2200 Mon-Sat,
1230-1430 & 1900-2100 Sun.
Garlic prawns, ribs, steaks, fish. E£. Themed linen restaurant and bar, spinning equipment, photographs.

Toffs ◔
6 Railway St. ☎ 671369.
0930-1630 Mon-Sat. Curry, lasagne, quiche.

Tormore
Temple Shopping Centre, Carryduff Rd. ☎ 638633.
1000-1800 Mon-Wed,
0930-1900 Thur-Sat. Ulster fry, steak pie, pastries, coffee.

★ **THE WALLACE** ♀
12 Bachelor's Walk.
☎ 665000. 1200-1500
Tues-Fri & Sun, 1800-2230
Tues-Sat. A la carte. Duck, turbot, fish, steaks.

MALLUSK

Good Evening Roughfort ♀
230 Mallusk Rd. ☎ (018494) 32963. 1200-1500 Thur-Sat. Grills, snacks.

NEWTOWNABBEY

Bumper's
1 Abbey Centre, Longwood Rd. ☎ (01232) 868058.
0900-1730 Mon, Tues & Sat,
0900-2100 Wed-Fri. Fish & chips, apple pie, doughnuts.

Cloughfern Arms ♀
214 Doagh Rd. ☎ (01232) 862387. 1200-1430 Mon-Sat. Pub grub.

Corr's Corner ♀
Ballyhenry. ☎ (01232) 849221. 1130-2230 Mon-Sat. Set lunch. A la carte, carvery. E££.

Cottonmount Arms ♀
128 Mallusk Rd. ☎ (01232) 832006. 1200-1430 Mon-Sat, 1700-2100 Mon-Fri, until 2200 Sat & 2030 Sun. Toasties, grills.

Co. ANTRIM — Newtownabbey

Fern Lodge
76 Doagh Rd.
☎ (01232) 867394.
1200-1430 Mon-Sat.
Ploughman's lunch, scampi.

The Gallery
28 Mallusk Rd. ☎ 838457.
1130-2200 Mon-Sat, 1230-1430 Sun. A la carte.

★ **GINGER TREE**
29 Ballyrobert Rd.
☎ (01232) 848176.
1200-1430 Mon-Fri,
1900-2200 Mon-Sat.
Japanese. E£££.

Glenavna House Hotel
588 Shore Rd. ☎ (01232) 864461. Last orders 2200, Sun 1930. Masquerades: kebabs, stir fry ravioli, carpetbagger steak. ££.

Ivy Inn
Jordanstown Rd. ☎ (01232) 862429. 1200-1400 Mon-Sat. Grills, salads.

Lady Love
158 Antrim Rd. ☎ (01232) 771383. 1200-1400 & 1700-0030 Mon-Thur, until 0130 Fri, 1600-0130 Sat, 1300-2400 Sun. Chinese & European. E££.

Maggie's Kitchen
14 Abbotts Cross. ☎ (01232) 863045. 0900-1730 Mon-Sat. Breakfast, coffee.

Mulvenna's
607 Shore Rd, Jordanstown.
☎ (01232) 863206. 1200-1430 Mon-Sat. Pub grub.

Rory's Restaurant
611 Shore Rd, Whiteabbey.
☎ (01232) 865234. 1030-1430 & 1700-2100 Mon-Sat. Snacks or set meals. Steaks, beef stroganoff, vegetarian curries, quiches and burgers.

Skandia
Abbey Centre. ☎ (01232) 365960. 0900-1730 Mon & Tues, 0900-2130 Wed-Fri, 0900-1800 Sat. Salads, desserts. A la carte.

★ **SLEEPY HOLLOW**
15 Kiln Rd. ☎ (01232) 342042. 1900-2130 Wed-Sat. Set menu. Pigeon breasts in red wine, lamb with raisin & rum sauce. Art gallery. E£££.

Texas Pantry
Texas Homecare, Longwood Rd. ☎ (01232) 868886. 0900-1730 Mon-Sat, until 2100 Wed-Fri. Restaurant in DIY store.

Valley Leisure Centre
Church Rd. ☎ (01232) 861211. 1100-2200 Mon-Sat, until 1730 Sun. Grills, sandwiches.

Newtownabbey-Portglenone   **Co. ANTRIM**

Whittley's ⚜
401 Ballyclare Rd.
☎ (01232) 832438.
1200-1400 & 1700-2130
Mon-Fri, 1200-2130 Sat,
1900-2130 Sun. Steaks,
vegetarian dishes, garlic
prawns. E£££.

PORTBALLINTRAE

Bayview Hotel ⚜
Seafront. ☎ (012657) 31453.
Last orders 2200. Set meals.
A la carte. E££.

Beach House Hotel ⚜
Seafront. ☎ (012657) 31214.
Last orders 2100. Set meals.
A la carte. ££.

Sallie's Craft 'n' Coffee Shop
47 Beach Rd. ☎ (012657)
31328. 1100-1800 Fri-Sun
Easter-end June; 1100-1800
Tues-Sun July & Aug. Pizzas,
baked potatoes, pastries.

★ **SWEENEY'S WINE BAR** ⚜

6b Seaport Avenue.
☎ (012657) 32405. 1230-2200
Mon-Sat, 1230-1430 & 1900-
2100 Sun. Char grill steaks,
ribs, vegetarian dishes.

PORTGLENONE
(STD 01266)

Bann Restaurant
30 Main St. ☎ 821267.
0900-1800 Mon-Wed,
until 2000 Thur-Sat. Burgers,
pizza.

Golden Hill ⚜
11 Clady Rd. ☎ 822168.
1700-2400 Mon-Sun. Chinese
& European. E£.

Hawthorne Inn ⚜
54 Kilrea Rd. ☎ 821523.
1930-2145 Thur-Sat. Pub
grub.

Pat's Bar ⚜
71 Main St. ☎ 821231.
1130-2300 Mon-Sat, 1230-
1430 & 1900-2200 Sun. Steak,
chicken, trout.

Teague's Bar ⚜
Clady. ☎ 821288. 1800-2200
Thur-Sun. Grills.

Wild Duck ⚜
93 Main St. ☎ 821232.
1200-1400 & 1700-2145
Tues-Sat, 1200-1400 &
1700-2130 Sun. Set lunch,
à la carte, pub grub. E£.

Co. ANTRIM — Portrush

PORTRUSH
(STD 01265)

Alpha Bar
63 Eglinton St. ☎ 823889.
1130-2300 Mon-Sat,
1230-1430 & 1900-2200
Sun. Pub grub.

Bethel
7 Lansdowne Crescent.
☎ 822354. Lunch, dinner.
Booking essential.

Black Swan House
61 Coleraine Rd. ☎ 822205.
0830-2030 Mon-Sat. Ulster
fry, grills, salads.

Café-de-Lux
4 Main St. 1100-1900
Mon-Sun June-Sept. Fish &
chips, ice cream, cakes.

Carousel
6 Main St. ☎ 824411.
0900-2200 Mon-Sun in
summer, until 2100 winter.
Set lunches, chicken, grills.

Causeway Coast Hotel
36 Ballyreagh Rd. ☎ 822435.
Last orders 2200. A la
carte. ££.

China House
55 Eglinton St. ☎ 822889.
1700-2330 Tues-Sun.
Cantonese & European, set
lunch. E££.

Coffee Pot
Dunluce St. ☎ 823554.
0930-2300 Mon-Sun summer,
until 1700 winter. Savoury
pies, Irish stew.

Dionysus
53 Eglinton St. ☎ 823855.
1700-2230 Mon-Sat,
until 2130 Sun. Greek &
English. Souvlaki, mezze. E££.

Eglinton Hotel
49 Eglinton St. ☎ 822371.
Last orders 2130. Fresh
haddock, Ulster fry, black
pudding. A la carte. ££.

Graham's
48 Main St. ☎ 822427.
0930-2300 Mon-Sun summer.
1100-1730 Mon & Tues,
1300-1800 Thur-Sat winter.
A la carte in Tudor Room.

Harbour Inn
5 Harbour Rd. ☎ 825047.
1230-1500 & 1700-2030 mid
week, 1230-2100 Sat, 1230-
1430 Sun. Fresh seafood. E£.

Kentucky Fried Chicken
54 Main St. ☎ 824689.
1100-0230 Mon-Sun
July & Aug, until 2400
Mon-Wed, 0200 Thur-Sun rest
of year. Chicken, barbecued
ribs, coleslaw, apple pie.

Langholm Hotel
15 Eglinton St. ☎ 822293.
Last orders 2130. A la carte. £.

Portrush   **Co. ANTRIM**

★ MAGHERABUOY HOUSE HOTEL

41 Magheraboy Rd.
☎ 823507. Last orders 2130. Fresh baked salmon, grills. £££.

Ma-ring
17 Kerr St. ☎ 822765. Lunches, dinner. Booking essential.

Morelli's
7 Eglinton St. ☎ 824848. 1100-2200 Mon-Sun. Pizza, lasagne, toasties, home-made ice cream.

Mount Royal
2 Mount Royal. ☎ 823342. 1200-2100. A la carte. £.

Nibblers
50 Main St. ☎ 824017. 1100-0300 Mon-Sun July & Aug, earlier closing rest of year. Burgers, hot dogs.

Nobody's Inn
50 Ballyreagh Rd.
☎ 823509. 1130-2300, 1230-1430. 7 days. Snacks, pub grub.

Rathlin House
2 Ramore Avenue. ☎ 824834. 1500-1930 Mon-Sun. Booking advisable.

★ RAMORE
The Harbour. ☎ 824313. Wine bar 1200-1400 & 1730-2100 Mon-Sat. Restaurant 1830-2230 Tues-Sat. Tempura prawns, Thai chicken, hot fresh fruit & Grand Marnier souffle. £££.

Rascals
31 Main St. ☎ 822069. 1200-1430 Mon-Sat. Lasagne, quiche, burgers.

Rogues Wine Bar
54 Kerr St. ☎ 822076. 1200-1430 & 1700-2200 Mon-Sat, 1900-2130 Sun. Spinach flan, moussaka.

Rowland's
92 Main St. ☎ 822063. June-Sept 1200-2200, Oct-May 1700-2200, Mon-Sun. Lasagne, tagliatelli, pizza. A la carte. £££.

Royal Court Hotel
White Rocks. ☎ 822236. Last orders 2130, Sun 2100. Grill bar. Steak, open sandwiches, vegetarian. ££. A la carte. £££.

Shirley's Diner
26 Causeway St. ☎ 823581. 1100-2200 Mon-Sun in summer, more limited opening in winter. Scampi, lasagne, steaks.

Co. ANTRIM — Portrush-Randalstown

Silver Sands
27 Eglinton St. ☎ 824113.
0900-2300 Mon-Sun summer, until 1900 winter. Fish & chips, Ulster fry.

Some Plaice Else 🍴
21 Ballyreagh Rd.
☎ 824945. 1700-2130 Mon-Sat, 1230-1430 & 1700-2130 Sun. Seafood. E££.

Spinnaker ♀
25 Main St. ☎ 822348.
1000-2100 Mon-Sun Easter-Sept, more limited hours in winter. Set lunch, home-baked cakes. A la carte. E£.

Station Bar ♀
16c Eglinton St.
☎ 822112. 1730-2130.
Mon-Sat. Coffee, sandwiches. In nightclub.

Uncle Sams
35 Eglinton St. ☎ 824796.
0900-2100 Mon-Sun.
Chicken, steaks, salads.

The Victoriana
Dunluce Centre. ☎ 824400.
May-Aug 1000-2200 Mon-Sun; Sept 1100-1800 Mon-Thur, 1100-2200 Fri-Sun; Oct-April 1400-2100 Fri-Sun.
Ulster fry, chicken, fish. E£.

Waterworld
The Harbour. ☎ 822001.
1000-2200 Mon-Sat,
1400-2200 Sun in summer.
Lunch, coffee.

West Bay View
48 Mark St. ☎ 823375. 1230-1330 & 1730-1830 Mon-Sun. Booking essential.

West Strand Guest House
18 Kerr St. ☎ 822270.
1200-1800 Mon-Sun. Lunch, high tea. Vegetarian, fresh fish, home baking.

RANDALSTOWN
(STD 01849)

Cranfield Inn ♀
34 Cranfield Rd. ☎ 472342.
1800-2300 Mon-Fri,
1300-2300 Sat, 1230-1430 & 1900-2200 Sun. Fish, eel suppers, sausages.

Granagh House ♀
9 New St. ☎ 472758.
1100-2200 Mon-Sat,
1230-1430 & 1900-2200 Sun.
Lunch, grills. A la carte.

Marrion's ♀
10 Main St. ☎ 472487.
1130-2300 Mon-Sat,
1230-1430 & 1900-2200
Sun. Pies.

O'Kane's ♀
22 Main St. ☎ 473101.
1230-1430 & 2000-2200
Mon-Tues. 1230-1430 & 2030-2230 Wed, Thur, Fri, Sat. Ulster fry, plaice, hokey in breadcrumbs, toasties.
'Bushmills Bar of the Year 1991'.

Randalstown-Toomebridge — Co. ANTRIM

The Village
18 New St. ☎ 479740. 0900-1800 Mon-Sat. Gammon & pineapple, Irish stew, cheesecake.

Waves
56 Main St. ☎ 472680. 1130-2400 Mon-Thur, 1030-0100 Fri & Sat, 1630-2330 Sun. Fish & chips, curry.

RATHLIN ISLAND
(STD 012657)

Rathlin Guesthouse ♦
The Quay. ☎ 63917. Open Mon-Sun. Snacks, sandwiches, soup. High tea, dinner. Booking essential. E£.

Rathlin Restaurant ♦
The Harbour. ☎ 63939. 1100-1800 Mon-Sun June-Sept, weekends Easter-June. Speciality seafood.

STONEYFORD
(STD 01846)

Ballymac ♀
7a Rock Rd. ☎ 648313. 1130-2300 Mon-Sat, 1230-1430 & 1930-2200 Sun. Restaurant: 1230-1430 & 1830-2130 Mon-Sun. E££.
A la carte.

Stoneyford Inn ♀
68 Stoneyford Rd. ☎ 648288. 1500-2330 Mon-Sat, 1230-1430 & 1900-2200 Sun. Hamburgers, chicken, pies.

TEMPLEPATRICK
(STD 01849)

Airport Inn ♀
745 Antrim Rd. ☎ 432775. 1200-2145 Mon-Sat, 1700-2130 Fri-Sat, 1230-1600 & 1700-2130 Sun. Carvery, à la carte. ££.

Happy Inn ♀
Unit 8, Twelfth Milestone. ☎ 433717. 1200-1400 & 1700-2330 Mon-Sat, 1300-1500 & 1700-2400 Sun. ££.

Lyle Hill Tavern ♀
96 Lylehill Rd. ☎ 432451. 1200-1500 Thur-Sat. Ulster fry, stew, pies.

★ **TEMPLETON HOTEL** ♀
882 Antrim Rd. ☎ 432984. 1230-1345 Mon-Sun, Last orders 2145. A la carte. E£££.

Wayside Inn ♀
25 New Mill Rd, Ballywee. ☎ (0960) 324276. 1200-2300 Mon-Sat. Chicken, chips, salad, grills.

TOOMEBRIDGE
(STD 01648)

Drumderg Café
177 Moneynick Rd. ☎ (01648) 50306. 0800-1830, home-baked cakes. Mon-Sat. Grills, coffee, home-baked cakes.

Co. ANTRIM — Toomebridge-Whitehead

Elver Inn
100 Moneynick Rd.
☎ (01648) 50362. 1230-1430
Mon-Sat. Pub grub.

O'Neill Arms Hotel
Main St. ☎ 50202.
Last orders 2200. £.

T-Junction Café
62 Hillhead Rd. ☎ 50095.
0930-1900 Mon-Sat. Grills.
On A6.

WHITEABBEY
(STD 01232)

Knockagh Lodge
236 Upper Rd. ☎ 861444.
1200-1430 & 1700-2130
Mon-Sat, 1200-1430 & 1700-
2000 Sun. Bar snacks. Evening
à la carte.

WHITEHEAD
(STD 01960)

Coffee & Cream
10 King's Rd. ☎ 378757.
0900-1900 Mon-Sat. Chicken,
fish, salads, coffee, snacks.

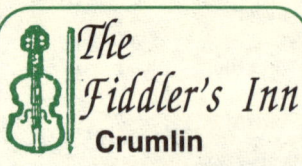

Pizza Plaice 'n' Chips
Marine Avenue. ☎ 353276.
1145-1400 Mon-Sat,
1700-2200 Tues-Thur, until
2400 Fri & Sat, 2000 Sun.
Pizzas, ribs, burgers.

The Fiddler's Inn
Crumlin

Bar and restaurant
For good food and service
Pleasant atmosphere
Live entertainment
every weekend

Sunday lunch
12 noon - 2.30 pm

Sunday dinner
6 pm - 9 pm

**36 Main Street
Crumlin**
☎ **(01849) 452221**

WYSNER'S
LICENSED RESTAURANT
16 ANN STREET BALLYCASTLE 012657 62372
FAX 012657 62372

**WYSNER'S
A TRADITION OF EXCELLENCE**

RECOMMENDED BY
"A TASTE OF ULSTER"
BRIDGESTONE GOOD FOOD GUIDE
AND THE HEALTHY EATING CIRCLE
NEED WE SAY MORE

COUNTY ARMAGH

AGHALEE

Greenhall ⚖
4 Airport Rd.
☎ (01846) 651997. 1200-1430 & 1730-2130 Mon-Sat, 1230-1430 & 1730-2100 Sun. A la carte, high teas. £.

ARMAGH
(STD 01861)

★ ARCHWAY

5 Hartford Place, The Mall.
☎ 522532. 1000-1700 Tues-Sat. Danish pastries, apple pie. Set lunch.

Armagh Fine Foods
24 Scotch St. ☎ 522805.
0900-1730 Mon-Sat. Morning coffee, sandwiches, salads. In delicatessen.

Barnaby's Restaurant at Harry Hoots ⚖
143 Railway St. ☎ 522103.
1230-1430 Mon-Sun, 1900-2130 Wed-Sun. Meatballs in Guinness sauce, smoked salmon & cream cheese pancake. E££.

Bramley Family Kitchen
Orchard Centre, Folly Lane.
☎ 522892. 1000-2200 Mon-Fri, until 1730 Sat, 1400-1730 Sun.
Burgers, chips, rolls.

Brigid's Café
Unit 1, Tullygoonigan.
☎ 526144.
0830-1700 Mon-Fri, 0830-1300 Sat. Braised steak, local vegetables. £.

Calvert's Tavern ⚖
3 Scotch St. ☎ 524186.
1200-1430 & 1800-2200 Mon-Sun. A la carte, seafood. E££.

Cellar Lounge ⚖
55 Thomas St. ☎ 525147.
1200-1500 Mon-Sat.
Pub grub.

Charlemont Arms Hotel ⚖
63 English St. ☎ 522028.
Last orders 2130. Seafood, duckling. Set lunch. A la carte. E£££.

Cottage Restaurant ☺
Gazette Arcade, Scotch St.
☎ 528582. 0830-1730 Mon-Sat, until 1400 Wed. Morning coffee, lunch, home baking.

Diamond Bar ⚖
21 Lower English St.
☎ 522645. 1200-1430 Mon-Sat. Soup, Irish stew, lunches.

Downtown Café
13 Dobbin St. ☎ 523538.
0900-1800 Mon-Sat, until 1400 Wed. Burgers, grills, fish.

Co. ARMAGH — Armagh

Drumsill House Hotel
35 Moy Rd. ☎ 522009. Last orders 2130. Salmon, lobster. Lunchtime carvery. £££.

Fat Sam's
7 Lower English St. ☎ 525555. 0845-1800 Mon-Fri, 0915-1700 Sat. Sandwiches, lasagne, salads.

Four Trees Lounge
2 Nursery Rd. ☎ 525393. 1300-1600 Mon-Sat. Pub grub.

Glencoe
72 Scotch St. ☎ 522994. 1130-2300 Mon-Sat. 1230-1430 & 1900-2200 Sun. Pub grub.

Hester's Place
12 English St. ☎ 522374. 0900-1730 Mon-Sat, closed Wed. Ulster fry, stew, grills.

Jodie's
37 Scotch St. ☎ 527577. 1200-1500 Mon-Sat, 1800-2200 Wed-Sat, 1730-2030 Sun. Steaks, à la carte. ££.

Johnston's Coffee Lounge
9 Scotch St. ☎ 522995. 0900-1730 Mon-Sat, closed Wed. Stew, lasagne.

Ken's
16 Barrack St. ☎ 525692. 0900-2100 Mon-Sat. Grills, snacks, pies.

Kerry Lynn Restaurant
3 Scotch St. ☎ 524186. 1200-1430 Mon-Sat, 1800-2200 Wed-Sat. Fillet of chicken with peppered sauce, salmon steaks, snacks.

Lantern
40 Scotch St. ☎ 524395. 0930-1700 Mon-Sat, closed Wed. Fish, chicken, salads.

Loudan's Cellars
49 English St. ☎ 522015. 2000-2130 Thur-Sat. Pub grub.

Calvert's Tavern and The Kerry Lynn Restaurant

* Lunches: 12 noon till 2.30 pm

* A La Carte nightly 6pm till 10pm

* Private Parties Catered for

* Live Entertainment *
Tuesday, Thursday,
Friday, Saturday and Sunday

3 SCOTCH STREET, ARMAGH
☎ **(01861) 524186**

Armagh **Co. ARMAGH**

McAnerney's
Irish St. ☎ 522468.
0900-1730 Mon-Sat.
Coffee, salads, rolls.

Mandarin House ♀
30 Scotch St. ☎ 522228.
1200-1400 Tues-Sat,
1700-2300 Tues-Sun. Chinese
& European. ££.

★ **NAVAN CENTRE**
Killylea Rd. ☎ 525550.
1000-1700 Mon-Fri, later start
on Sat & Sun. Coffee shop in
interpretive centre, offers
choice of hot meals and
snacks.

Northern Bar ♀
100 Railway St. ☎ 527316.
1130-1500 Mon-Sat.
Salads, scampi.

Orr's Corner ♀ ☉
36 Barrack St. ☎ 522052.
1230-1400 Mon-Sat.
Pub grub.

Palace Stables ☉
Palace Demesne. ☎ 522722.
1000-1900 Mon-Sat,
1300-1900 Sun, April-Sept;
1000-1700 Mon-Sat,
1400-1700 Sun, Oct-Mar.
Morning coffee, filled rolls,
lasagne, steaks. In heritage
centre.

Pub With No Beer
30 Thomas St. ☎ 523586.
0900-2230 Mon-Sat. Chips,
burgers, lasagne. Non-
alcoholic drinks.

Rainbow ☉
13 Upper English St.
☎ 525391. 0830-1730
Mon-Sat. Coffee, grills.

Restaurant No. 12
14 English St. ☎ 522374.
0900-1730 Mon-Sat, closed
Wed. Soup, salads.

St Patrick's Trian
The Pilgrim's Table,
38 English St. ☎ 527808.
Open daily. Steak hot pot,
potato & leek soup.

Shambles Bar ♀
9 Lower English St. ☎ 524107.
1230-1430 Mon-Sat. Soup,
sandwiches.

Station Bar ♀
3 Lower English St. ☎ 523731.
1230-1430 Mon-Sat. Pub
grub.

Strawberry Bar ♀
23 Lower English St.
☎ 523865. 1230-1430
Mon-Sat. Lasagne, chicken,
plaice.

Tino's
11 Thomas St. ☎ 523187.
0900-1800 Mon-Sat.
Pasta, chicken, fish.

Co. ARMAGH — Armagh-Craigavon

★ WHEEL & LANTERN
Market St. ☎ 522288.
1000-1700 Mon-Sat, closed Wed. Quiche, pies, pastries. Coffee lounge in department store.

BELLEEKS

Glenside Bar & Lounge ☲
15 Main St. ☎ (01693) 878280. 1900-2200 Mon-Sat. Soup, steak, chips, salads, sweets.

Mountain House ☲
Drumilly. ☎ (01693) 838766. 1900-2200 Thur-Sat, 1230-1430 Sun. A la carte.

BESSBROOK
(STD 01693)

Country Folk Inn ☲
Drumnahuncheon, 114 Tullyah Rd, Whitecross.
☎ 830230. 1130-2300 Mon-Sat. Hamburgers, pies.

Millvale ☲
Millvale. ☎ 830306.
1130-2300 Mon-Sat, 1230-1430 & 1900-2200 Sun. Pub grub.

BLACKWATERTOWN

Portmor House ☲
44 Main St.
☎ (01861) 548053. 1230-1430 Wed-Sun, 1800-2200 Fri-Sun. Hamburgers, pies. A la carte. ££.

CAMLOUGH

Doyle's ☲
22 Main St.
☎ (01693) 830269. 1130-2300 Mon-Sat, 1230-1430 & 1900-2200 Sun.
Stew, pies, pub grub.

Finnegan's ☲
25 Main St.
☎ (01693) 830044. 1230-1430 Mon-Sat. Pub grub.

Village Inn ☲
21 Main St.
☎ (01693) 838537. 1200-1430 & 1700-2100 Mon-Sat. Pub grub. A la carte.

CRAIGAVON
(STD 01762)

Brownlow Centre ◉
Brownlow Rd. ☎ 341333.
1200-1400 & 1700-2130 Mon-Fri, 1000-1700 Sat. Fish & chips, curries, hamburgers. Café in recreation centre.

Craigavon-Crossmaglen — Co. ARMAGH

Captain's Table
Craigavon Lakes. ☎ 342669.
1000-2100 Mon-Fri,
1000-1700 Sat & Sun,
June-Sept & Easter. Ice cream, coffee.

Cove Inn ♀
Craigavon Shopping Centre.
☎ 341044. 1130-2300
Mon-Sat, 1900-2200 Sun.
Pub grub.

Drumgor Tavern ♀
Drumgor. ☎ 342187.
1130-2300 Mon-Sat,
1230-1430 & 1900-2200
Sun. Pub grub.

Irwin's
Craigavon Shopping Centre.
☎ 342629. 0900-1730
Mon-Sat, until 2100 Thur & Fri. Self-service, snacks.

Laganview ♀
Donacloney. ☎ 881232.
1130-2300 Mon-Sat.
Sandwiches, coffee.

Loughside Café
Lough Neagh Discovery Centre, Oxford Island.
☎ 322205. 1000-1430
Mon-Sun. Soup, pies, lasagne.

Mr Pickwick's Kitchen
Craigavon Shopping Centre,
15 Market Lane. ☎ 341025.
0900-1730 Mon-Wed & Sat,
until 2100 Thur & Fri. Baked potatoes (20 fillings), pizzas.

Number 7
Craigavon Shopping Centre,
15 Market Lane. ☎ 342629.
0845-1730 Mon-Tues & Sat,
0845-2100 Wed-Fri. Stuffed steak, Ulster fry, scones.

Pinebank Centre
Tullygully Rd. ☎ 341033.
0830-1700 & 1930-2300
Mon-Sat. Coffee, snacks.

Tannaghmore Gardens
Tannaghmore. ☎ 341199.
1400-1730 Mon-Sun
July-Aug. Self-service, snacks.

CROSSMAGLEN
(STD 01693)

Ashfield Golf Club ♀
Freeduff, Cullyhanna.
☎ 868180. 1400-2100 Mon,
1200-2100 Tues-Sun. Grills, salads.

Cartwheel ♀
20 The Square. ☎ 861285.
1800-2300 Mon-Sat.
Pub grub. E£.

Chums ♀
46 The Square. ☎ 868413.
1230-1430 Mon-Sat.
Steaks, grills.

Conalig House ♀
124 Concession Rd.
☎ 861517. 1900-2200
Mon-Sat. Pub grub.

Co. ARMAGH — Crossmaglen-Keady

★ HEARTY'S FOLK COTTAGE
Glassdrummond. ☎ 861916. 1400-1900 Sun. Coffee, home-baked scones. Live music. Antiques/crafts sales.

Keenan's Bar ⚱
42 The Square. ☎ 868071. 1900-2230 Fri-Sat. Daily specials.

Kerryman ⚱
36 The Square. ☎ 861589. 1900-2200 Mon-Sun. A la carte.

Lima Country House
16 Drumalt Rd. ☎ 861944. 1800-2200 Mon-Sat. American. Booking essential.

Lite & Easy ⚱
Tullynavall Rd. ☎ 868262. 1300-1800 Mon-Sat. Pub grub.

McConville's Place ⚱
12 The Square. ☎ 861212. 1200-1500 Mon-Sat. Pub grub.

Murtaghs Bar ⚱
15 North St. ☎ 861378. 1230-1500 Mon-Sat. Pub grub.

FORKHILL
(STD 01693)

The Forge ⚱
100 Carrickasticken Rd. ☎ 888175. 1130-2300 Mon-Sat, 1230-1430 & 1900-2200 Sun. Pub grub.

Welcome Inn ⚱
35 Main St. ☎ 888273. 1130-2300 Mon-Sat, 1230-1430 & 1900-2200 Sun. Soup, sandwiches.

HAMILTONSBAWN

Bawn Inn ⚱
25 Main St. ☎ (01762) 871239. 1130-2330 Mon-Sat. Bar snacks.

Corner Bar ⚱
Main St. ☎ (01762) 871070. 1130-2300 Mon-Sat. Hamburgers, stew, pies.

KEADY
(STD 01861)

Arthur's ⚱
Bridge St. ☎ 539708. 1200-1400 Mon-Sat. Pub grub.

Callan River Inn ⚱
2 The Square. ☎ 539679. 1230-1500 Mon-Sat. Chicken, scampi, plaice.

Keady-Lurgan   **Co. ARMAGH**

Carnwood Lodge Hotel ♤
121 Castleblaney Rd.
☎ 538935. Last orders 2130. ££.

Old Mill
Kinelowen St.
0930-1730 Mon-Sat.
Home cooking. In Keady
Heritage Centre.

Rock Bar ♤
Granemore. ☎ 531992.
2000-2200 Mon-Sat.
Pub grub.

The Trap ♤
37 Kinelowen St. ☎ 538889.
1230-1430 Mon-Sun.
Pub grub. A la carte.

KILLYLEA

Digby's & Red Grouse ♤
53 Main St.
☎ (01861) 568330. 1230-1430
Mon-Sun, 1830-2400 Fri-Sun.
Steaks, kebabs. A la carte. ££.

LOUGHGALL
(STD 01762)

★ **THE FAMOUS GROUSE** ♤

6 Ballyhegan Rd. ☎ 891778.
1200-2100 Mon-Sat,
1900-2200 Wed-Sat,
1230-1430 & 1730-2015 Sun.
Poached Irish salmon, steaks,
duckling. Bar lunches. E££.

LURGAN
(STD 01762)

Alpine Lodge
Ski Centre, Turmoyra Lane,
Silverwood. ☎ 326606.
1100-1900 Mon-Fri,
0900-1800 Sat & Sun.
Chicken, salads, vegetarian.

Andrea's Coffee House
64 Belfast Rd. ☎ 324950.
1000-1630 Mon-Sat. Scones,
pastries, salads, lunch.

Ashburn Hotel ♤
81 William St. ☎ 325711. Last
orders 2045, Fri & Sat 2145.
A la carte. £.

Bradley's
36 Edward St. ☎ 321551.
1200-2400 Mon-Sun. Fresh
fish, filled rolls, pizza.

Brindle Beam Tea Rooms
20 Windsor Avenue.
☎ 321721. 1000-1700
Mon-Sat. Chicken & broccoli
crunch, home-made savoury
pies, salads. M£.

Byrne's ♤
Main St, Magheralin.
☎ (01846) 611506.
1200-1430 & 1700-2000
Mon-Sat. Sandwiches, grills.

Cafolla
51 Church Place. ☎ 324022.
1000-1800 Mon-Sat, until
1430 Wed. Fish & chips,
chicken, grills.

Co. ARMAGH — Lurgan

Cafolla
2 Carnegie St. ☎ 323331.
1000-1730 Mon-Sat. Snacks, grills, fish & chips, ice cream.

Castle Park Inn ♀
Robert St. ☎ 322726.
1200-1430 Mon-Thur,
1700-1930 Fri & Sat.
Pub grub.

Cellar Lounge ♀
50 Church Place. ☎ 327994.
1230-1430 Mon-Sat.
Pub grub.

Centrepoint Leisure
Portadown Rd. ☎ 321997.
1230-1430 Mon-Sun, later opening weekends. Kebabs, garlic bread, pancakes & maple syrup. Cinema, bowling alley. E£.

Coasters
35 Union St. ☎ 325452.
1030-2330 Mon-Sat.
1700-2300 Sun. Fish & chips

Corner House ♀
93 Silverwood Rd,
Derrymacash. ☎ 341817.
1200-1430 Mon-Sat,
1900-2200 Thur-Sat,
1200-1500, 1900-2130 Sun.
Soup, baked ham, pork chops, gateaux. A la carte. E£.

Gemini
2 Church Place. ☎ 327323.
0900-1730 Mon-Wed, until 1900 Thur, 2000 Fri & Sat.
Set lunch. A la carte.

Kebab King
62 William St. ☎ 325200.
1200-2400 Mon-Sun.
Indian food, fish, snacks.

Long Hall
22a High St. ☎ 328974.
0930-1700 Mon-Sat, closed Wed. Grills, afternoon tea.

The Mall ☺
Waves Complex, Robert St.
☎ 322906. 1000-2130 Mon-Sat. Closed Thur. Home-made pies, Irish stew, salads.

The Newsroom
32 Market St. ☎ 322121.
0830-1700 Mon-Sun.
Vegetarian, pitta pockets, home-baked scones.

Old Yard ♣
Edenmore House,
70 Drumnabreeze Rd.
☎ (01846) 619199.
0930-1630 Mon-Sat.
Caribbean chicken, seafood crunch. At golf course.

Peking Chinese ♀
86 William St. ☎ 342290.
1700-2200 Tues-Sun.
Chinese & European. E££.

Pizza Pasta Hut ♣
42 Church Place. ☎ 326444.
1700-2300 Mon-Sat, until 2200 Sun. Pizza, pasta.
A la carte.

Lurgan-Markethill   **Co. ARMAGH**

Rumpoles
High St. ☎ 321747.
0900-1730 Mon-Sat, until
1400 Wed. Burgers, fish.

Silverwood Hotel ♀
Kiln Lane. ☎ 327722. Last
orders 2130, Sun 2030. Beef
stroganoff, steaks. Set lunch,
à la carte. E£.

Spades
Grattans Centre. ☎ 343558.
0900-1730 Mon-Wed & Sat,
until 2100 Thur & Fri.
Quiche, lasagne, pie.

Stables ♀
Old Portadown Rd.
☎ 323974. 1200-1430
Thur-Sun. Pub grub.
Grills, salads.

Truffles
44a Market St.
0800-1700 Sun-Sat. Stew,
quiche, snacks.

Vintage ♀
31 Church Place. ☎ 328757.
1230-1430 & 1900-2100 Sat.
Pies, pub grub.

Wellworths
Market St. ☎ 325842.
0900-1730 Mon, Wed & Sat,
until 2100 Thur & Fri.
Breakfast, grills, salads.

White Wren
45 Market St. ☎ 325418.
0900-1800 Mon-Sat. Grills.

Wilton Cross ♀
38 Church Place. ☎ 322076.
1230-1500 Mon-Thur,
all day Fri-Sat. Daily special. A
la carte. £.

Woodville Arms ♀
111 Lake St. ☎ 324005.
1230-1430 Fri & Sat.
Pub grub.

MARKETHILL
(STD 01861)

Buttery ♀
103 Main St. ☎ 551237.
1930-2230 Wed-Sat.
A la carte. E£.

Corner Bar ♀
110 Main St. ☎ 551887.
1230-1500 Tues-Fri,
1900-2200 Fri & Sat.
A la carte. Pub grub.

Gosford Forest Park
☎ 551277. Open weekends
Easter-September, every day
July, August. Closed in winter.
Scones, pastries, home-made
chocolate cake. Tea shop in
forest park. Off B28.

Old Barn
5 Mowhan Rd. ☎ 551082.
0900-2300 Mon-Sat. Coffee
shop & restaurant. A la carte.
£.

113

Co. ARMAGH — Markethill-Portadown

★ OLD THATCH
3 Keady St. ☎ 551261.
0900-1300 & 1400-1700
Mon-Fri, 0900-1700 Sun.
Home-made jam, chocolate
fudge cake, carrot cake.
Coffee shop in Alexander's
department store.

MIDDLETOWN

Commercial Bar
Main St. ☎ (01861) 568407.
1230-1430 Mon-Sat.
Pub grub.

Fedara's
4 Main St. ☎ (01861) 568189.
1030-2230 Mon-Sat, until
2100 Sun. Steaks, salmon,
grills, stroganoff, sandwiches.
A la carte.

Longnancy's Bar
Tamlaght, Madden.
☎ (01861) 568437. 1130-2300
Mon-Sat, 1230-1430 &
1900-2200 Sun. Pub grub.

MOUNTNORRIS

Port Bar
Main St. ☎ (01861) 507204.
1130-2200 Mon-Sat.
Pub grub.

NEWTOWNHAMILTON
(STD 01693)

Canteen
The Commons. ☎ 878250.
1000-1500 Thur, 1000-2000
alternate Sats (market days).
Irish stew, sandwiches, Ulster
fry, pastries.

Slane's
Dundalk St. ☎ 878249.
1230-1400 Mon-Sat.
Snacks, grills.

South Side
47 Dundalk St. ☎ 878620.
1130-2300 Mon-Sat,
1230-1430 & 1900-2200
Sun. Pub grub.

Vallendale
16 The Square ☎ 878984.
1200-1430 Mon-Sat. Pub
grub.

PORTADOWN
(STD 01762)

Abra-Kebabra
Magowan Buildings, Borough
Place. ☎ 335075. 1100-2400
Mon-Sat, 1600-2400 Sun.
Indian & European.

Bengal Tandoori
121 Bridge St. ☎ 350922.
1200-1400 & 1700-2400
Mon-Sat, 1700-2300 Sun.
Indian & European. ££.

Portadown   **Co. ARMAGH**

Bennett's Bar ♎
46 Mandeville St. ☎ 350778. 1200-1430 Mon-Sat. Soups, salads, roasts.

Brambles
2 Borough Place, Magowan Buildings. ☎ 351000. 0900-1700 Mon-Sat. Lasagne, shepherd's pie, quiche.

Buttercup
47 William St. ☎ 333388. 0900-1730 Mon-Sat. Home-made quiche, chicken & ham pies. Also delicatessen.

Carn Restaurant
21 Craigavon Enterprise. ☎ 338801. 0900-1600 Mon-Fri. Set lunch, afternoon tea.

Carngrove Hotel ♎
2 Charlestown Rd. ☎ 339222. Last orders 2130, Sun 2100. Duckling, paella. A la carte £££.

Carol's
15 Mandeville St. ☎ 337814. 0900-1700 Mon-Sat, 0900-2200 Sat. Grills, set lunch, coffee.

Cascades
Swimming Pool, Thomas St. ☎ 332802. 1500-2030 Mon-Fri, 0930-1730 Sat. Café in swimming pool complex.

Chalet ♎
111 Armagh Rd. ☎ 336980. 1230-1430 Mon-Sat. Set lunch, steak & kidney pie, roasts.

Cookery Nook
42 High St. ☎ 351535. 0900-1700 Mon-Sat. Home-made soup, pies, quiches.

Cosy Corner ♎
Teagy Rd. ☎ 852211. 1230-1430 & 1830-2130 Thur-Sat. Salads, grills.

Dragon Inn ♎
34 Carleton St. ☎ 350761. 1700-2400 Mon-Sun, 1200-1500 & 1700-2400 Sun. Chinese & European. ££.

Ells ♎
42 Dobbin Rd. ☎ 336326. 0900-2200 Mon-Sat. Breakfast, grills. Set lunch. A la carte ££.

Ferguson's Bar ♎
91 Markethill Rd. ☎ 840230. 1130-2300 Mon-Sat. Hamburgers, pies.

Fifi's
44 Meadow Lane. ☎ 330321. 0800-1900 Mon-Sat. Ulster fry, frog's legs, steaks, soups.

Gallery Tea Shop
16 Church St. ☎ 331796. 0900-1730 Tues-Sat, until 2000 Thur. Cream teas, dietary meals.

Co. ARMAGH — Portadown

Gaynor's
3 Church Lane. ☎ 337117.
0800-1830 Mon-Sat.
Speciality fish, steak.

Golden Bridge ☼
71 Bridge St. ☎ 333028.
1200-1400 & 1700-2400
Mon-Thur, 1200-0100 Fri &
Sat, 1300-2400 Sun. Chinese
& European. E£.

Green Pepper
16 West St. ☎ 337581.
0830-1700 Mon-Sat. Pizza,
curry, soup, fruit tarts.

Hanging Sign ☼
8 Birches Rd. ☎ 851988.
1130-2130 Mon-Thur,
1230-1430 & 1900-2200 Fri-
Sat. Grills, scampi, steak.

JR's Restaurant
16 Loughgall Rd. ☎ 330332.
1700-2100 Thur, Fri, Sun.
1700-2200 Sat. E£.

Killycomain Inn ☼
Killycomain Rd. ☎ 337304.
1130-2300 Mon-Sat.
Set lunch. A la carte.

Lunch Box
1 Carleton St. ☎ 337663.
0945-1700 Mon-Fri. Toasties,
baked potatoes, burgers.

McCann's
250 Obin St. ☎ 332668.
0900-2400 Mon-Sat,
until 2100 Sun.
Fish & chips, chicken.

Meeting Place
20 Woodhouse St. ☎ 332735.
1230-1430 Mon-Sat.
Grills, salads.

Minella
22 Market St. ☎ 355911.
0900-1700 Mon-Sat,
until 1400 Thur.
Grills, sandwiches.

New Mandarin House ☼
34 West St. ☎ 351034.
1200-1400 & 1700-2330
Mon-Thur, until 0030 Fri-Sat,
1730-2300 Sun. Cantonese &
European. E££.

No. 7
7 High St. ☎ 350808.
0900-1730 Mon-Sat. Lasagne,
curries, home-baked pastries.

Park Lanes
Mandeville Mews. ☎ 358388.
1500-2300 Mon-Thur,
0900-2400 Fri & Sat,
1500-2300 Sun. Steaks, chilli,
snacks. Bowling, adventure
playground.

Parkside Inn ☼
Garvaghy Rd. ☎ 330260.
1800-2330 Mon-Sat.
Pub grub.

Pie Man
74 Woodhouse St.
☎ 330743. 0930-1645
Mon-Sat. Savoury & sweet
pies (28 varieties), pizza,
vegetarian, afternoon tea.

Portadown-Whitecross **Co. ARMAGH**

Queen's
1 Thomas St. ☎ 334644.
1230-1400 Mon-Thur, until
1700 Fri & Sat. Pies,
hamburgers, grills.

Railway Arms
28 Woodhouse St.
☎ 332054. 1200-1500
Mon-Sat. Pub grub, set lunch.

Seagoe Hotel
Upper Church Lane.
☎ 333076. Last orders 2200.
Irish brotchan, planter's beef,
seafood, local vegetables.
Carvery. A la carte. E££.

Spades
Portadown Shopping Centre.
☎ 339420. 0900-1730
Mon-Sat, until 2100 Fri.
Breakfast, Irish stew, sweets.

Upper Crust
16 West St. ☎ 332114.
0900-1730 Mon-Sat.
Snacks, grills, sweets.

Whistles Coffee Lounge
43 High St. 0900-1700
Mon-Sat. Lunch, coffee.

RICHHILL
(STD 01762)

Ballynahinch House
47 Ballygroobany Rd.
☎ 870081. 1900-2200
Mon-Sat. Buffets, party
functions. Booking essential.

Normandy Inn
6 Main St. ☎ 871386.
1230-1430 Mon-Sat,
1800-2100 Fri & Sat. Open
sandwiches, grills, burgers.

Ye Olde House Bar
9 Irish St. ☎ 871616.
2000-2200 Fri-Sat. Pub grub,
scampi. E£.

TANDRAGEE
(STD 01762)

Farmer's Inn
2 Mill St. ☎ 840928.
1130-2300 Mon-Sat,
1230-1400 & 1900-2200
Sun. Toasties, hamburgers.

Huntsman
65 Market St. ☎ 841115.
1230-1430 Mon-Fri,
1800-2100 Mon-Sun. Pork in
barbecue sauce, prawns,
steaks. A la carte. E£.

Park View Bar
12 Church St. ☎ 840219.
1200-1430 & 1900-2115. Pub
grub.

WHITECROSS

Rockerfellas
114 Tullyah Rd. ☎ (01693)
830230. 1800-2300
Fri & Sat. Pub grub.

Whitecross Bar
☎ (0186157) 642.
1900-2200 Fri-Sat. Steaks,
roast beef, chicken.

THE VISCOUNT *of* CLANDEBOYE

—— BANGOR ——

Where you'll find the liveliest entertainment all through the week

plus a varied and mouth-watering menu of the finest food-
<u>LUNCH AND EVENING!</u>

SPRINGHILL SHOPPING CENTRE, BANGOR.
☎ **(01247) 271545**

ADELBODEN LODGE COUNTRY HOUSE INN

FULLY LICENSED

Open Tuesday to Saturday for:
Lunches 12-2.30pm, High Tea 5-7pm,
Dinner 7-9pm

Bar snack menu also served
Excellent facilities for wedding receptions,
conferences and functions

☎ Bangor 464288   Fax: 01247 270053

38 Donaghadee Road, Groomsport,
Co Down BT19 2LH

ANNALONG
(STD 013967)

Halfway House 🍷
138 Glassdrumman Rd.
☎ 68224. 1230-1430 & 1900-2100 daily. Scampi, plaice.

Harbour Inn 🍷
6 Harbour Drive. ☎ 68678.
1200-1500 Mon-Thur,
1200-2100 Fri & Sat. Fish, steaks, stuffed turkey, desserts. £.

Marlino's
224 Glassdrumman Rd.
☎ 67080. 1030-2230 Mon-Sun Apr-Sept, 1100-1800 Mon-Sun Oct-Mar. Soup, sandwiches, toasties, ice cream.

Mill Coffee Shop
Marine Park. ☎ 68736.
1000-2000 Mon-Sun in summer, 1000-1700 Sat & Sun in winter. Snacks.

Shirley's
21 Main St. ☎ 68468.
1000-2200 Mon-Sat in summer,1200-1400 & 1700-2200 Mon-Sat in winter. Irish stew, salads.

ARDGLASS
(STD 01396)

Aldo's 🍷
7 Castle Place. ☎ 841315.
1700-2200 Wed-Sun,
1230-1430 Sun in summer,
1800-2200 Thur-Sun in winter.
A la carte. Steak chasseur, chicken kiev, seafood. E££.

Angus Cochrane's
The Harbour. ☎ 841551.
0800-2200 Mon-Sun.
Sandwiches, prawns, potted herrings, cockles, mussels.

Harbour Restaurant
4 Quay St. ☎ 842200.
0930-2400, Mon-Sun. Steak, chicken, scampi.

Roadside Tavern 🍷
83 Strangford Rd, Chapeltown.
☎ 841341. 1830-2230 Mon-Fri, 1130-2300 Sat. Pub grub.

BALLYGOWAN
(STD 01238)

Deerstalker Inn 🍷
15 The Square. ☎ 528712.
1200-1430 Mon-Sun, 1700-2200 Mon-Sat. Steaks, open sandwiches, spring rolls. A la carte.

Co. DOWN — Ballynahinch

BALLYNAHINCH
(STD 01238)

Coffee Nook
17 Main St. ☎ 563152. 0945-1630 Tues-Fri, 0930-1700 Sat. Sandwiches, pastries.

Connoisseur
51 High St. ☎ 561797. 0900-1700 Tues-Sat. Shepherd's pie, minced beef pie, salads, coffee.

Corner Restaurant ⌾
1 Main St. ☎ 562264. 0900-1400 Mon, until 1800 Tues-Thur, 2300 Fri & Sat. Grills, self-service.

Foo Kwai
25 Dromore St. ☎ 563214. 1700-2400 Mon-Fri, until 0100 Sat & Sun. Cantonese.

Fortune ♀
25 High St. ☎ 561030. 1200-1400 Thur-Sat, 1700-2400 Mon-Wed & Sun. Chinese & European. E££.

Ginesi ♠
34 Main St. ☎ 562653. 1130-2330 Mon-Sat, 1400-2330 Sun, closed Tues. Steak, scampi, fish & chips.

Graham's
37 Dromore St. ☎ 563868. 2000-2400 Mon, until 2300 Tues-Thur, 1700-2430 Fri & Sat, 1800-2300 Sun. Grills, fish.

Hideaway
19 Main St. ☎ 565450. 0945-1630 Tues-Fri, 0930-1700 Sat. Coffee, scones, quiche.

Millbrook Lodge Hotel ♀
5 Drumaness Rd. ☎ 562828. Last orders 2115. A la carte. M£, E££.

Pharaoh
10 Main St. ☎ 565252. 1200-1400 & 1630-2300 Mon-Sat, 1630-2030 Sun. Pizzas, pasta, fish, chicken, kebabs.

★ **PRIMROSE** ♀ ⌾
30 Main St. ☎ 563177. 1200-2200 Mon-Sat. Casseroles, shellfish, trout, salmon, home-made bread. E£.

Primrose Pop In
30a Main St. ☎ 563872. 0900-1730 Mon-Sat. Afternoon tea, quiche, pies.

Ramery Inn ♀
45 Windmill St. ☎ 562171. 1230-1400 & 2200-2400 Thur-Sat. Daily specials.

White Horse Hotel ♀
17 High St. ☎ 562225. Last orders 2115. A la carte. E££.

Windmill
5 Windmill St. ☎ 561111. 1200-1430 Mon-Sun, 1730-2130 Mon-Sat. Roasts, beef, pork, gammon.

BALLYWALTER
(STD 012477)

Country Cake Shop
38 Main St. ☎ 38215.
0830-1730 Mon-Sat. Ulster
fry, sandwiches, pastries.

Greenlea Farm
Dunover Rd. ☎ 58218.
Evening meals. Booking
essential. Farmhouse cooking.

BANBRIDGE
(STD 018206)

Banbridge Motor Company
101 Dromore Rd. ☎ 28241.
1000-2000 Mon-Sat,
1230-1430 & 1700-2000 Sun.
Mixed grill, baked potatoes.
E££.

Banbridge TIC
Octagon Restaurant. Off A1.
1000-1700, winter,
1000-2000, summer. Ulster
fry, scones, daily specials. £.

Bann Restaurant
43 Newry St. ☎ 24382.
0900-1700 Mon-Sat,
until 1430 Thur.
Breakfast, lunch, grills.

Banville House ♀
174 Lurgan Rd. ☎ 24267.
1230-1400 & 1730-2130
Sun. 1730-2130 Wed-Sat.
Closed Good Fri,
25 Dec. Set lunch, high tea.
Fresh salmon, duckling.
A la carte. E££.

Belmont Hotel ♀
Rathfriland Rd. ☎ 62517.
Last orders 2130 Mon-Fri,
Sun 2030. Pub lunch. Scampi
provençale, garnished steaks,
melon in port wine.
A la carte. ££.

Captain Cooks
17 Castlewellan Rd. ☎ 62112.
1130-2400 daily. Fish,
sausage, milk shakes.

Coach Inn ♀
13 Church Square. ☎ 22763.
1200-2300 Mon-Sat. Set
meals. Beef stroganoff,
duckling. E£.

Downshire Arms Hotel ♀
95 Newry St. ☎ 62343.
Last orders 2030. A la carte.
Set meals. E££.

Friar Tucks
57 Bridge St. ☎ 28282.
1130-2400 daily. Fish
sausages.

Gall Bog ♀
4 Gall Bog Rd. ☎ (01846)
692546. 1130-2300
Mon-Sat, 1230-1430 &
1900-2200 Sun. Pub grub.

Golden Bloom
Scarva St. ☎ 25411. 0830-
1730 Mon-Sat. Ulster fry,
quiche, pastries.

Goodfellas ♀
28 Scarva St. ☎ 62394.
1200-1500 Mon-Sat.
Pub grub.

Half Way House ♀
80 Half Way Rd. ☎ (01846)
692351. 1230-1430
& 1830-2100 Mon-Sat.
Grills, snacks. Buffet.

Hallsmill Inn ♀ ☉
Banbridge Rd, Lawrencetown.
☎ 25565. 1200-2200 Mon-Sat,
1730-2100 Sun. A la carte,
high tea. ££.

Harry's ♀ ☉
7 Dromore St. ☎ 22794.
1200-1430 Mon-Sat,
1730-2030 Tues-Sat,
1900-2130 Sun. Pies, snacks.

Imperial Inn ♀
38 Bridge St. ☎ 22610.
1230-1430 Mon-Sat.
Fish, omelettes, salads.

Jamies ♀
Peggy's Loaning, Scarva Rd.
☎ 26714. 1800-2100
Mon-Sat. Grills, salads.

Jockey Club ♀
21 Church Square. 1130-2300
Mon-Sat. Pub grub.

Majestic Café
52 Newry St. ☎ 23602.
0900-2200 Mon-Sun.
Fish, grills.

Patrisse Coffee Lounge
48 Newry St. 0800-1630
Mon-Sat, 0800-1330 Thur.
Soup, burgers.

Rosamar
12 Bridge St. ☎ 22263.
0900-1730 Mon & Wed,
until 1630 Thur, 1800 Fri &
Sat. Fish & chips, grills.
Self-service.

Sami's ♀
4 Rathfriland St. ☎ 25725.
1130-2300 Mon-Sat,
1230-1430 & 1900-2200 Sun.
Toasties, burgers, stew.

Strings ♀
41 Newry St. ☎ 62446.
1100-1430 Mon-Sat, 1730-
2130 Tues-Thur, 1730-2200
Sat & Sun. A la carte. E£.

Superbite
3 Shopping Centre
Scarva St. ☎ 62200.
0900-1700 Mon-Sat, until
1900 Fri. Irish stew, home-
made soup, pork chop
casserole, gammon.

Ulster Bar ♀
72 Newry St. ☎ 22266.
1130-2300 Mon-Sat.
Pub grub.

BANGOR
(STD 01247)

★ BACK STREET CAFÉ ♦
14 Queen's Parade.
☎ 453990. 1900-2230
Tues-Sat. A la carte. Baked
turbot, Barbary duck fillets,
home-made bramble ice
cream. E££.

Bangor   **Co. DOWN**

Bamboo Tree ♀
22 High St. ☎ 467826.
1200-1400 Mon-Sat, 1700-0030 Mon-Thur & Sun, until 0130 Fri & Sat. Cantonese & European. E£.

Bewley's ☻
Bloomfield Shopping Centre, South Circular Rd. ☎ 272079. 0900-2100 Mon-Fri, 0900-2000 Sat. All home-made stews, soups, sweets. Bewley's coffee.

Bryansburn ♀
151 Bryansburn Rd. ☎ 270173. 1200-1400 Mon-Sun, 1700-2130 Mon-Sat, 1700-1900 Sun. Home cooking. A la carte. E££.

Bunjy Jump ♀
99 Main St. ☎ 461529. 1200-2300 Mon-Sat, 1200-2100 Sun. Tapas, cannelloni, trout with stilton, vegetarian. E££.

The Canteen ♀
119 High St. ☎ 274423. 1700-1900 Grill menu, 1900-2130 à la carte. Game sausage, spring onion potato bread in port wine sauce, marinated chump of lamb.

Castle Garden
Heritage Centre, Town Hall. ☎ 270371. 1100-1630 Tues-Sat, 1400-1630 Sun, until 1730 summer, earlier closing winter. Morning coffee, afternoon tea.

Charlie Heggarty's ♀
17 High St. ☎ 271285. 1230-1400 & 1700-2000 Mon-Sat. Set lunch. E£.

Cineplex
1 Valentine Rd. ☎ 454729. 1000-1500 & 1700-2200 Mon-Sat, 1000-2130 Sun. Lasagne, pies.

Clandeboye Lodge Hotel ♀
10 Estate Rd, Clandeboye. ☎ 852500. 0700-2200 breakfast. 1200-1500 & 1800-2100 Sun. Late breakfast with jazz.

Coffee Pot
88a Groomsport Rd. ☎ 271765. 0930-1700 Mon-Sat. Soup, salads, sandwiches.

Donegan's ♀
44 High St. ☎ 270362. 1230-1430 & 1700-2200 Mon-Sat, 1900-2100 Sun. A la carte. E££.

Dragon House
76 High St. ☎ 459031. 1700-0030 Mon-Thur, 1700-0130 Fri & Sat, 1700-2400 Sun. Chinese & European. Vegetarian.

Esplanade ♀
Esplanade, Ballyholme. ☎ 473294. 1215-1415 & 1830-2130 Mon-Sat, 1230-1400 Sun. Set meals. A la carte. E£.

123

Co. DOWN — Bangor

Ganges 🍴
9 Bingham St. ☎ 453030.
1200-1400 & 1730-2330
Mon-Sat, 1700-2300 Sun.
Indian. E££.

★ THE GEORGE 🍷 ☻
10 Estate Rd, Clandeboye.
☎ 853311. 1230-1430 &
1700-2130 Mon-Sat. Set
meals. E££.

Gray's Bistro ☻
20a Gray's Hill. ☎ 270339.
0900-1700 Mon-Sat,
1100-1900 Sun. Sandwiches,
toasties.

Green Bicycle
6 Hamilton Rd. ☎ 271747.
1000-1630 Mon-Sat.
Vegetarian, afternoon tea.

Gryphon ☻
12 The Esplanade, Ballyholme.
☎ 473294. 1200-1415 Mon-
Sun, 1900-2115 Tues-Sat,
1700-1900 Fri & Sat. A la
carte. High tea. E££.

★ HEATHERLEA TEA ROOMS ☻
94 Main St. ☎ 453157.
0900-1730 Mon-Sat. Quiche,
pies, salads, pizza, desserts.

Honey Tree Chinese Restaurant 🍷
5 Crosby St. ☎ 457817.
1200-1400 & 1700-2400
Mon-Sat. 1700-2330 Sun.
Chinese & European. ££.

Imperial 🍷
Central Avenue. ☎ 271133.
1200-1700 Mon-Sat,
1230-1430 & 1900-2200 Sun.
Pub grub.

International at Bangor 🍷
2A Castle Square. ☎ 272049.
1030-2230 Mon, Tues &
Thur-Sat, 0800-2230 Wed,
1130-1600 Sun. Carvery
lunches & teas. 12 ethnic
restaurants under one roof.
Russian salad, Zanzibar
prawns, oysters, sole in
chablis. £.

Jamaica Inn 🍷
188 Seacliff Rd. ☎ 274674.
1130-1500 & 1700-2130
Wed-Sat, 1230-1430 Sun.
Warm beef salad, pork
marsala, char-grilled
swordfish. E££.

Jenny Watt's 🍷
41 High St. ☎ 270401.
1200-2130 Mon-Sat,
1230-1430 & 1900-2100 Sun.
A la carte. Stir fry, ribs. £.

Kentucky Fried Chicken
1 Main St. ☎ 452686.
1100-2400 Sun-Thur, until
0200 Fri & Sat. Chicken,
barbecued ribs, coleslaw,
apple pie.

Bangor **Co. DOWN**

King Jade ♀
22 Dufferin Avenue.
☎ 270662. 1200-1400 &
1800-2130 Tues-Sat, 1700-
2330 Sun. Cantonese &
European. Chinese banquets.
E££.

Knuttel's 🍴
7 Gray's Hill. ☎ 274955.
1800-2130 Tues-Sat. Pork in
sherry & cream sauce,
mignons of fillet scallops. E££.

Leisure Centre
Castle Park. ☎ 270271.
0930-2200 Mon-Fri,
0930-1800 Sat, 1400-1800
Sun. Hamburgers, chips,
salads.

**Marerosa Chinese
Restaurant** ♀
14 Abbey St. ☎ 471106.
1200-1400 & 1700-2400
Mon-Sat. 1700-2400 Sun.
Chinese & European. E£.

Mrs Bun's Coffee Shop
108 Abbey St. ☎ 466294.
0900-1730 Mon-Sat. Ulster
fry, stew, toasties, milk shakes.

★ **O'HARA'S ROYAL
  HOTEL** ♀
26 Quay St. ☎ 271866.
Last orders 2130. Salads,
quiche. Sunday carvery, ££.
A la carte. Fresh prawns in
lobster sauce. E££.

Oriental Palace ♀
2a King St. ☎ 452439.
1200-1430 & 1700-2400
Tues-Thur, until 0100
Fri & Sat, 1700-2330 Sun.
Chinese & European. E££.

Penguin Coffee Shop
5 King St. ☎ 271682. 0900-
1700. Pies, toasties, baked
potatoes.

Penny Whistle ♀
13 High St. ☎ 473943.
1200-1500 Mon-Thur, until
1900 Fri-Sat, 1230-1430 Sun.
Pub grub, scampi, lasagne. £.

Pizza Hut ♀
115 Main St. ☎ 271272.
1200-2400 Mon-Sat, until
2300 Sun. Pizza, pasta,
desserts. E£.

Rose & Chandlers ♀
2 High St. ☎ 271540.
1200-1500 Mon, 1200-2100
Tues-Sat. Lunch, high tea, pub
grub, home-made soup.

Sampan ♀
2a Market St. ☎ 460470.
1200-1400 & 1700-2330
Mon-Sat, 1700-2300 Sun.
Cantonese. E££

Sands Hotel ♀ ☻
10 Seacliff Rd. ☎ 270696.
Last orders 2115, Sun 2000.
Garlic mushrooms, Portavogie
prawns. Set meals, à la carte.
E££.

The Refectory

Comber's newest restaurant

Venison with wild mushrooms and rosemary jus, or perhaps scallops with a spinach and balsamic vinegar

Just two dishes from our menu to whet the appetite.

A warm welcome and a relaxing evening are assured at The Refectory. Our aspiration is to provide you with an unforgettable gastronomic experience.

Using the best of local produce to enjoy with soft music and relaxing decor.

For reservations ☏
Mike or Steve (01247) 870870

46 Mill Street, Comber, Co Down

The Smuggler's Table

**Experience
The best in seafood**

Dining times

11 am - 5 pm Tues

11 am - 10.30 pm Wed - Sat

Sunday lunch from

12.30 pm - 2.30 pm

**The Harbour
Killyleagh, Co. Down**
☏ **(01396) 828778**

The Villager Restaurant

**3 Downpatrick Street, Crossgar.
(01396) 830385**

Fully Licensed Restaurant & Bars

* Open Sundays *

Knuttels

RESTAURANT

Overlooking the Marina

for fine international cuisine with a local flavour
SERVED IN A RELAXED INFORMAL SETTING
PARTIES CATERED FOR

OPENING TIMES
Lunch by arrangement
Dinner Tues - Sat 6 pm - 9.30 pm

For further details or reservations:-

☏ **(01247) 274955**

(Proprietors)
Stephen or Esther Hylands

7 Gray's Hill, Bangor

Bangor-Carrowdore **Co. DOWN**

Simas Indian Cuisine
9 Crosby St. ☎ 271722.
1200-1400 Mon-Sat,
1700-2330 Mon-Sun,
1230-1430 Sun. Indian &
European. ££.

Springers
Springhill Shopping Centre.
☎ 469802. 0900-1730
Mon-Sat, until 2100
Thur & Fri. Mince steak pie,
quiche.

Steamer Bar
30 Quay St. ☎ 467699.
1200-1430 & 1730-2130
Mon-Thur, until 2200 Fri &
Sat. 1230-1400 Sun. Seafood,
à la carte. E£.

Tedworth Hotel
Lorelei, Princetown Rd.
☎ 463928. Last orders 2115.
Garlic prawns, snails, trout.
A la carte. E££.

Victor's
6 Dufferin Avenue.
☎ 271088. 1100-2300
Mon-Sat. Fish & chips.

Viscount of Clandeboye
Springhill Shopping Centre.
☎ 271545. 1200-1500
Mon-Sat, 1900-2200
Thur-Sat. Set meals. A la carte.

Warwick
41 Queen's Parade.
☎ 271462. 1230-1430
Mon-Fri, 1200-1900 Sat. Pub
grub.

★ **WHEATEAR**
108 Main St. ☎ 467489.
0830-1730 Mon-Sat. Lasagne,
chicken special, Irish stew.

Windsor
Quay St. ☎ 473943.
1200-2130 Mon-Sat,
1230-1430 & 1900-2400 Sun.
Jazz Tues. A la carte. E££.

Winston Hotel
19 Queen's Parade.
☎ 454575. Last orders 2200,
Sun 1900. A la carte. E£.

Wolsey's
24 High St. ☎ 460495.
1200-1900 Mon-Thur & Sun,
until 2000 Fri & Sat, 2130-
2330 - bookings. Lasagne,
pizza.

Wongs
37 Queen's Parade.
☎ 452893. 1200-1400 Mon-
Sat, 1700-2400 Mon-Thur,
until 0100 Fri & Sat, 1700-
2400 Sun. Chinese &
European. Set lunch. E£.

CARROWDORE

Tavern
38 Main St. ☎ (01247)
861222. 1130-2300 Mon-Sat,
1230-1430 & 1900-2200 Sun.
Pub grub.

Co. DOWN — Carrowdore-Castlewellan

White Horse Inn
39 Main St. ☎ (01247) 861212. 1230-1430 Mon-Sun, 1730-2030 Mon-Fri & Sun, until 2230 Sat. Pub grub.

CARRYDUFF
(STD 01232)

★ **IVANHOE**
556 Saintfield Rd. ☎ 812240. 1230-1400 & 1700-2130 Mon-Sat, until 2030 Sun. Set meals. A la carte. E££.

Little Chef
Town & Country Shopping Centre. ☎ 812097. 0930-2200 Mon-Sat. Chicken, salads, sweets.

Old Saint Coffee House
5 Old Saintfield Rd. ☎ 815141. 1000-1800 Mon-Sat. Sandwiches, ice cream parlour.

Oriental Garden
Town & Country Shopping Centre. ☎ 812755. 1700-2400 Mon-Sun. Chinese & European. E£.

Pizza Hut
Town & Country Shopping Centre. ☎ 815060. 1200-2400 Mon-Sat, 1200-2300 Sun. Pizzas, garlic bread, salads. £.

Rick's
Carryduff Shopping Centre. ☎ 814558. 0900-1730 Mon-Sat, until 2100 Wed-Fri. Breakfast, afternoon tea. Home baking.

Royal Ascot
Hillsborough Rd. ☎ 813477. 1200-2400 Mon-Sat, 1200-1430 & 1900-2100 Sun. Set meals, à la carte. E£.

CASTLEWELLAN
(STD 013967)

Castlewellan Forest Park
Grange Coffee House. From Easter-Oct daily. From Oct weekends only. Teas, snacks.

Chestnut Inn
28 Lower Square. ☎ 78247. 1200-2100 Mon-Sat, 1200-1400 & 1700-2200 Sun. Steak, scampi, pub grub. E£.

Dolly's Brae Inn
15 Gargary Rd. ☎ (08206) 50213. 1700-2230 Mon-Sat, 1900-2130 Sun. Pub grub.

McElroy's
151 Ballylough Rd. ☎ 78238. 1800-2330 Mon-Sat. Soup, stew, pub grub.

Maginn Bros
9 Main St. ☎ 78359. 1230-1430 Mon-Sun. Scampi, chilli, salads.

Castlewellan-Comber — Co. DOWN

Rose Bar ♀
7 Upper Square ☎ 71500.
1200-1430 Mon-Sun. Pub grub.

Ulster Arms ♀
2 Moneyslane Rd.
☎ (0820650) 724. 1230-1430 Sun-Sat & 1730-2200 Mon-Sat, 1900-2130 Fri-Sun. Ulster fry, open prawn sandwich.

CLOUGH

Clough Inn ♀
28 Main St. ☎ (0396811) 209.
1200-1400 & 1700-1930 Sun-Mon.

COMBER
(STD 01247)

★ CASTLE ESPIE

78 Ballydrain Rd. ☎ 872517.
1030-1700 Mon-Sat, 1400-1800 Sun. Coffee, home-made soup, fisherman's pie, scones.

Country Fayre ☕
Castle Arcade. ☎ 873728.
0900-1630 Mon-Sat.
Quiche, salads, pies.

Donnell's
12 The Square. ☎ 878307.
0900-1700 Mon-Thur, until 2100 Fri & Sat. Home baking. Bistro.

Harry Fraser's
11 Castle St. ☎ 872546.
0830-2230 Tues-Fri, until 1900 Sat. Breakfast, set lunch, fish & chips.

Kate's
47 Ballyhenry Rd. ☎ 874577.
1000-1700 Mon-Fri, 0930-1730 Sat, 1230-1730 Sun.
Bistro, set meals. £.

Lisbarnett House ♀
Lisbane. ☎ (0238) 541589.
1130-2300 Mon-Sat. 1900-2200 Sun.

McBride's
1 The Square. ☎ 878703.
1200-1430 Mon-Sat. Stuffed steak, ham & parsley, stuffed pork sultana.

Mayflower ♀
47 Castle St. ☎ 873254.
1200-1400 & 1700-2400 Mon-Sat, 1630-2330 Sun.
Chinese & European. ££.

North Down House ♀
Belfast Rd. ☎ 872242.
1200-1400 Mon-Fri,
1900-2230 Mon-Sat. Pub grub, prawn sandwiches, baked potatoes.

★ OLD SCHOOL HOUSE ♀

100 Ballydrain Rd.
☎ (01238) 541182. 1900-2200 Tues-Sat, 1200-1500 Sun.
A la carte. £££.

Co. DOWN — Comber-Cultra

Refectory ♇
46 Mill St. ☎ 870870. 1830-2200 Tues-Sat & 1230-1500 Sun. Fresh fish, game, baked hake with asparagus and champagne sauce. E£££.

Salems Gallery
29 Mill St. ☎ 873624. 1000-1630 Mon-Sat. Salads, baked potatoes, daily specials. Beside antiques gallery.

Ulster Arms ♇
3 The Square. ☎ 878703. 1200-1430 Mon-Sat. Pub grub.

CONLIG

Grapevine Restaurant ☉
105 Main St. ☎ (01247) 820219. 0930-1700 Mon-Sat. Soup, lasagne, pies, salads.

CRAWFORDSBURN

Conservatory Restaurant ☉
Crawfordsburn Country Park. ☎ (01247) 852725. 1000-1830 in summer, earlier closing in winter. Sandwiches, soup, coffee.

★ **OLD INN** ♇
15 Main St.
☎ (01247) 853255.
Last orders 2130, 2000 Sun. Roast beef, sole, Portavogie scampi, salmon, sherry trifle. A la carte, 18th-century minstrels' gallery. E££.

CROSSGAR
(STD 01396)

Hill House
53 Killyleagh Rd. ☎ 830792. Steaks, home-made soups. Pre-booking essential.

Magee's ♇
Downpatrick St. ☎ 830281. 1200-1400 Mon-Sat. Pub grub.

★ **ROSEMARY JANE TEA ROOM**

20 Downpatrick St.
☎ 831335. 0930-1730 Mon-Sat. Home baking, afternoon tea.

Villager ♇
3 Downpatrick St.
☎ 830385. 1230-1430 & 1730-2130 Mon-Sat, 1230-1430 & 1700-2030 Sun.

CULTRA
(STD 01232)

★ **CULLODEN HOTEL** ♇
Craigavad. ☎ 425223.
Last orders 2145, Sun 2030. A la carte. E£££.

Cultra Inn ♇
Culloden Hotel, Craigavad.
☎ 425840. 1230-1415 & 1800-2145 Mon-Sat. Salmon, turkey, steak & kidney pie. Set lunch. A la carte. E£££.

Cultra-Donaghadee   **Co. DOWN**

Manor House ♀
Cultra Manor, Ulster Folk & Transport Museum. ☎ 427097. 1100-1700 Mon-Sat, 1400-1800 Sun. Open later in summer. Carvery Sun, snacks.

DONAGHADEE
(STD 01247)

Bow Bells
5 Bow St. ☎ 888612. 1000-1630 Mon-Sat. Home baking.

Captain's Table
22 The Parade. ☎ 882656. 1200-1400 & 1630-2100 Mon-Fri, closed Wed, 1200-2100 Sat & Sun. Fish & chips.

★ **COFFEE PLUS**
Market House, New St. ☎ 882641. 0930-1630 Mon-Sat. Pies, lasagne.

Copelands Hotel ♀
60 Warren Rd. ☎ 888189. Last orders 2130. Sunday lunch. A la carte. E££.

Deans
52 Northfield St. ☎ 882204. Evening dinner. Booking essential.

Dunallan Hotel ♀
27 Shore St. ☎ 883569. Last orders 2030. Steaks, à la carte. E£.

★ **GRACE NEILL'S** ♀
33 High St. ☎ 882553. 1130-2300 Mon-Sat. Pub grub, potted herrings. Beer garden at rear. 17th-century bar.

Harlequin
5a Shore St. ☎ 883840. 1000-1730 Mon-Sat, 1400-1800 Sun. Tray bakes, sausage rolls, scones.

Moat Inn ♀
102 Moat St. ☎ 883297. 1230-1430 & 1730-2130 Mon-Sat, 1230-1400 & 1900-2100 Sun. Garlic steaks, curry, spaghetti. ££.

Moorings ☺
26 The Parade. ☎ 882239. 0930-1730 Mon-Thur, until 2100 Fri & Sat. Breakfast, set lunch, afternoon tea.

Old Pier Inn ♀
33 Manor St. ☎ 882397. 1230-1430 & 1700-2100 Mon-Sat, 1230-1430 & 1900-2200 Sun. Set lunch. A la carte. E£.

Tivoli Bar ♀
32 Manor St. ☎ 882961. 1230-1430 & 1630-2100 Mon-Sun. Roast lamb, steak & kidney pie, open sandwiches.

Co. DOWN — Downpatrick

DOWNPATRICK
(STD 01396)

Abbey Grill
38 Market St. ☎ 613039.
0930-1730 Mon-Sat,
0930-1400 Wed. Grills.

Abbey Lodge Hotel ♀
Belfast Rd. ☎ 614511.
Last orders 2130. Fresh
oysters, trout, kebab, crêpe
suzette. A la carte. M£, E££.

Aldo's Coffee Lounge
Downtown Shopping Centre.
☎ 615414. 0900-1730
Mon-Sat, until 1500 Wed.
Stew, pastries, coffee.

Arts Café
Down Arts Centre, Irish St.
☎ 615283. 0930-1630 Mon-
Sat. Soup, salads, pastries,
freshly baked bread.

Bon Appetit ♀
1c English St. ☎ 613364.
1200-1400 Mon-Sat,
1700-2400 Mon-Thur & Sun,
1700-0100 Fri & Sat. Chinese
& European. E£.

Brendan's ♀
94 Market St. ☎ 615311.
1200-1500 & 1700-2100
Mon-Sat. 1200-1400, 1900-
2100 Sun. Soup, stew, scampi.

Castle Inn ♀
109 Ballynoe Rd. ☎ 612116.
1230-1430 & 1800-2100
Mon-Sat. Basket meals.

Countryside Inn ♀
37 Mearne Rd, Saul.
☎ 615750. 1230-1430 Mon-
Sun, 1700-2100 Mon-Sat,
1900-2130 Sun. Daily
specials. A la carte, high tea.

De Courcy Arms ♀
14 Church St. ☎ 612522.
1200-1430 Mon-Sat, 1700-
2000 Wed-Sat. 1230-1430
Sun. E££.

Dick's Cabin ♀
40 Church St. ☎ 612800.
1200-1430 Mon-Fri. Ulster
fry, Irish stew.

Golden Dragon
21 Scotch St. ☎ 613364.
1200-1400 & 1700-2400
Mon-Thur, 1700-0100
Fri & Sat, 1700-2400 Sun.
Chinese & European.

Oakley Fayre ۞
Market St. ☎ 612500.
0930-1730 Mon-Sat. Quiche,
lasagne, salads.

Pepper Pot
38 St Patrick's Avenue.
☎ 615165. 0900-1900
Mon-Sat, 1300-2000 Sun in
summer. Set lunch, à la carte.

Downpatrick-Dundrum — Co. DOWN

Rea's ♀
78 Market St. ☎ 612017.
1200-1500 Mon-Sat. Fresh seafood. E££.

Russell ♀
7 Church St. ☎ 614170.
1200-1400 Mon-Fri.
Soup, salads, savouries.

Slaney Inn ♀
Raholp. ☎ 612093. 1230-1430 Mon-Sun, & 1800-2100 Wed-Sat, 1800-2000 Sun. Carvery. A la carte E£.

Tyrella House
Clanmaghery Rd. ☎ 851422.
2000-2200 Mon-Sat.
Set meals. Booking essential. Parties of 6 plus only.

Brewery Inn ♀
4 Meeting St. ☎ 692476.
1200-1430 & 1730-1930 Mon-Sat. Steak, scampi, lasagne. E££.

Castle Bar ♀
8 Castle St. ☎ 692378.
1130-2300 Mon-Sat, 1230-1430 & 1900-2200 Sun. Pub grub.

Wendy's
36 Market Square. ☎ 693149.
0900-1700 Mon-Sat. Ulster fry, shepherd's pie, chicken, baguettes.

Winstaff
45 Banbridge Rd. ☎ 692252.
1900-2200 Mon-Sat. Set meals. Booking essential.

DROMARA
(STD 01238)

O'Reilly's ♀
7 Rathfriland Rd. ☎ 532209.
1130-2200 Tues-Sat, 1230-1430 & 1900-2100 Sun.
Lobster, crab, salmon. Set meals. E£££.

DROMORE
(STD 01846)

Boss Hoggs
9 Market Square. ☎ 692852.
0900-2400. Pizzas, chicken.

DUNDRUM
(STD 013967)

Bay Inn ♀
169 Main St. ☎ 51209.
1230-1400 & 1700-2200 Mon-Sat, 1230-1400 & 1900-2200 Sun. Snacks.
A la carte.

★ BUCK'S HEAD ♀

77 Main St. ☎ 51868/51859.
1200-1430 & 1800-2130 Mon-Sat, 1200-1430 & 1800-2000 Sun. Seafood, steaks, vegetarian. High tea.

DOWN

A landscape inscribed with legendary names and beautiful places...

- **Newcastle**
- Mountains of Mourne
- Delamont Country Park
- Tollymore Forest Park
- Tyrella Beach
- Murlough Nature Reserve

...steeped in history

- Down Museum
- Down Cathedral
- Struell Wells
- St Patrick's Grave
- Inch Abbey

...with activities for everyone

- Golfing
- Walking
- Fishing
- Equestrian
- Tropicana Pool/Play Area
- CoCo's Adventure Playground

...so, why not take time to find time in Down

For further information contact:
Down Tourist Information Centre
74 Market Street, Downpatrick,
Co. Down BT30 6LZ
Tel: 01396 612233; Fax: 01396 61235

DOWN
DISTRICT COUNCIL

The Bucks Head Inn

77 MAIN STREET : DUNDRUM

Enjoy a friendly drink in a relaxing atmosphere and dine in convivial surroundings choosing from an extensive menu which includes Vegetarian and Seafood Dishes, Steaks etc.

Lunches and snacks: 12.00 noon - 2.30 pm Mon to Sat.
Evening meals: 6.00 pm - 9.30 pm Mon to Sat.
Sunday lunch: 12.00 noon - 2.30 pm.
High teas: until 7 pm Mon to Sat
Sundays until 8pm.

**We can also cater for small weddings, cocktail parties and christening parties etc.
(up to 50 persons)**

Please call for reservations
DUNDRUM (013967) 51868 or 51859

Dundrum-Greyabbey **Co. DOWN**

Marina Bar
59 Main St. ☎ 51284.
1130-2200 Mon-Sat,
1230-1430 & 1900-2200 Sun.
Pub grub, steak, scampi.

Murlough Tavern
143 Main St. ☎ 51211.
1200-1430 & 1700-2200
Mon-Sat. Set lunch. Open
sandwiches, quiche, lasagne,
home-made soup.

GILFORD
(STD 01762)

★ **GILBERRY FAYRE** ⊙

92 Banbridge Rd. ☎ 832098.
0900-1630 Mon-Sat.
Afternoon tea, quiche, salads,
home baking.

Gilford Inn
4 Dunbarton St. ☎ 831801.
1200-1400 Mon-Sun.
Pub grub.

Honey Pot
Dunbarton St. ☎ 831497.
0900-1700 Mon-Sat.
Breakfast, home-made soup,
Irish stew.

The Loft
4 Dunbarton St. ☎ 831801.
1200-1400 Mon-Sat & 1900-
2300 Sat-Sun. Pub grub. E££.

Pheasant Lodge
34 Mill St. ☎ 832293. 1200-
1430 Fri-Sun. Pub grub.

Pot Belly
59 Banbridge Rd, Tullylish.
☎ 831404. 1830-2330
Tues-Sat, 1230-1430 & 1800-
2100 Sun. A la carte. E££.

Sarah Moon's
Bridge St. ☎ 831543/831636.
1900-2200 Tues-Sat. Oysters,
sherried mushrooms, garlic
steak. ££.

GREYABBEY
(STD 012477)

Boley Hill Farm
10 Cardy Rd. ☎ 88252.
1000-2100 Mon-Sun
July-Aug. Scones, biscuits,
gateaux, home-made ice
cream. On a fruit farm.

Hoops
7 Main St. ☎ 88541.
0930-1730 Wed, Fri & Sat.
Sandwiches, pizza, stew.
Craft & antique shop.

Mount Stewart House
Ark Club tea room. ☎ 88387.
Open same times as National
Trust house. Quiche, lasagne.

Poacher's Inn
23 Main St. ☎ 88330.
1200-1430 & 1700-2200
Mon-Sun. A la carte, seafood,
duck with raspberries,
venison. E££.

Co. DOWN — Greyabbey-Hillsborough

Wildfowler ♀
1 Main St. ☎ (012477) 88260.
1200-1500 & 1700-2130
Mon-Sat, until 2200 Sun.
High tea, pub grub. A la carte.
E££.

GROOMSPORT
(STD 01247)

★ **ADELBODEN LODGE** ♀ ◉
38 Donaghadee Rd.
☎ (01247) 464288.
1200-1430 & 1700-2330
Tues-Sat. High tea, vegetarian.
A la carte. E£.

★ **THE STABLES** ♀
26 Main St.
☎ (01247) 464229. 1230-1430 & 1700-2130 Mon-Sat, 1230-1430 & 1900-2115 Sun.
Lasagne, steak.
A la carte. E£.

HELEN'S BAY
(STD 01247)

★ **DEANE'S ON THE SQUARE** ♀
Station Square. ☎ 852841.
1900-2200 Tues-Sat & 1230-1430 Sun. A la carte. £££.

HILLSBOROUGH
(STD 01846)

Carriage Restaurant ♀
41 Old Coach Rd. ☎ 689624.
1730-2130 Mon-Sat,
1230-1430 Sun. Pheasant,
trout, steak. E££.

Cornmill ♀
19 Lakeland Rd, Annahilt.
☎ (01238) 532818.
1700-2130 Wed-Sat,
1230-1430 & 1700-2030
Sun. A la carte, high tea. E££.

★ **HAMPTON'S COFFEE SHOP**
Harry's Rd. ☎ 682500.
0930-1700 Mon-Sat. Home-baking, cakes, scones.

★ **HILLSIDE** ♀ ◉
21 Main St. ☎ 682765.
1230-1430 & 1900-2130
Mon-Sat, 1230-1400 & 1900-2045 Sun. Oysters, salmon & sole plait, duck breast in sweet brandy. E££.

Marquis of Downshire ♀
48 Lisburn St. ☎ 682095.
1230-1430 & 2000-2200
Mon-Sat. Pub grub.
Grills, salads.

Plough Inn ♀
3 The Square. ☎ 682985.
1200-1415 & 1800-2030
Mon-Sat, 1230-1415 & 1900-2100 Sun. Home-made soup, pies, seafood, steaks, sweets.

Hillsborough-Holywood — Co. DOWN

★ RED FOX
6 Main St. ☎ 682586.
1015-1400 & 1445-1700
Tues-Sat. Salads, quiche,
sweets, coffee. Home baking.

Ritchie's
3 Ballynahinch St. ☎ 683601.
1200-1430 Mon-Sat. Club
sandwiches, lasagne, pies.

Shambles Coffee Shop
1 Dromore Rd. ☎ 689022.
1000-1600 Mon-Sat, 1400-
1700 Sun, Home-baked
snacks, scones, desserts.

Traveller's Kitchen
163 Dromore Rd. ☎ 683956.
0745-1900 Mon-Fri, until
1700 Sat. Ulster fry, gammon,
fish.

★ WHITE GABLES HOTEL
14 Dromore Rd. ☎ 682755.
Last orders 2115, 2030 Sun.
Local vegetables, game in
season. A la carte. M£, E££.

HILLTOWN

The Downshire Arms
Main St. ☎ (018206) 38899.
1230-1430 Mon-Sun, 1830-
2200 Mon-Thur, 2230 Fri-Sat,
1900-2100 Sun. Salmon,
chicken, steaks. Set meals, à la
carte. E££.

Mourne Rambler
22 Main St. ☎ (018206)
30749. 1800-2300 Mon-Fri,
1130-2300 Sat, 1900-2200
Sun. Pub grub.

Shamrock
Main St. ☎ (018206) 30045.
1600-2200 Tues-Thur, 1130-
2330 Fri-Sat, 1200-1430 Sun.
Pub grub.

Village Inn
43 Main St. ☎ (018206)
38649. 1230-1430 & 1800-
2200 Mon-Sat, 1900-2200
Sun. A la carte.

HOLYWOOD
(STD 01232)

★ BAY TREE COFFEE HOUSE
Audley Court, 118 High St.
☎ 426414. 1000-1630
Mon-Sat. Cinammon scones,
vegetarian dishes, salmon
plait. Restaurant open from
1930 last Fri each month.
Booking essential. E££.

Bear Tavern
62 High St. ☎ 426837.
1200-1500 Mon-Fri. Quiche,
pies, burgers.

Bell's
8 Shore St. ☎ 423203.
0900-1600 Mon-Fri.
Home-made soup, pastries,
set lunch. In bakery.

Co. DOWN — Holywood

Bokhara ♧
149 High St. ☎ 427989. 1700-2300 Mon-Thur & Sun, until 2330 Fri-Sat. Indian. £££.

★ CARMICHAEL'S ♧
Hibernia St. ☎ 424759. 1200-1430 & 1700-2030 Mon-Sat. A la carte. E££.

Claudia's Patisserie ♦
49B High St. ☎ 427552. 1900-2400 Tues-Sat. Salmon & spinach tart, stuffed pork rolled in smoked ham. Coffee shop 1100-1500.

Empress Oriental International ♧
49 High St. ☎ 422333. 1200-1400 & 1700-2400 Mon-Sat, 1700-2300 Sun. Chinese, European & Thai. ££.

Herbert Gould & Co
Church Rd. ☎ 427916. 0915-1730 Mon-Sat, 1400-1730 Sun (Nov/Dec only). Scones, soup.

★ IONA ♦
27 Church Rd. ☎ 425655. 1830-2400 Mon-Sat. Beef with garlic beans, pork with peppercorns, coffee ice cream with hazelnuts. ££.

Old Priory Inn ♧
Main St. ☎ 428164. 1230-1430 & 1900-2200 Mon-Sat, until 2100 Sun. Bistro: pâté, soup, salads. £. Restaurant: steaks. ££.

★ RAYANNE HOUSE ♧
50 Demesne Rd. ☎ 425859. Pear stuffed with stilton in port & redcurrant sauce, lamb with roast peppers & rosemary. A la carte. Booking essential.

Seaside Tavern ♧
19 Stewart's Place. ☎ 423152. 1130-1430 & 1730-2000 Mon-Fri, 1130-2000 Sat. 1230-1430 Sun. Home cooking. A la carte.

Silver City
124 High St. ☎ 428766. 1700-2400 Tues-Sun. Chinese & European. E£.

Sullivan Coffee Shop
117 High St. ☎ 427467. 0900-1700 Mon-Sat. Lasagne, pies.

★ SULLIVANS ♦
Sullivan Place. ☎ 421000. 1000-1600 Mon-Sun, 1900-2130 Tues-Sat. Seafood with leeks and saffron. Game. E£££.

Waterfront Wine Bar & Bistro ♧
2 Kinnegar Rd. ☎ 425533. 1230-1430 Mon-Sat, 1230-1400 Sun, 1800-2100 Mon-Wed, 1800-2200 Thur-Sat. Grills.

Wilson's
58 High St. ☎ 427419. 0800-1630 Mon-Sat. Snacks, coffee.

Katesbridge-Kilkeel **Co. DOWN**

KATESBRIDGE
(STD 018206)

Angler's Rest ♀
42 Aughnacloy Rd. ☎ 71515. 1800-2200 Mon-Sat. Pub grub, baked potatoes.

KILKEEL
(STD 016937)

Archways ♀
23 Newry St. ☎ 64112. 1230-1400 Mon-Sat. Pub grub.

Captain's Table
24 Newcastle St. ☎ 64555. 1100-1800 Mon-Fri, until 2100 Sat. Fish, chicken, chips.

Coffee Shop
25a Greencastle St. ☎ 64370. 0930-1730 Mon-Sat, open 0830 in summer. Quiche, pies, lasagne.

Coffee Shop
Silent Valley. 1130-1830 Mon-Sun in summer. Home baking.

Cranfield House Hotel ♀
57 Cranfield Rd. ☎ 62327. Last orders 2045, Sun 2000. Set lunch, high tea, pub grub. E££.

Fisherman ♀
68 Greencastle St. ☎ 62130. 1230-1430 Wed-Sat, 1800-2130 Thur & Fri, 2230 Sat, 1700-2030 Sun. Open Wed evening during summer. Local prawns, clams, lobster, salmon, turbot, stuffed mushrooms. E££.

Harbour Café
5 Harbour Rd. ☎ 62207. 1030-1900 Mon-Wed, 1030-2000 Fri & Sat. Fish, chicken.

Jacob Hall's ♀
8 Greencastle St. ☎ 64751. 1200-1430, 1700-2000, summer only. Mon-Sat. Starters, grills.

Kilmorey Arms Hotel ♀
Greencastle St. ☎ 62220. Last orders 2100, Sat 2200. A la carte. E££.

Mourne Grange
169 Newry Rd. ☎ 62228. 1000-1230 Mon-Sat, 1400-1700 Mon-Sun. Scones, cakes, coffee. Craft shop.

Old Mill
12 Knockchree Avenue. ☎ 62112. 1000-1830 Mon-Sat, until 2300 in summer. Barbecued beef, scampi, seafood platter.

Port Inn
3 The Square. ☎ 62453. 1130-2300 Mon-Sat. Pies, burgers.

DEERSTALKER INN

15-19 The Square,
Ballygowan.

☎ 01238 528712

NOW OPEN

Co. Down's HOTTEST & NEWEST NIGHTSPOT!

* Resident Live Bands
* Beer Garden
* Off-Sales Beside Bar
* Games Room - Pool etc.
* Functions catered for

All this and much, much more at the newly opened ...

DEERSTALKER INN

NOW BOOKING FOR WEDDINGS ...

NEWRY & MOURNE

Enjoy

Hill Walking • Horseriding • Golfing

Windsurfing • Fishing • Caravanning

Camping and Exploring our Heritage

in the beautiful South Down,

South Armagh countryside:

For further information contact:
Tourist Office
Newry & Mourne District Council
Greenbank, Warrenpoint Road, Newry, Co. Down, Northern Ireland BT34 2QU

☎ (01693) 68877 Fax: (01693) 68833

Kilkeel-Killyleagh — Co. DOWN

Port O Call
13 Bridge St. ☎ 62621.
0930-1730 Mon-Wed, until
1400 Thur, 1800 Fri, 2030 Sat.
Ulster fry, steaks, chicken.

Riverside Tavern ♀
2 Bridge St. ☎ 65316.
1900-2200 Mon-Sat. Grills.

Silver Herring ♀
4 The Square. ☎ 62491.
1200-1415 Mon-Sat, 1900-
2100 Sat. Pub grub.

KILLINCHY
(STD 01238)

Balloo House ♀
☎ 541210. 1230-2200
Mon-Sun. Grilled salmon. Hot
& cold buffet. A la carte. E££.

Daft Eddy's ♀ ☺
Sketrick Island, Whiterock.
☎ 541615. 1200-1500, 1700-
2130 Mon-Sat, 1230-1430,
1900-2100 Sun. Salmon,
steaks. Pub on island across
causeway. E£.

★ LISBARNETT HOUSE ♀
Lisbane. ☎ 541589. 1200-
1430 Mon-Sat, à la carte,
1800-2130. 1230-1430 &
1900-2100 Sun. Sizzling
dishes, seafood, steak,
Mexican chicken.

KILLOUGH

Old Inn ♀
36 Castle St.
☎ (01396) 841067.
1200-1430 Mon-Sun.
Ploughman's lunch, fish.

KILLYLEAGH
(STD 01396)

Anchor Inn ♀
16 Catherine St. ☎ 828700.
1130-2300 Mon-Sat,
1230-1430 & 1900-2200
Sun. Pub grub.

★ DUFFERIN ARMS ♀
35 High St. ☎ 828229.
1230-1430 Mon-Sun, 1730-
2100 Mon-Wed, -2400 Thur-
Sat. Steak, fish. A la carte. Live
music.

Siglu
Delamont Country Park.
☎ 821091. 1300-1700
weekends only Easter to
September. Sandwiches,
crepes, home-made cookies.

Smuggler's Table ♀
2 Bridge St. ☎ 828778.
1130-2230 Tues-Sat, 1230-
1430 & 1730-2000 Sun.
Salmon, lobster, monkfish,
garlic prawns. E££.

KIRCUBBIN
(STD 012477)

Saltwater Brig ♀
43 Rowreagh Rd. ☎ 38435.
1230-1430 Mon-Sun,
1700-2100 Mon-Sat,
1900-2100 Sun.
Bistro menu. £.

LOUGHBRICKLAND

Bronte Steakhouse
Ballynafoy Rd, Ballinaskeagh.
☎ (018206) 51338. 1730-2300
Tues-Sat. Steaks, Barbary Duck
with Cointreau sauce, chicken
stir fry. E£.

Road Chef
Dublin Rd. ☎ (01762) 318366.
0800-2000 Mon-Sat, 1230-
2130 Sun. Breakfast, lunch.
Grills, toasties, sweets. E£.

Seven Stars ♀
4 Main St. ☎ (018206) 26461.
1230-1430 & 1800-2200
Mon-Sat, 1230-1430 & 1900-
2100 Sun. A la carte. Steak,
chicken, pavlova, gateaux. £.

MILLISLE
(STD 01247)

Dorothy's
53 Main St. ☎ 861852.
1130-2100 Mon-Sun in
summer. 1200-1400 & 1700-
2000 Mon-Fri, 1130-2030 Sat,
1400-2000 Sun in winter.
Fish, burgers, ice cream.

First Last ♀
37 Main St. ☎ 862644. 1130-
2300 Mon-Sat, 1230-1430 &
1900-2200 Sun. Roast beef,
pies, burgers.

Kingfisher ♀
26 Main St. ☎ 861304.
1800-2300 Tues-Fri in winter.
1230-1430 Sat. 1230-1430 &
1700-2300 in summer.
Seafood, steak. Set meals. A la
carte. E£.

Windmill Grill
57 Main St. ☎ 861461.
1000-2400 Mon-Sun. Grills.

Woburn Arms ♀
69 Main St. ☎ 861272.
1200-2000 Mon-Sun.
Pub grub.

MOIRA
(STD 01846)

Ballycanal Manor
2 Glenavy Rd. ☎ 611923.
Traditional cooking, dinner.
Booking essential.

Bon Appetit
87 Main St. ☎ 619718. 1130-
2330 Mon-Wed, until 0030
Thur-Sat, 1700-2300 Sun.
Chicken, sausages.

Chestnut Lodge ♀
6 Chestnuthill Rd.
☎ 611409. 1200-1430
Mon-Sat, 1700-2200
Wed-Sat, 1230-1430 &
1900-2200 Sun. A la carte. E£.

Moira-Newcastle   **Co. DOWN**

Cork & Cleaver ♀
4 Rawdon Court, Main St.
☎ 611853. 0930-1630 Mon-Sat, 1700-2130 Thur, Fri, Sat. Steaks, lamb with apple & cider sauce. A la carte. E££.

Country Kitchen
21 Main St. ☎ 612787. 1000-1700 Mon-Sat, Thur & Fri 2045. Snacks, salads, home-made sweets. Coffee shop in textile-cookshop store.

Glenavy Road Restaurant ⊙
Glenavy Rd Service Station, Airport Rd. ☎ 611909. 0830-1930 Mon-Sat, until 2130 Sun. Set lunch. Ulster fry, chicken, fish.

Halfpenny Gate Inn ♀
Halfpenny Gate Rd.
☎ 621280. 1130-2300 Mon-Sat, 1230-1430 & 1900-2200 Sun. Burgers, scampi.

Maghaberry Arms ♀
23 Maghaberry Rd.
☎ 611852. 1130-1430 & 1730-2130 Mon-Fri, 1130-1900 Sat. Scampi, pork chops, salad.

Midnight Haunt ♀
90 Main St. ☎ 611391. 1700-2400 Mon-Thur, until 2430 Fri & Sat, 1700-2300 Sun. Chinese & European. E£.

Nina's Pizzeria
74 Main St. ☎ 611185. 0900-1800 Mon-Sat. Pizzas, soups, salads.

★ **NO. 1 GALLERY**
101 Main St. ☎ 619788. 0930-1730 Tues-Sat. Casseroles, salads, sweet & savoury pancakes.

Norman Inn ♀
Main St. ☎ 611318. 1230-1430 Mon-Sat. Pub grub, snacks.

NEWCASTLE
(STD 013967)

Anchor Bar ♀
9 Bryansford Rd. ☎ 23344. 1200-1430 Mon-Fri, 1200-1730 Sat. Curries, lasagne.

Arkeen Hotel ♀
59 Central Promenade.
☎ 23473. Last orders 1930. A la carte. £.

Armours Cove House
26 Ballagh Rd. ☎ 23814. Dinner. Booking essential.

Avoca Hotel ♀
93 Central Promenade.
☎ 22253. Last orders 2100. A la carte. £.

Co. DOWN — Newcastle

Brambles
4 Central Promenade.
☎ 26888. Winter 1000-1800 Fri-Sun. Summer 1000-1800 Mon-Fri, until 2300 Sat & Sun. Apple pie, Canadian cheesecake & pancakes.

Brook Cottage Hotel ♆
58 Bryansford Rd. ☎ 22204. Last orders 2100, Sun 2030. A la carte. ££.

★ **BURRENDALE HOTEL** ♆
51 Castlewellan Rd.
☎ 22599. Last orders 2100, Sun 2000. A la carte. £££.

Central Park ♆
121 Central Promenade.
☎ 22487. 1230-1430 & 1700-2100 Mon-Sat, 1900-2100 Sun. Grills, salads, daily specials.

Cookie Jar ☻
Main St. ☎ 22427.
0900-1730 Mon-Sat.
Home-baked cakes.

Country Fried Chicken
119 Main St. ☎ 23900.
1100-2400 Mon-Fri & Sun, until 0130 Sat. Chicken, burgers.

Cup 'n' Saucer
87 Central Promenade.
☎ 22753. 1030-2000 Mon-Sun July-Sept, until 1700 Fri-Sun Easter-June. Open sandwiches, snacks, sweets, home baking.

The Cygnet ☻
2 Savoy Lane. ☎ 24758.
Winter 1000-1700 Mon-Sat, 1100-1700 Sun. Summer 1000-1800 Mon-Sat, 1100-1800 Sun. Soup, stew, scones.

Donard Hotel ♆
27 Main St. ☎ 22203. Last orders 2115. Closed Jan & Feb. A la carte. ££.

Enniskeen Hotel ♆
98 Bryansford Rd. ☎ 22392. Last orders 2030. Closed Dec-Feb. A la carte. £££.

Harbour House Inn ♆
4 South Promenade. ☎ 23445.
1200-1500 & 1700-2130 Mon-Sat, 1230-1430 & 1700-2200 Sun. Chicken curry, pâté, rainbow trout. £.

Lunch Box Café
133a Main St. ☎ 68284.
1030-1700 Mon-Sun.
Burgers, fish.

McGlennon's Hotel ♆
61 Main St. ☎ 22415. Last orders 2200. A la carte. ££.

Mario's ♆
65 South Promenade.
☎ 23912. 1230-1430 Tues-Sun, 1830-2200 Tues-Sat, 1700-2100 Sun. Italian. Minestrone, pasta, zabaglione. A la carte.

Newcastle — **Co. DOWN**

Newcastle Centre
Central Promenade. ☎ 22222.
1100-1900 Mon-Sat, 1400-1900 Sun summer only.
Sausage rolls, sandwiches.

Oaks ⌇
62 Main St. ☎ 26400.
1230-1500 Mon-Sat. Chicken, lasagne, pork dishes.

Pavilion ⌇
36 Downs Rd. ☎ 26239.
Restaurant: 1000-2200 Mon-Sat, 1000-2000 Sun.
Salmon, steaks, gateaux. E££.
Sandwiches, scones, lasagne, plaice, salads.

Percy French ⌇
Downs Rd. ☎ 23175.
1230-1430 & 1730-2130 Mon-Sat, 1200-1400 & 1730-2100 Sun. Chicken chasseur, poached haddock, ploughman's lunch. A la carte.

Pizza Palazzo
98 Main St. ☎ 26444.
1700-2400 Mon-Thur & Sun, until 0200 Fri & Sat. Pizzas, fish, garlic bread.

Shimna Diner ⌇
14 Railway St. ☎ 23010. 1000-1900 Mon-Sun. Kilkeel fish, steaks, toasted sandwiches.

Slieve Donard Hotel ⌇
Downs Rd. ☎ 23681.
Last orders 2130. Booking essential Sept-Feb. A la carte. Grill bar. E££.

Strand Coffee Shop
3 Main St. ☎ 23924. 0830-1800 Mon-Sat July & Aug, 0900-1730 Mon-Sat rest of year. Sandwiches, soup.

Strand Palace
53 Central Promenade.
☎ 23472. 1000-2300 Mon-Sun summer, limited hours rest of year. Pancakes. A la carte. Restaurant beside bakery.

Tollymore Teahouse
Tollymore Forest Park.
☎ 24067. 0900-2030 Mon-Sun Mar-Sept, 1200-1800 Sat & Sun rest of year. Scampi, chicken, grills.

Top of the Town
1 Main St. ☎ 24328.
1000-0030 Mon-Wed, 1000-0130 Thur-Sun.
Fish, burgers.

Toscano ⌇
47 Central Promenade.
☎ 22263. 1230-2200.
Mon-Sun Easter-Oct. Ice cream, snacks, high tea. A la carte.

Wadsworths
42 Main St. ☎ 22626.
0930-1700 Mon-Sat, closed Thur in winter. Snacks, lunch. In department store.

Co. DOWN — Newry

NEWRY
(STD 01693)

Ambassador
81 Hill St. ☎ 65307.
0800-1900 Mon-Wed,
0800-2000 Thur-Sat. Set
meals. A la carte.

Arts Centre
1a Bank Parade. ☎ 61244.
1100-1600 Mon-Fri.
Sandwiches, coffee.

The Boulevard
1 Margaret Square, Hill St.
☎ 66555. 0800-1830 Mon-
Wed & Sat, until 2000 Thur &
Fri. Chicken curry, fish, roast
beef.

Boyd's
Hill St. ☎ 62424.
0900-1700 Mon-Sat. Snacks,
grills, lunch.

★ **BRASS MONKEY** ♙
Trevor Hill. ☎ 63176.
1230-1430 & 1800-2200
Mon-Sat. Bar snacks, steaks,
chicken. M£. E£££.

Brenda's Kitchen
Island Arcade, Sugar Island.
☎ 67987. 0900-1730
Mon-Sat. Set lunch.

Bridge Bar ♙
53 North St. ☎ 62240.
1230-1500 & 1800-2100
Mon-Sat. Pub grub.

Cavern ♙
28 Church St. ☎ 62124.
1230-1500 & 1700-2200
Mon-Sat. Pub grub.

Clarke's ♙
73 Kilmorey St. ☎ 63960.
1230-1500 Mon-Sat. Pub grub.

Crown Bar ♙
59 Lower North St. ☎ 62494.
1130-2300 Mon-Sat.
Hamburgers, pies.

Crusty Corner
22 Margaret St. ☎ 67708.
0830-1730 Mon-Sat. Quiche,
snacks.

Cupids ♙
25 Merchants Quay.
☎ 63221. 1230-1500 Mon-Sat.
Grills, pizzas. Set lunch,
buffet.

**Dominic's &
Hill Street Blues** ♙
8 John Mitchell Place.
☎ 62413. 1130-1500 & 2000-
2230 Mon-Sat. Grills, salad,
pizzas.

Donnelly's ♙
Silverbridge. ☎ 861410.
1230-1430 Mon-Sat. Pub
grub.

Friar Tuck's
3 Sugar Island. ☎ 69119.
1100-2400 Mon-Sat,
1500-2400 Sun. Burgers.

Newry — **Co. DOWN**

Glenside House
22a Tullynavall Rd. ☎ 861075.
1200-1430 & 1800-1930
Mon-Sat. Steaks, home baking.

Hermitage Bar ♀
1 Canal St. ☎ 64594.
1230-1430 Mon-Sat. Grills.

Hillside
1 Rock Rd. ☎ 65484/61430.
1630-1930 Mon-Sat. Set meals. Booking essential.

Kylemore Café
10 Buttercrane Centre.
☎ 65555. 0900-1730
Mon, Tues & Sat, until 2100
Wed-Fri. Grills, snacks.

Lido
23 Hill St. ☎ 62626.
0930-1730 Mon-Sat, until 1400 Wed. Sandwiches, fried fish.

Lite 'n' Easy ♀
Tullynavall Rd, Cullyhanna.
☎ 868262. 1300-1800 Mon-Sat. Set meals, pub grub.

Little Italy
Kildare St. ☎ 65111.
1130-2430 Mon-Wed, until 0100 Thur, 0230 Fri & Sat.
Pizzas, burgers.

★ **McLOGAN'S** ♀
55 Merchant Quay.
☎ 62143. 1230-1500 & 1830-2215 Mon-Sun. Carvery, steaks. A la carte. E£.

Mall View
60 Lower Mill St. ☎ 66236.
0900-1800 Mon-Sat. Snacks.

Mister B's ♀
8 Water St. ☎ 62193.
1200-1800 Mon-Sat. Pub grub.

Murtaghs ♀
25 Bridge St. ☎ 62558.
1230-1430 Mon-Sat. Baked potatoes, toasties, grills.

Newry Golf Inn
11 Forkhill Rd. ☎ 63871.
1230-1400 & 1700-2100
Mon-Fri, 1130-2300 Sat.
A la carte. E£.

Orchard Bar ♀
114 Rathfriland Rd. ☎ 64911.
1930-2130 Mon-Sat. Pub grub.

Riverside ♀
3 Kildare St. ☎ 2170.
1200-1430 & 1900-2330 Sun-Thur. 1200-1430 & 1700-0030 Fri & Sat. Cantonese & Peking.

Rose Garden ♀
3 Sugar Island. ☎ 68702.
1200-1400 Mon-Fri,
1700-2330 Mon-Thur, until 2430 Fri & Sat, 1700-2315
Sun. Chinese & European. E£.

The Halfway House
138 Glassdrumman Road
Annalong, Co. Down
☎ (013967) 68224

Bar Snacks - daily
Lunches - 12.30 pm to 2.30 pm
High Tea - 7.00 pm to 9.00 pm
Sunday Lunch - 12.30 pm - 2.30 pm
Special Evening Meal
Fri-Sat-Sun - 7.00 pm to 9.00 pm

Located in the heart of the Mournes, this 18th-century pub & restaurant offers a wide range of ales and a selection of fine wines, beers & spirits. The front bar is known for its traditional music. In the restaurant we serve excellent home cooked meals with fresh vegetables and a selection of fresh fish. Come along and enjoy anything from a bar snack to full à la carte.

Welcome to upstairs at

Bellamy's

(licensed restaurant)
& downstairs at

HUDSON'S

(cellar bistro bar)

For a unique dining out experience.
Lunch - high tea - à la carte and bistro (open 7 days a week)

**96-98 Frances Street,
Newtownards**
☎ **(01247) 813480**

DEANES
on the
SQUARE

Licensed Restaurant
HAYDN J H DEANE
and
MICHAEL DEANE
Chef
Dorchester Hotel • Belfast Castle
Nick's • Santé
Michael Deane Chef of the Year
Salon Culinaire NIFEX 1993
ARE DELIGHTED TO INVITE YOU
TO ENJOY
SPLENDID FOOD
with
FINE WINES
in a
UNIQUE ATMOSPHERE
AT THEIR RESTAURANT IN
STATION SQUARE, HELEN'S BAY
(01247) 852841/(01247) 273155
FOR RESERVATIONS
Lunch by arrangement
*Tuesday - Saturday Dinner from 7.00pm
Sundays with a difference
Mondays - Cookery Workshop*

DAFT EDDY'S LTD
Sketrick Island, Killinchy

Unique Island Setting

Bar meals served
Mon - Sat 12.00 pm - 3 pm
Sunday 12.30 pm - 2 pm

A la Carte
Tues - Sat 7 pm - 9.30 pm
Sunday Lunch 12.30 pm - 2 pm

☎ **Killinchy
(01238) 541615**

Newry-Newtownards — **Co. DOWN**

Satellite
13 Kilmorey St. ☎ 62657.
1200-2330 Mon-Sat,
1700-2430 Sun. Fish, chicken, pies.

Shakespeare ☲
48 Monaghan St. ☎ 60006.
1130-2300 Mon-Sat. Pub grub.

Sheepbridge Inn ☲
143 Belfast Rd. ☎ 60000.
1200-1500 & 1800-2130
Mon-Sat, 1230-1430 & 1730-2030 Sun. High tea, fish, steaks, pub grub.

Shelbourne
69 Hill St. ☎ 62006.
0900-1730 Mon-Sat, closed Wed. Soup, stews, pies.

Snaub's Coffee Shop ☲ ☉
15 Monaghan St. ☎ 65381.
0930-1730 Mon-Sat. Home cooking, salads. Hot & cold buffet. A la carte.

Speakeasy ☲
5 Cornmarket. ☎ 68614.
1130-2230 Mon-Sat.
Grills, baked potatoes, sweets.

Sports Centre
61 Patrick St. ☎ 67322.
0900-2200 Mon-Fri. Snacks.

Tall Man ☲
2 Water St. ☎ 68654.
1200-1800 & 1900-2200
Mon-Sat. Pub grub.

Terrace
6 Marcus St. ☎ 65396.
0900-1730 Mon-Sat.
Breakfast, lunch.

Texas Pantry
Merchant Quay. 1000-1900
Mon-Tues, until 2000
Wed-Fri. Limited hours at weekend. Scones, pizzas, baked potatoes.

Three Steps ☲
75 Finegan's Rd, Drumintee.
☎ 888543. 1130-2300
Mon-Sat, 1230-1430 &
1900-2200 Sun. Pub grub.

Timoney's
6 Canal St. ☎ 67189.
0900-2100 Mon-Sun. Ice cream parlour.

Yewtree ☲ ☉
1 Trevor Hill. ☎ 64888.
1230-1500 Mon-Sun, 1730-2200 Mon-Sat, 1900-2200
Sun. Burgers, lasagne, plaice.
£

NEWTOWNARDS
(STD 01247)

Ballyharry Roadhouse ☲
151 Donaghadee Rd.
☎ 820808. 1200-2200
Mon-Sat, 1230-1430 & 1700-2200 Sun. Ribs, garlic bread, garlic shrimps, mushroom & pepper stroganoff. E£.

Co. DOWN   Newtownards

Beechill Farm
10 Loughries Rd. ☎ 818404.
Home grown produce, dinner.
Booking essential.

Bellamy's ⚲ ☺
Hudson's (cellar/bistro bar),
96 Frances St. ☎ 813480.
1200-1430 Mon-Sat, 1730-
2200 Mon-Sat, 1200-1430 &
1700-2000 Sun. Seafood,
lamb. E£.

Cafolla
15 Conway Square. ☎ 812185.
0800-1730 Mon-Sun. Fish &
chips, ice cream parlour.

Castle Garden ⚲
90 Upper Greenwell St.
☎ 818577. 1200-1430 Tues-
Thur, 1230-1700 Fri & Sat.
Basket meals.

Connors ⚲
12 Regent St. ☎ 813359.
0900-1700 Mon-Sat. Baked
potatoes, rice dishes,
sandwiches.

Eastern Tandoori ⚲
16 Castle St. ☎ 819541.
1200-1400 & 1700-2400
Mon-Sat, 1630-2300 Sun.
Indian & European. E££.

Edit Smyth's Café
134 Frances St. ☎ 810655.
1200-1400 & 1600-2400
Mon-Sat. Fish & chips, scampi.

Flyer ⚲
1 Court Sq. ☎ 823353.
1200-1500 Mon-Wed, 1700-
2100 Thur-Sat. Pub grub,
specials, steaks, fish, home-
made soup.

Gallery ☺
5 South St. 0900-1700
Mon-Sat. Set lunch, grills,
salads.

Ganges ⚲
69 Court St. ☎ 811426.
1200-1400 & 1730-2330
Mon-Thur, until 2400 Fri &
Sat, 2300 Sun. Indian. E££.

★ **GASLAMP** ⚲

47 Court St. ☎ 811225.
1830-2200 Tues-Sat. Rack of
lamb with red wine, trout in
lime & walnut sauce,
langoustine in cream &
chablis. E£££.

Guiseppe's Ristorante ⚲ ☺
31a Frances St. ☎ 812244.
1700-2300 Tues-Sun. Italian.
E£.

Huntsman ⚲
10 Castle St. ☎ 813073.
1200-1430 Mon-Sat,
1830-2130 Thur-Sat. Pub
grub, curry, plaice.

Ivy Bar ⚲
14 Castle St. ☎ 813063.
1230-1500 & 1900-2230
Mon-Sat. Grills, savouries.

Newtownards **Co. DOWN**

Jack Murphy's ⚲
Ards Shopping Centre.
☎ 817211. 1200-1430
Mon-Sat. Pub grub.

Jolly Judge ⚲
54 Regent St. ☎ 819895.
1200-1415 Mon-Thur & Sun,
1700-1930 Mon-Thur, 1200-2030 Fri & Sat. High
tea, à la carte.

Knightsbridge Inn ⚲
Scrabo Rd. ☎ 813221.
1200-2230 Mon-Sat,
1230-1500 & 1900-2200 Sun.
A la carte. Sunday carvery. ££.

★ **KNOTT'S COFFEE SHOP** ☉
45 High St. ☎ 819098.
0900-1700 Mon-Sat, closed
Thur. Coffee, quiche, salads,
pastries, home baking.

Menary's Café
99 East St. ☎ 812870.
1200-1400 & 1600-2400
Mon-Thur, 1600-0100 Fri &
Sat, 1230-2300 Sun. Fish &
chips.

★ **MING COURT** ⚲
63 Court St. ☎ 815073.
1200-1400 & 1730-2330
Mon-Fri, 1200-2400 Sat,
1230-2300 Sun. Chinese. £££.

Minstrels
7 Lower Mary St. ☎ 811760.
0900-1645 Mon-Sat. Set
lunch, baked potatoes, open
sandwiches.

Mount Stewart Ark Tea Rooms
Mountstewart. ☎ (012477)
88387. 1200-2000 Tues-Sun
in summer. Coffee, cakes.

Old Cross Inn ⚲ ☉
3 Castle Place. ☎ 820212.
1200-1500 Mon-Thur, 1730-2000 Wed, Thur, until 1900
Fri-Sat. Steaks, fish.
A la carte. E£.

Oscars ⚲
9 High St. ☎ 815041.
1200-1430 Mon-Thur, 1200-1700 Fri-Sat. Steak, lasagne.

Peach Tree ⚲
4 North St. ☎ 822185.
1200-2200 Mon-Sat, 1230-1430 & 1900-2200 Sun.
Ulster fry, lasagne, burgers. £.

Peking Garden ⚲
17 Castle St. ☎ 813903. 1200-1400 & 1700-2400 Mon-Sat,
1630-2300 Sun. Chinese &
European. £££.

Pied Piper
11 High St. ☎ 818140.
0930-1730 Mon-Sat. Pies,
lasagne.

Scrabo Café
187 Mill St. ☎ 810963.
1230-1430 & 2000-2300
Mon-Sat. Fish & chips.

Co. DOWN — Newtownards-Portaferry

Smyth's
31 West St. ☎ 812732.
1130-2300 Mon-Thur,
1130-0030 Fri & Sat. Fish &
chips, Ulster fry, chicken.

Steeplechase Inn ⚲
48 South St. ☎ 812019.
1130-1430 Mon-Sat,
1730-2100 Fri & Sat. Set
lunch, high tea. £.

Strangford Arms Hotel ⚲
92 Church St. ☎ 814141.
Last orders 2130, Sun 2030.
Oysters. Set lunch, Sunday
carvery. A la carte. £££.

Take Five ☺
25 High St. ☎ 819591.
0815-1700 Mon-Sat. Full
lunch menu, home-cooked
hams, chocolate & mandarin
gateau.

Temptations ☺
31b Frances St. ☎ 882565.
0930-1700 Mon-Sat. Baked
potatoes, seafood vol-au-vents,
home-made sweets.

That's Entertainment ⚲
South St. ☎ 820201.
1200-1530 & 1800-2300
Mon-Sat. Fish soup with
croutons and crème fraiche.
Grilled swordfish with puy
lentils and orange butter
sauce.

Tower Court
8 Court St. ☎ 815332.
0900-1730 Mon-Sat,
1200-1800 Sun. Ulster fry,
set lunch.

Tudor Tavern ⚲
6 Georges St. ☎ 815453.
1130-2300 Mon-Sat,
1230-1430 & 1900-2200
Sun. Pub grub.

Wellworths ☺
Ards Shopping Centre.
☎ 815577. 0900-1730
Mon-Sat, until 2100 Wed-Fri.
Ulster fry, liver & onion,
stuffed sausage & bacon, fish.
Restaurant in chainstore.

The Willows
101b Victoria Avenue.
☎ 812116. 0900-1700 Tues-
Thur Sept-June. Lasagne, pies.
College training restaurant.

PORTAFERRY
(STD 012477)

Coach Inn ⚲
1 Ann St. ☎ 28409.
1130-2300 Mon-Sat,
1230-1430 & 1900-2200 Sun.
Sausage rolls, hamburgers.

Coffee Pot
3 The Square. ☎ 28971. 0945-
1700 Mon-Sat, later opening
in summer. Ulster fry, home-
baked pastries, teas.

Elaine's ♦
22 Church St. ☎ 28915.
1000-1800 Mon-Sun. Lunch.
A la carte.

Portaferry-Rathfriland **Co. DOWN**

Exploris
Rope Walk, Castle St.
☎ 28062. 1200-1700
Mon-Sun in summer,
1200-1700 at weekends.
Snacks.

Ferry Grill
3 High St. ☎ 28448.
1200-2400 Mon-Sat,
1700-2230 Sun in summer,
limited hours in winter. Fish
& chips.

★ **PORTAFERRY HOTEL** ♀
10 The Strand. ☎ 28231.
Last orders 2100, 2030 Sun.
Bar lunches. Stuffed mussels,
fried oysters, turbot. A la carte.
E££.

Scotsman ♀
156 Shore Rd. ☎ 28024.
1230-1430 Mon-Sun, 1730-
2030 Mon-Tues, until 2100
Wed-Fri & until 2130 Sat,
2030 Sun. High tea, à la carte.

RATHFRILAND
(STD 018206)

Country Fayre
1A Church Square. ☎ 38177.
0900-1730 Mon-Sat. Early
closing Thur. Breakfast, fish,
sausages, open Danish
sandwiches.

Harp & Crown ♀
The Square. ☎ 30369.
1130-2300 Mon-Sat. Soups,
pies, burgers.

Home Cooking
19 Downpatrick St.
☎ 30530. 0930-1730
Mon-Wed, until 1400 Thur,
2200 Fri & Sat. Lunch,
afternoon tea, snacks.

Maple Leaf Café
4 John St. ☎ 30788.
1130-2300 Tues-Sat. Fish,
chicken, scones, pastries.

Monterey ♀
10 Downpatrick St. ☎ 30286.
1230-1430 Mon-Sat. Pies,
burgers.

Mourne Sauna
37 Downpatrick St.
☎ 30808. 0900-2100 Mon-Fri.
0900-2400 Sat. Salads, coffee.
In health club.

Old George ♀
Caddell's Lane. ☎ 30836.
1230-1900 Mon-Sat. Set
lunch. A la carte. £.

Pat's Bar ♀ ☻
Lenish. ☎ 30439. 1900-2100
Tues-Fri, 1800-2130 Sat,
1700-2030 Sun. A la carte. E£.

Rafferty's Bar ♀
1 Caddell's Lane. ☎ 30575.
1700-2300 Mon-Thur, 1130-
2300 Fri & Sat, 1230-1430 &
1900-2200 Sun. Pub grub.

Ye Olde Bar ♀
40 Downpatrick St. ☎ 30395.
1130-2300 Mon-Sat, 1230-
1430 & 1900-2200 Sun. Pub
grub.

153

Co. DOWN — Rostrevor-Saintfield

ROSTREVOR
(STD 016937)

Cloughmor Inn ♀
2 Bridge St. ☎ 38007. 1930-2230 Mon-Sat. Pub grub.

Corner House ♀
1 Bridge St. ☎ 38236. 1200-1430 & 1830-2130 Mon-Sat, except Wed. Pub grub.

Kilbroney Park ⌒
☎ 38026. May-Oct 1100-1730 Mon-Fri, until 1900 Sat & Sun. Earlier closing rest of year. Café in forest park.

Patrick K ♀
The Square. ☎ 38969. 1230-1530 & 1900-2130 Tues-Sun. Buffet lunch. Grilled duck & walnut sausage, monkfish gratinée with fresh prawns. £££.

Top of the Town
31 Church St. ☎ 38276. 1130-2200 Mon-Sat, 1230-1400 & 1900-2030 Sun. Steak, scampi.

Ye Olde Corner House ♀
The Square. ☎ 38236. 1900-2200 Mon-Sun. Salads, baked potatoes.

SAINTFIELD
(STD 01238)

★ **BARN** ♀
120 Monlough Rd. ☎ 510396. 1900-2200 Wed-Sat. Salmon & prawn mousse, roast duck in orange & vermouth sauce, honey & walnut flan. £££.

MARINE TAVERN
Orient Express

OPEN 7 DAYS
5.30 pm - 10.00 pm
Monday - Saturday

SUNDAY-
CARVERY & LUNCH
SUNDAY LUNCH
12.30 - 2.30 pm
Sunday, 4.30 pm - 9.00 pm

BAR SNACKS
12.30 - 2.30 pm and
5.30 - 9.00 pm

MARINE BAR
'Friends' each Wednesday night

TELEPHONE
WARRENPOINT: (016937) 54147

Saintfield-Strangford **Co. DOWN**

Caroline's Parlour
66 Main St. ☎ 511108.
0900-1700 Mon-Sat. Set lunch, afternoon tea.

Rosy Bar ♀
14 Main St. ☎ 510388.
1900-2300 Mon-Thur,
1130-2300 Fri & Sat,
1900-2200 Sun. Pub grub.

Rowallane Gardens
Rowallane. ☎ 510131.
May-Aug 1400-1800
Mon-Sun, closed Fri. April & Sept 1400-1800 Sat & Sun. Cream teas. Edwardian tea parlour.

Rowallane Inn ♀
Belfast Rd. ☎ 510466.
1800-2200 Mon-Sat, 1730-2100 Sun. Pub grub. A la carte. ££.

White Horse Inn ♀
49 Main St. ☎ 510417.
1130-2230 Mon-Sat. Garlic steaks, home-baked gammon.

SCARVA
(STD 01762)

Scarva Visitor Centre
Main St. ☎ 832163. 1100-1700 Tues-Fri, 1400-1600 Sat-Sun March-Oct. Coffee shop at visitor centre.

SEAFORDE
(STD 01396)

Seaforde Butterfly House
☎ 811225. Summer & Easter 1200-1700 Mon-Sun, weekends only May, Sept & Oct. Afternoon tea, snacks.

Seaforde Inn ♀
24 Main St. ☎ 811232.
1900-2130 Mon-Sat. Cold buffet, garnished steaks. A la carte. ££.

STRANGFORD
(STD 01396)

Castleward Tea Rooms
Strangford. ☎ 881204. Open during Castle Ward House viewing hours (National Trust). Lunch, scones, cakes.

Cuan Bar & Restaurant ♀ ☻
6 The Square. ☎ 881222.
1230-1430 & 1830-2200 Mon-Sat, 1900-2200 Sun. Hot & cold buffet lunch, daily specials. ££.

★ LOBSTER POT ♀
9 The Square. ☎ 881288.
1230-2130 Mon-Sat,
1230-1430 & 1730-2100 Sun. Lobster, clams, fresh salmon. ££.

Co. DOWN — Temple-Warrenpoint

TEMPLE

Laurel House 🍾
99 Carryduff Rd. ☎ (01846) 638422. 1230-1430 & 1730-2000 Mon-Sun. Lunches & high tea. £.

WARINGSTOWN
(STD 01762)

★ THE GRANGE ♀
Mill Hill, Main St. ☎ 881989. 1930-2230 Tues-Sat, 1230-1430 Tues-Fri & Sun. Baked salmon, whiskey steak, chocolate mousse. A la carte. Booking essential. £££.

Grange Restaurant ♀
☎ 881232. 1230-1430 Mon-Sat. Pub grub.

Joy's Kitchen
51 Main St. ☎ 882557. 1100-2200 Mon-Sat. Chicken, fish, ice cream.

Planters Tavern ♀
4 Banbridge Rd. ☎ 881510. 1200-1430 Mon-Sun, 1730-2030 Thur-Sat, 1900-2100 Sun. Burgers, curry, salads, scampi.

The Village Inn ♀
51 Main St. ☎ 881495. 1230-1430 & 1900-2200 Mon-Sat. Pub grub.

WARRENPOINT
(STD 016937)

★ AYLESFORTE HOUSE ♀ 🅗
44 Newry Rd. ☎ 72255. 1230-1430 & 1800-2200 Mon-Sat, 1230-1430, 1730-2030 Sun. Carvery. A la carte. £££.

Balmoral ♀
13 Seaview. ☎ 54093. 1230-1430 & 1800-2130 Mon-Sat. Pub grub, pies.

Four Roads Inn

Friendly atmosphere

Situated 1 mile approx from Tyrella beach

* Open all day for pub grub *

☎ **(01396) 851267**

15 Carricknab Road, Ballykinler

Warrenpoint — **Co. DOWN**

Bennett's ♀ ☺
21 Church St. ☎ 52314.
1230-1430 & 1700-2130
Mon-Sat. Seafood, steaks.

Carlingford Bay Hotel ♀
Osborne Promenade.
☎ 73521. Last orders 2130. £.

Central Café
32 Church St. ☎ 72693.
0930-1800 Mon-Sat,
0930-1400 Wed. Set lunch,
sweets.

Coffee House
40 Church St. ☎ 72718.
0930-1800 Mon-Sat,
1430-1800 Sun. Closed Wed.
Coffee, cakes.

The Crown ♀
7 The Square. ☎ 52917.
1230-1430 & 1730-2100
Mon-Sun. Steaks, afternoon
tea. A la carte. E£.

The Diplomat ♀
6 Seaview. ☎ 53629.
1215-1415 & 1715-2130
Mon-Sun. A la carte, pub grub.

Donmir Inn ♀
The Square. ☎ 52001.
1230-1430 & 1730-2130
Mon-Thur & until 2200 Fri &
Sat. Bar lunch. A la carte, set
menu.

Duke of Mourne ♀
7 Duke St. ☎ 53149.
1700-2300 Tues-Thur, until
2400 Fri-Sat & 2200 Sun.
Grills, daily specials.

Mac's Bar ♀
1 Marine Parade. ☎ 52082.
1200-1500 & 1700-2130
Mon-Sat, 1230-1430 &
1900-2200 Sun. Pub grub.

Marine Tavern ♀
4 Marine Parade. ☎ 54147.
1230-1430 & 1730-2200
Mon-Sat, 1230-1430 & 1630-
2100 Sun. Set meals, à la
carte, high tea. E££.

Ship Lounge ♀
14 The Square. ☎ 52685.
1230-1430 Mon-Sat. Pub
grub. Evenings on request.

Silvana
29 Church St. ☎ 72714.
1000-2200 Mon-Sun. Grills,
salads. A la carte.

Ulster Bar ♀
The Square. ☎ 72892. 1200-
2200 Mon-Sat, 1230-1430 &
1730-2100 Sun. A la carte.

Mulligans

BAR & RESTAURANT

33 Darling Street, Enniskillen, Co Fermanagh, N. Ireland BT74 7DP

''Traditional Irish Hospitality and Superb Cuisine''.... ....That's what Mulligan's is all about. Set in the West End of the Island Town of Enniskillen, a short stroll from most of the jetties, Mulligan's offers you the warmest of welcomes, and the rare chance to enjoy the most delectable cuisine in beautifully relaxed yet elegant surroundings. Under the personal supervision of Jill and Billy Mulligan, the finest local and International cuisine awaits you here, with tender Irish steak, sumptuous seafood fresh from the Atlantic, vegetarian options, and a selection of ... mouthwatering desserts. Add the cosy ambience in our bar, recently awarded the prestigious title 'Bushmills Bar of the Year Northern Ireland 1994' and the picture is complete. Lunch is served from midday till late afternoon and dinner from 7 pm till late. Give us a call - we're looking forward to meeting you!

☎ **(Reservations) 01365 322059 Fax. 325319**

COUNTY FERMANAGH

BALLINAMALLARD
(STD 01365)

Country Store
Main St. ☎ 388321. 0900-1700 Mon-Sun. Home-made soup, scones, crunchy chicken pie, Café in gift shop.

Encore Steak House ♀
66 Main St. ☎ 388606. 1730-2200 Wed-Sun. Steak, Italian beef, duck, trout. £££.

BELCOO
(STD 01365)

Border Diner
11 Main St. ☎ 386464. 0900-0100 Mon-Sat, 1400-2400 Sun. Grills.

Leo's ♀
Main St. ☎ 386228. 1930-2200 Thur-Sat. Pub grub.

BELLANALECK

The Moorings ♀
☎ (01365) 348328. 0930-2130 Sun-Sat. Lunch, snacks, à la carte, children's menu. £.

★ **THE SHEELIN** ♀
☎ (01365) 348232. 1030-1830 Mon, 1030-2130 Tues-Thur, 1030-2230 Fri-Sat, 1230-2130 Sun. Booking essential. Gourmet. ££££.

BELLEEK
(STD 013656)

Belleek Pottery Tea Rooms ☉
☎ 58501. 0930-1800 Mon-Sat, 1400-1800 Sun. Lasagne, quiche, baked potatoes.

Cleary's Corner Bar ♀
5 Main St. ☎ 58403. 1200-2200 Mon-Sat. Pub grub.

Fiddlestone Café
Castle Caldwell Forest Park. ☎ 58236. 1000-1900 Mon-Sun Easter-Sept. Quiche, vol-au-vents, salads. Craft shop.

Rooney's Bar ♀
Main St. ☎ 58279. 1200-1500 Mon-Sat. Pub grub.

BROOKEBOROUGH
(STD 013655)

Castle Hill Bar ♀
58 Main St. ☎ 31424. 1200-2300 bar snacks, Mon-Sat, 1230-1430 Sat-Sun. Pub grub.

Forest Inn ♀
73 Main St. ☎ 31636. 1130-2400 bar snacks, Mon-Sat, 1200-1800 Sun. Pub grub.

Co. FERMANAGH — Derrygonnelly-Enniskillen

DERRYGONNELLY
(STD 013656)

Bond Store ♀
Main St. ☎ 41254. 1300-2400 Mon-Sat. Pub grub.

Cozy Bar ♀
Main St. ☎ 41636. 1130-2300 Mon-Sat, 1900-2200 Sun. Pub grub.

Drumary Farm
Glenasheever Rd. ☎ 41420. 0800-2000 Mon-Sun. Breakfast, scones. Dinner - booking essential. E£.

McGovern's ♀
66 Main St. ☎ 41212. 1130-2300 Mon-Sat, 1900-2200 Sun. Pub grub.

Tir Navar ♀
Creamery St. ☎ 41673. 0800-2030 Mon-Thur, until 2230 Fri-Sun. Stir fry vegetables, home-made garlic bread. Breakfast.

DERRYLIN
(STD 013657)

Blake's ♀
Main St. ☎ 48203. 1230-1430 & 1830-2130 Mon-Sat. Burgers, scampi.

Knockninny ♦
Corraclare. ☎ 48339. 0930-2200 Mon-Sun. Home cooking, lunches, à la carte. E££.

Mountview Inn ♀
☎ 48226. 1200-1430 & 1800-2100 Mon-Sat. Set meals. A la carte. M£. E££.

EDERNEY

Gallen's Café
Market St. ☎ (013656) 31506. 1230-2400 Mon-Sat, 1230-2200 Sun, closed Wed. Fries, burgers, fish.

ENNISKILLEN
(STD 01365)

Aisling Centre
37 Darling St. ☎ 325811. 1000-1700 Mon-Fri & 1000-1400 Sat. Scones, pastries, light lunches in coffee shop.

Ardhowen Theatre ☺
Dublin Rd. ☎ 325254. 1100-1600 Mon-Sat. Coffee, lunches, salads.

Barbizon
5 East Bridge St. ☎ 324456. 0800-1800 Mon-Sat. Home baking.

Blake's of the Hollow ♀
6 Church St. ☎ 322143. 1130-2300 Mon-Sat. Sandwiches, soup in Victorian pub. Live music.

Bush ♀
26 Townhall St. ☎ 325210. 1230-1430 & 1700-1900. Mon-Sat. Pub grub.

Enniskillen — **Co. FERMANAGH**

Concorde
14 Tempo Rd. ☎ 322955.
1000-2400 Mon-Sat, 0900-2230 Sun. A la carte. Set lunch. E££.

County Bar
14 Forthill St. ☎ 327484.
1230-1430 & 1800-2100.
Toasted sandwiches, hamburgers.

Crow's Nest
12 High St. ☎ 325252.
1130-2100 Mon-Sat,
1230-1430 Sun. A la carte. E£.

Devenish Bar
24 Darling St. ☎ 325350.
1130-2300 Mon-Sat. Toasted sandwiches, hamburgers, salads.

Fort Lodge Hotel
72 Forthill St. ☎ 323275.
Last orders 2100 Mon-Wed, until 2200 Thur-Sun.
A la carte. E£££.

★ **FRANCO'S**
Queen Elizabeth Rd.
☎ 324424. 1200-2330 Mon-Sat, 1700-2200 Sun.
Pasta, pizza, kebabs. Italian. ££.

Golden Arrow
23 Townhall St. ☎ 322259.
1000-1800 Mon-Sat, closed Wed. Fish & chips, snacks.

Johnston's
6 Townhall St. ☎ 322277.
0900-1730 Mon-Sat.
Sandwiches, lasagne, home-made pastries.

Kamal Mahal
1 Water St. ☎ 325045
1700-2100 Sun-Mon & Wed-Sat. Indian ££.

Killyhevlin Hotel
Dublin Rd. ☎ 323481.
Last orders 2100, Sun 2000.
A la carte. E£££.

Lakeland Forum
Broad Meadow. ☎ 325534.
Same hours as sports centre.
Health food bar, main meals.

★ **LE BISTRO**
Erneside Centre. ☎ 326954.
0900-1730 Mon-Sat, until 2100 Thur & Fri. Breakfast, coffee, grills.

Leslie's
10 Church St. ☎ 324902.
0830-1700 Mon-Sat. Coffee, savouries, cakes.

Lily's Bakery
Head St. ☎ 325100.
0830-1730 Mon-Sat. Home-baked scones, pastries, pizza, filled rolls. Café in bakery.

Lough Erne House
St Catherines, Blaney.
☎ (013656) 41216. 1200-2200 Mon-Sun. Snacks, afternoon tea. Home cooking.

**Welcome to
Saddler's Restaurant
Bars and Lounge • Off Sales**

66 BELMORE ST, ENNISKILLEN,
CO FERMANAGH

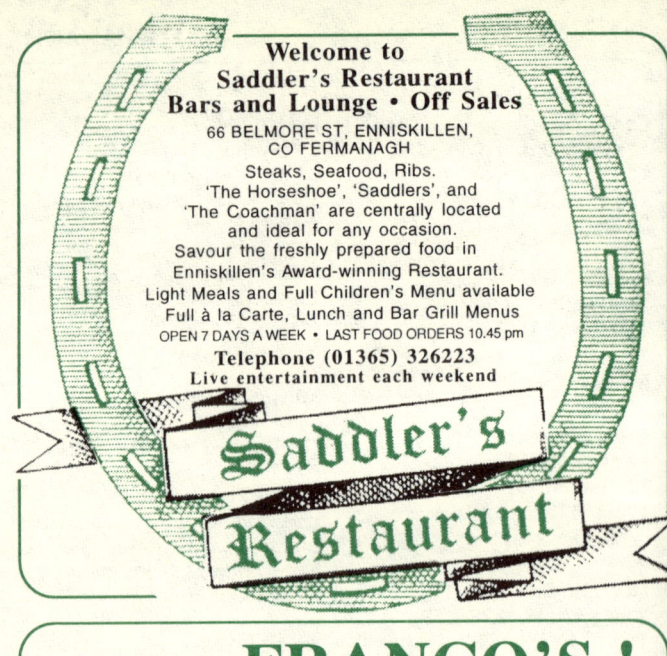

Steaks, Seafood, Ribs.
'The Horseshoe', 'Saddlers', and
'The Coachman' are centrally located
and ideal for any occasion.
Savour the freshly prepared food in
Enniskillen's Award-winning Restaurant.
Light Meals and Full Children's Menu available
Full à la Carte, Lunch and Bar Grill Menus
OPEN 7 DAYS A WEEK • LAST FOOD ORDERS 10.45 pm

Telephone (01365) 326223
Live entertainment each weekend

Saddler's Restaurant

FRANCO'S !

francos **PIZZERIA**

A warren of nooks and crannies
serving authentic Mediterranean
food, warm and atmospheric.

Regular live music sessions - Jazz,
Traditional, etc.

Mentioned in Bridgestone Guide,
Routiers, Daily Telegraph,
The Independent and other local and national press.
Fresh fish, shell fish including oysters,
mussels and lobster from west
coast of Ireland daily.

***Queen Elizabeth Road, Enniskillen,
Co Fermanagh.*** ☎ ***(01365) 324424***

Enniskillen   **Co. FERMANAGH**

McCartney's Inn
17 Belmore St. ☎ 322012.
1215-1500 Mon-Sat. Home-made broth, Irish stew. Dinner. Booking essential.

Manor House Hotel
Killadeas. ☎ Irvinestown (013656) 21561. Last orders 2200. M£, E£.

Melvin Bar
Townhall St. ☎ 327462.
1200-1800 Mon-Sat. Salad, toasties. Bar lunches.

★ **MELVIN HOUSE**
Townhall St. ☎ 322040.
1000-1800 Mon, Tues & Thur, 1000-1500 Wed, 1000-2200 Fri-Sat. Coffee, set lunch, teas. A la carte. E£££.

Mulligan's
33 Darling St. ☎ 322059.
1200-1730 Mon-Sat, 1900-2300 Mon-Sun. Steaks, seafood. £.

Oscar's
29 Belmore St. ☎ 327037.
1700-2300 Mon-Sun. Curries, baked potatoes, seafood. £.

Pat's Bar
Townhall St. ☎ 327462.
1200-1500 & 1900-2200 Mon-Sun. Salads, grills. Live music Sun pm.

Peppercorn
15 Townhall St. ☎ 324834.
0930-1730 Mon-Sat. Fish, chicken, lasagne.

Railway Hotel
34 Forthill St. ☎ 322084.
Last orders 2100. A la carte. E£.

Rebecca's
Buttermarket, Down St.
☎ 324499. 0930-1730 Mon-Sat. Sandwiches, salads, pastries.

Round 'O' Tea Room
Brooke Park. ☎ 322882.
0900-1900 Mon, Wed, Fri & Sat, until 2200 Tues, Thur & Sun. Pancakes, sandwiches, pastries.

Saddler's Restaurant
66 Belmore St. ☎ 326223.
1200-1430 & 1730-2300 Mon-Sun. Pub grub. Sunday lunch. A la carte. E£.

Silver Lough
64 Belmore St. ☎ 325243.
1700-2400 Mon-Sun.
Chinese & European. E£.

Silver Swallow
Drumawill, Sligo Rd.
☎ 322051. 1130-2300 Mon-Sat, 1230-1430 & 1900-2200 Sun.
Hamburgers, rolls, pies.

Three Way Inn
Ashwoods, Sligo Rd.
☎ 327414. 1230-1430 Mon-Sat. Soup, plaice, salads.

Co. FERMANAGH — Enniskillen-Garrison

Tippler's Brook ♀
1 The Brook. ☎ 322048.
1130-2300 Mon-Sat,
1230-1430 & 1900-2200
Sun. Pub grub.

Tippler's Inn ♀
Skea, Arney. ☎ 348492.
Evenings as required. Light
grills, fried foods.

Village Inn ♀
Sligo Rd. ☎ 323132.
1230-1430 Mon-Sat.
Chicken, plaice, roast beef.

Vintage ♀
13 Townhall St. ☎ 324055.
1200-1900 Mon-Sat. Set
lunch, high tea, self-service
buffet. E£.

Waterfront ♀
Rosigh, Killadeas.
☎ (013656) 21938. 1730-2100
Wed-Sat, 1200-2200 Sun,
1100-2200 Sun-Sat July/Aug.
Soup, sandwiches.

Watergate ♀
1 Ann St. ☎ 327447.
1130-1800 Mon-Fri.
Hamburgers, sandwiches, pies.

Welcome Inn ♀
10 Sligo Rd. ☎ 323734.
1700-2430 Mon-Thur, until
0130 Fri & Sat, 0100 Sun.
Chinese & European. E££.

FLORENCECOURT
(STD 01365)

Florence Court House
☎ 348249. 1200-1800 Mon &
Wed-Sun July & Aug. 1400-
1800 April-Sept. Quiche, meat
loaf, stew, wheaten bread.

Le Bistro
Marble Arch Caves.
☎ 348855. 1100-1630
Mon-Sun Mar-Sept. Coffee,
sandwiches, pastries.

Regal Bar ♀
2 Mullanaveay Rd. ☎ 348264.
1230-1430 & 1500-2200
Mon-Sat. Grills, salads.

★ **TULLYHONA** 🍾

59 Marble Arch Rd.
☎ 348452. 1000-1900 Mon-
Sun Easter & June-Aug only.
Buffet salad, snacks, coffee,
home baking. A la carte.

GARRISON

Heather Grove
Meenacloybane. ☎ (013656)
58362. Dinner. Booking
essential. Lough Melvin trout. £.

Lough Melvin Holiday Centre ⌂
☎ (013656) 58142. 0800-2100
April-Oct, 0800-1800 Nov-
March, Sat & Sun. Set lunch,
afternoon tea, evening
meal. Fresh fish.

Irvinestown   **Co. FERMANAGH**

IRVINESTOWN
(STD 013656)

Ann's Coffee Shop
Main St. ☎ 28089.
0900-1730 Mon-Sat, closed
Thur. Quiche, cakes.

Bawnacre Centre
Castle St. ☎ 21177. 1300-2230
Mon-Fri, 1400-1800 Sat-Sun.
Soups, hot chocolate,
sandwiches. Café in leisure
centre.

Castle Archdale Café
☎ 21345. 0900-2230
Mon-Sun July & Aug, earlier
closing June & Sept.
Lasagne, quiche, scampi.

★ **CEDARS** ♀
Drumall, Castle Archdale.
☎ 21493. 1800-2130 Wed-Sat,
1730-2130 Sun. Set meals,
à la carte.

Central Bar ♀
Main St. ☎ 21249.
1230-1530 Thur-Sat. Basket
meals.

Corner Café
Church St. ☎ 21696.
0900-1900 Mon-Sat, closed
Thur. Fish & chips, chicken.

★ **HOLLANDER** ♀
5 Main St. ☎ 21231.
1130-2300 Mon-Sat, 1900-
2200 Sun in summer. 1230-
1430 Mon-Sat, 1730-2200
Sun in winter. Bar lunches.
A la carte. E££.

Lily House ♀
54 Main St. ☎ 21880.
1700-2400 Mon-Thur, until
0100 Fri & Sat, 1600-2400
Sun. Chinese & European.
E££.

Mahon's Hotel ♀
Enniskillen Rd. ☎ 21656.
Last orders 2100. Garlic steak,
stuffed mushrooms. E£.

Railway Engine Bar ♀
Mill St. ☎ 21392.
1800-2130 Mon-Sat.
American brunch, mini
waffles, fish.

Robinson's Corner Bar ♀
Church St. ☎ 21572.
1130-2300 Mon-Sat.
Pub grub.

Woodhill Hunting Lodge ♀
Derrynanny. ☎ 21863.
1700-2300 Wed-Sun, until
0100 Sat. A la carte. E£££.

GLENCAR BAR

Extensive à la carte menu
Bar snacks served daily

For the best in food
and entertainment
every Friday & Saturday

Now open Sat & Sun
6 pm - 9.30 pm

Booking essential

Main Street, Lisbellaw

☎ (01365) 387818

The Sheelin
Licensed Restaurant

*Bellanaleck, Enniskillen,
Co Fermanagh*

**Open each day for morning
coffee, lunches and
afternoon teas**
**Snacks and salads served
throughout the day**
**Gourmet dinner each
Saturday evening
(booking necessary)**
• **A la carte menu** •
Friday evening from 7 pm

We are open every evening
except Monday during June,
July and August.

*Cosy relaxed atmosphere
Home cooking at its best!*

Enquiries and reservations

☎ *(01365) 348232*

McCartney's Inn

Fermanagh Locals - Visitors
Enjoy yourself at
McCartney's Inn
17 Belmore Street • Enniskillen
Good food served daily at very
keen prices
Lots of entertainment in our
traditional Public Bar or Cellar
Lounge
Disco Music - Live Bands
Karaoke Nights -
Special Promotion Nights
Late Bar every night.
Happy hour Thursday nights
8.30 pm - 9.30 pm
Forthcoming events will
be advertised in the bar.

Give us a call-you'll enjoy it
☎ **(01365) 322012**

Kesh-Lisbellaw — Co. FERMANAGH

KESH
(STD 013656)

Bettany
Boa Island Rd. ☎ 31157.
1000-1800 Mon-Fri & 1000-2000 Sat-Sun. Soup, baked potatoes, lasagne.

Drumrush Lodge ♀
Boa Island Rd. ☎ 31578.
1730-2130 Mon-Sun June-Sept, 1730-2130 Fri-Sun Oct-May. Grills, à la carte. E££.

Hunting Lodge ♀
Lusty Beg, Boa Island.
☎ 31342. 1800-2100 Wed-Fri, 1200-2100 Sat-Sun. Grills.

Irene's Café
23 Main St. ☎ 31014.
1100-0100 Mon-Thur, 1800-2400 Sun, until 0200 Fri, 0300 Sat. Shorter hours in winter. Snacks.

Lough Erne Hotel ♀
Main St. ☎ 31275. Last orders 2100. A la carte. E££.

May Fly ♀
Main St. ☎ 31281.
1200-1430 Mon-Sat, 1800-2200 daily.
Pub grub. A la carte. E£.

Mullynaval Lodge ♦
Boa Island. ☎ 31995.
Home-baked bread, dinners. Booking essential.

Sarah Jane's
41 Main St. ☎ 31940.
1030-1700 Mon-Sat, 1200-2000 Sun. Home baking.

Willow Pattern Pantry
Clareview House, Crevenish Rd. ☎ 31278. 1030-2000 Mon-Sat July & Aug, 1100-1700 Sat Easter-June. Irish stew, pavlova, coffee.

KINAWLEY

Corrigans ♀
39 Main St. ☎ (01365) 348285. 1900-2300 Mon-Sat. Pies, grills. £.

LETTERBREEN

Half Way Inn ♀
☎ (01365) 341367. 1230-1430 Mon-Sat. Grills, curries, salads.

LISBELLAW
(STD 01365)

Carrybridge Hotel ♀
☎ 387282. Last orders 2200.
A la carte. E£.

Glencar Bar ♀
Main St. ☎ 387818.
1230-1430 Mon-Sun, 1800-2130 Sat-Sun.
A la carte. Booking essential.

Co. FERMANAGH — Lisbellaw-Newtownbutler

Wild Duck Inn ♀
Main St. ☎ 387258.
1130-2300 Mon-Sat,
1230-1430 & 1900-2200
Sun. Pub grub.

LISNARICK

★ **DRUMSHANE HOTEL** ♀
☎ (013656) 21146. Last orders
2000. Lamb kebab Drumshane,
shark steaks, flambéd Irish
coffee. A la carte. E£.

LISNASKEA
(STD 013657)

Corner House ♀
169 Main St. ☎ 21172.
1230-1430 grills, 1230-1700
snacks Mon-Sat.
Pub grub.

FDH Coffee Shop ☕
Main St. ☎ 21276. 1000-1700
Mon-Wed & Sat, until 2030
Thur & Fri. Quiche, pizza,
desserts.

Horse & Hound ♀
133 Main St. ☎ 21298.
1230-1430 & 1900-2230
Mon-Sat. Pub grub.

Moate
78 Lower Main St. ☎ 22598.
1000-2200 Mon-Sat,
1800-2200 Sun.
Breakfast, set lunch.

Ortine Hotel ♀
Main St. ☎ 21206. Last orders
2130. Pub grub, gateaux.
A la carte. E££.

Stag's Head ♀
112 Main St. ☎ 21968.
1130-2300 Mon-Sat,
1230-1430 & 1900-2200
Sun. Pub grub.

Teach a' Ceili
Inishcorkish. ☎ 21360.
Booking essential for hot
meals. Grills & snacks
for holidaymakers on
boats. On island.

Wyvern Inn ♀
Main St. ☎ 21248.
1200-2200 Mon-Sat.
Pub grub, buffet.

NEWTOWNBUTLER
(STD 013657)

Crom Estate
☎ 38118.
1400-1700 April-Sept
weekends, July-Aug daily. Tea
shop (National Trust) in visitor
centre. Admission charge to
estate.

★ **RAFTERS**
30 High St. ☎ 38165.
0800-2000 Mon-Sat.
Traditional Irish cooking.

Roslea-Tempo   **Co. FERMANAGH**

ROSLEA
(STD 013657)

Roslea Arms ☴
Main St. ☎ 51343. 1230-1500 & 1800-2100 Mon-Sat. Daily specials.

Roslea Heritage Centre
Monaghan Rd. ☎ 51750. 0900-1700 Mon-Fri, April-Sept 1600-1800 Sat & Sun. Scones, pastries, coffee.

TEMPO
(STD 013655)

Milltown Manor ☴
61 Main St. ☎ 41779. 1230-1430 Mon-Sat. 1900-2130 Fri-Sat. Toasties, grills, daily specials, à la carte.

The best of all worlds for the touring traveller-

THE YORK

2 STATION ROAD
PORTSTEWART
CO LONDONDERRY,
NORTHERN IRELAND
BT55 7DA
TEL: (01265) 833594

Situated on the world famous Causeway Coast with its excellent golf courses, beaches and many local attractions.

Continental style luxury self-catering apartments with traditional pub serving nationally renowned food.

* Entertainment weekly *

MOYOLA LODGE

A LA CARTE MEALS

WEDDINGS

FUNCTIONS

PRIVATE PARTIES

CONFERENCES

ACCOMMODATION

Pleasant surroundings

Warm welcome

Relaxing atmosphere

High standard of food & service

RESTAURANT GUESTHOUSE

Castledawson, Magherafelt, Co Londonderry
Tel:(01 648) 68224 Fax: (01648) 68955

R·A·F·T·E·R·S
Award Winning Restaurant

**OPEN EVERY NIGHT
FROM 5 pm - 10.45 pm**
Monday, Tuesday, Wednesday,
Thursday, Friday and Saturday;
also each lunchtime
from 12.00 noon-3.00 pm

SUNDAY EVENING
7 - 9.30 pm Lunch 12.30 - 2.30 pm

NORTHLAND ROAD, DERRY -
TELEPHONE: (01504) 266080

COUNTY LONDONDERRY

AGHADOWEY
(STD 01265)

★ BROWN TROUT GOLF & COUNTRY INN ♆

209 Agivey Rd, Mullaghmore. ☎ 868209. 0700-2130 Mon-Sun June-Sept, 0700-1500 & 1700-2130 Mon-Sun rest of year. Grills, steaks. Last orders 2130. A la carte, set lunch. E£.

BALLYKELLY

Drummond Hotel ♆
481 Clooney Rd. ☎ (015047) 22121. Last orders 2130. A la carte. E£.

Helen's Restaurant ♆
440 Clooney Rd. ☎ (015047) 62098. 1700-2330 Sun-Thur, until 0030 Fri & Sat. Chinese & European. ££.

Marmadukes ♆
63 Main St. ☎ (015047) 63266. 1230-1430 & 1900-2130 Mon-Sat. Baked crab & prawn soufflé, beef with green peppercorn & mushroom cream sauce, seasonal fruit pie. E££.

Weavers ♆
450 Clooney Rd. ☎ (015047) 62999. 1230-1430 & 1900-2130 Mon-Sat. Steak, curry, lasagne.

CASTLEDAWSON
(STD 01648)

Ditty's Home Bakery ☻
44 Main St. ☎ 68243. 0900-1730 Mon-Sat. Vegetarian pies, lasagne, sandwiches.

Moyola Lodge ♆
9 Broagh Rd. ☎ 68224. 1700-2130 Mon, Thur & Fri, 1600-2130 Sat & Sun. Set meals. A la carte. E£.

Shillgray Lounge ♆
1 Bridge St. ☎ 68951. 1230-1330 Mon-Fri. Lunches, scampi, chicken.

Thatch Inn ♆
116 Hillhead Rd. ☎ 68322. 1230-1430 & 1800-2200 Wed-Sat, 1230-1430 Sun. Steak, fish. £.

Co. LONDONDERRY — Castledawson-Coleraine

T-Junction Café
62A Hillhead Rd. ☎ 50095.
0800-2130 Mon-Sun.
Breakfast, sandwiches, fish &
chips. Café in newsagents.

CASTLEROCK
(STD 01265)

Copper Kettle
4 Main St. ☎ 848229.
1000-1730 Tues-Sat in
summer, 1000-1700 Thur-Sat
Easter-Sept. Home baking.

Golf Hotel
17 Main St. ☎ 848204. Last
orders 2030. A la carte. E££.

Marine Inn
9 Main St. ☎ 848456.
1230-1930 Mon-Sat,
1230-1500 & 1700-2200
Sun. £.

Pool Café
Main St. ☎ 42232. 1030-2200
Mon-Sun Easter-Sept. Fish &
chips, chicken.

Temple Lounge
17 Sea Rd. ☎ 848423.
1200-1500 & 1900-2200
Mon-Sat. Roast meat, fish,
chicken.

CLAUDY
(STD 01504)

Beaufort House
☎ 338248. 1230-2030
Mon-Sat. Snacks.

Claudy Inn
Main St. ☎ 338515.
1200-1430 Mon-Sat. Pies,
burgers.

Connolly's
68 Main St. ☎ 338546.
1130-2300 Mon-Sat,
1230-1430 & 1900-2200 Sun.
Grills, pies, hamburgers.

McGonigle's
64 Main St. ☎ 338819.
1200-1400 & 1700-2400
Mon-Thur, 1200-0100 Fri &
Sat, 1700-2200 Sun.
Sandwiches, grills, Ulster fry.

Rio Grande
Park. ☎ (015047) 81210.
1900-2100 Mon-Sat. Pub
grub.

COLERAINE
(STD 01265)

Beau Brummel
18 Bridge St. ☎ 55145.
1000-1730 Mon-Sat.
Pizzas, burgers, grills.

Belfry Restaurant
Church Lane. ☎ 44646.
0900-1730 Mon-Sat. Quiche,
salad.

Bertie's
108 Long Commons. ☎ 42874.
1200-1430 Mon-Sat. Pub
grub, stew, pies.

Coleraine **Co. LONDONDERRY**

Big 'O'
11 New Row. ☎ 44777.
0900-1700 Mon-Sat.
Hamburgers, pizzas. Set lunch.

Blackthorn Inn ♀
16 New Market St. ☎ 44514.
1200-1430 Mon-Sat. Stew, lasagne.

Bohill Hotel & Country Club ♀
69 Cloyfin Rd. ☎ 44406.
Last orders 2100, Sun 2000.
Grill bar, poached salmon. ££.

Brook's Wine Bar ♀
21 Park St. ☎ 42552.
1200-1500 & 1730-2100
Mon-Sat. Burgers, steaks, baked potatoes.

Bull's Eye ♀
Lime Market St. ☎ 43485.
1230-1500 Mon-Sat,
1730-2100 Wed-Sat. Savoury pies, open sandwiches.

Bushtown House Hotel ♀
283 Drumcroone Rd.
☎ 58367. 1200-2130 Mon-Sun. Set lunch. A la carte. £££.

Buttery ☕
31 Kingsgate St. ☎ 52127.
0745-1745 Mon-Sat. Carvery, casseroles, quiche, lasagne, salads. Home baking.

Charly's ♀
34 Newbridge Rd. ☎ 52020.
1200-2200 Mon-Sun. Closed 1500-1700 in winter. Beef, pork, chicken, lamb.

Chew Chews
21 Railway Rd. ☎ 55504.
1030-1900 Mon & Tues, until 2400 Wed-Fri, 0200 Sat,
1300-2400 Sun. Hot dogs, burgers.

Clyde Bar ♀
40 Railway Rd. ☎ 42791.
1200-1430 Mon-Fri. Pub grub.

Coffee Cup
Queen St. ☎ 43810.
0900-1715 Mon-Sat, until 1600 Thur. Home-made pies, scones, gateaux, milk shakes.

Coffee Dock ☕
20 New Row. ☎ 52565.
0900-1700 Mon-Sat. Baked potatoes, salads. Home baking.

Copper Room
4 Railway Rd. ☎ 53184.
1000-1700 Mon-Sat, closed Thur. Pizza, pies.

Dolphin
26 Railway Rd. ☎ 56247.
1200-2300 Mon-Sat. Set lunch. Steak, hamburgers, scampi.

Eileen's Diner
Station Square. ☎ 57386.
0830-1730 Mon-Sat. Quiche, salads, toasties.

Co. LONDONDERRY — *Coleraine*

Erin Eating House
5 Long Commons. ☎ 43612.
1000-1730 Mon-Sat,
0900-1400 Thur. Set lunch.
Salads, curry, baked potatoes.

Forum ⊙
15 Church St. ☎ 52638.
0930-1700 Mon-Sat. Coffee
shop in department store.

Grandma Smyth's
9 Railway Rd. ☎ 51150.
0900-1700 Mon-Sat. Lunch,
snacks.

★ **KITTY'S OF COLERAINE**
3 Church Lane. ☎ 42347.
0900-1730 Mon-Sat, closed
Thur. Sandwiches, sausage
rolls, coffee.

Lacy's Wine Bar ⌑
Beresford Rd. ☎ 43755.
1200-1430 & 1700-2100
Mon-Sat. Lasagne, chicken
kiev.

Connor's Coffee Shop
2 Church St. ☎ 42996. 0900-
1730 Mon-Sat. Breakfast, hot
pot, savoury pancakes.

★ **LITTLE TEA SHOP** ⊙
Diamond Arcade.
1030-1730 Mon-Sat (ex Thur)
July-Aug. Afternoon tea, set
lunches.

Lodge Hotel ⌑ ⊙
Lodge Rd. ☎ 44848. Last
orders 2100, Sun 1930.
A la carte. £££.

Lombard Café
Queen St. ☎ 43041.
0900-1730 Mon-Sat. Set
lunch. Soup, sandwiches,
scones.

★ **MACDUFF'S** ⌑
112 Killeague Rd, Blackhill.
☎ 868433. 1900-2130
Tues-Sat. Game in season,
seafood, local country
produce. £££.

Mary Craig's ⌑
30 New Market St. ☎ 52461.
1200-1400 Mon-Sat. Pub
grub.

Old Forge Inn ⌑
6 New Market St. ☎ 52931.
1200-1500 & 1700-2100
Mon-Sat. Grills, à la carte. ££.

The Pantry
Right Price Carpets, Bushmills
Rd. 0900-1700 Mon-Sat.
Lasagne, shepherd's pie,
salads.

Pine Tree Country Club
1 Somerset Rd. ☎ 58002.
1200-1430 Mon-Sat. Snacks.

Racquets
Leisure Centre, Railway Rd.
☎ 56432. 1000-2130 Mon-Fri,
until 1800 Sat, 1400-1800
Sun. Soup, sandwiches, rolls.

Red Cross Café
43 Kingsgate St. ☎ 58250.
1000-1600 Mon-Sat. Lasagne,
pies, high tea.

Coleraine-Dungiven   **Co. LONDONDERRY**

Restaurant Twenty Two
22 Church St. ☎ 43761.
0900-1730 Mon-Sat. Salads, quiche, lasagne.

Roost ♀
2 Shuttle Hill. ☎ 42516.
1130-2300 Mon-Sat,
1230-1430 & 1900-2200
Sun. Pies, burgers.

★ **SALMON LEAP** ♀
53 Castleroe Rd. ☎ 52992.
1130-2300 Mon-Sat, 1230-1430 & 1900-2200 Sun. Buffet lunch, game in season, smoked fish, salmon. A la carte. M£, E££.

Sun Do
66 New Row. ☎ 53022.
1200-1400 & 1700-0030
Mon-Sat, 1700-2400 Sun.
Chinese & European.

Teddy & Son
12 Railway Rd. ☎ 53211.
0900-1700 Mon-Sat.
Sandwiches, snacks.

Water Margin at the Boathouse ♀
Hanover Place. ☎ 42222.
1730-2330 Mon-Sat, 1300-1500 & 1700-2330 Sun.
Chinese. Seafood dishes when available. Vegetarian. E££.

Wellworths ☺
2 Ring Rd. ☎ 58446.
0900-1730 Mon, Tues & Sat, until 2100 Wed-Fri. Afternoon tea, salad bar.

DRAPERSTOWN
(STD 01648)

Mary Pats ♀
2 St Patrick St. ☎ 28051.
1200-1430 Mon-Sun, 1200-2130 Fri-Sat, 1800-2130 Sun.
A la carte.

Market Inn ♀
27 St Patrick St. ☎ 28250.
1230-1430 Mon-Sat.
Pub grub.

Shepherds ♀
220 Sixtowns Rd. ☎ 28517.
1200-1430 Mon-Sat. Snacks.

DUNGIVEN
(STD 015047)

Carraig Rua ♀
40 Main St. ☎ 41682.
1200-1430 Mon-Sat,
1800-2130 Mon-Sun. E££.

Castle Inn ♀
Upper Main St. ☎ 41369.
1200-2130 Mon-Sat,
1230-1430 & 1830-2100
Sun. Lunch, snacks.
A la carte.

Cosy Inn ♀
84 Main St. ☎ 41781.
1230-1430 & 1800-2200
Mon-Sat. Pub grub.

Dolphin Bar ♀
Gortnaghey Rd. ☎ 41289.
1000-0100 Sat, 1800-2200 &
1230-1430 Sun. Pub grub.

Co. LONDONDERRY — Dungiven-Kilrea

Ponderosa ♀
Glenshane Rd (top of Glenshane Pass). ☎ 41987. 1130-2130 Mon-Sat, 1230-1430 & 1900-2200 Sun. A la carte. Steak, seafood.

EGLINTON
(STD 01504)

Longfield Inn ♀
Longfield Rd. ☎ 810211. 1230-1430 Mon-Sun. Pub grub, chicken, fish, pies.

Station Inn ♀
37 Station Rd. ☎ 810470. 1200-1400 Mon-Sat, 1730-2200 Mon & Wed, until 2300 Thur-Sat, 1230-1430 & 1900-2100 Sun. Grills, set meals.

The Villager ♀
4 Main St. ☎ 810206. 1230-1430 & 1700-2100 Mon-Thur, until 2200 Fri & Sat, 1900-2200 Sun. Pub grub. A la carte. E£.

GARVAGH
(STD 012665)

The Café
Main St. ☎ 58374. 1000-1700 Mon-Sat. Café in grocery shop. Set lunch.

Imperial Hotel ♀
38 Main St. ☎ 58218. Last orders 2200. Trout. £.

Tasty Bite
37 Main St. ☎ 58262. 0800-2300 Mon-Wed, until 0100 Thur-Sat. Fish & chips.

Turn Inn ♀
33 Main St. ☎ 58257. 1130-2300 Mon-Sat, 1900-2200 Sun. A la carte.

GREYSTEEL

Foyle View Bar ♀
161 Clooney Rd. ☎ (01504) 810560. 1230-2200 Mon-Sun. Pub grub.

Rising Sun ♀
105 Killylane Rd. ☎ (01504) 810959. 1230-1430, 1630-1930 Mon-Sun. Pub grub. A la carte.

KILREA
(STD 012665)

Bridge Way Café
4 Bridge St. ☎ 41247. 1000-1800 Mon-Wed, until 2130 Thur-Sat. Ulster fry, sandwiches, pies.

The Manor ♀
69 Bridge St. ☎ 40205. 1200-1500 Mon-Sat, 1600-2100 Mon-Wed, until 2200 Thur-Sat, 1230-1430 & 1900-2100 Sun. Garlic mushrooms, curry, lasagne, home-made apple pie.

Kilrea-Limavady   **Co. LONDONDERRY**

Pointers ♉
The Diamond. ☎ 40404.
1230-1430 & 1800-2100
Tues-Sat. Bar snacks.

Old Point Inn ♉
80 Drumagarner Rd.
☎ 40330. 1230-1430 & 1800-2100 Thur-Sat, 1230-1430 & 1900-2130 Sun. Pies, hamburgers.

KNOCKCLOGHRIM

Fireside Inn ♉
☎ (01648) 42635. 1400-2000 Thur-Sat. Pub grub.

Fox & Pheasant Inn ♉
69 Glenmaquille Rd.
☎ (01648) 69463. 1300-1400 & 1800-2100 Thur-Sun. Grills, set meals. A la carte.

Knockcloghrim Windmill
On A6 near Maghera. 1030-1630 Easter to October. Sandwiches, pastries. Tea room in windmill/craft shop.

LIMAVADY
(STD 015047)

Alexander Arms ♉
Main St. ☎ 63443. 0800-1000, 1200-1430 & 1700-2230 Mon-Sat. A la carte.

Beehive
21 Market St. ☎ 63692.
0900-1800 Mon-Sat. Grills, snacks, chicken, steak.

Belmont ♉
24 Linenhall St. ☎ 22514.
1130-2300 Mon-Sat. Pub grub.

Coasters ♉
148 Seacoast Rd. ☎ 63562.
1230-1500 Mon-Sun, 1900-2200 Mon-Sat, 1900-2100 Sun. Steak, pizza.

Crown Bar ♉
24 Irish Green St. ☎ 62402.
1900-2300 Fri & Sat. Pies, hamburgers.

Crumpet ☺
43 Market St. ☎ 22886.
0900-1730 Mon-Sat, until 1400 Thur. Breakfast, grills, salads, pastries.

Gentry's ♉
18 Main St. ☎ 22017.
1230-2230 Sun-Wed,
1200-2400 Thur-Sat. Indian, European. E£.

Gorteen House ♉
Deerpark, 187 Roe Mill Rd.
☎ 22333. Last orders 2230, 2100 Sun. A la carte. E££.

Lucille's Kitchen ☺
17c Catherine St. ☎ 68180.
0900-1730 Mon-Sun. Curries, soup, scones.

Co. LONDONDERRY — Limavady-Londonderry

Oven Door
Hunter's Bakery, 5 Market St.
☎ 63411. 0800-1730
Mon-Sat, closed 1630 Thur
Oct-May. Beef & pepper
casserole, wheaten bread,
coffee cake.

**Radisson Roe Park Hotel &
Golf Resort**
☎ 722313. Hotel opening
1995.

Rajmahal
17 Main St. ☎ 22097. 1900-
2300 Mon-Sat. Indian,
European.

Rivolli Pizzeria
4a Ballyclose St. ☎ 66663.
1700-2300 Mon-Sun. Pizza,
pasta, salads.

Rendezvous
15 Catherine St. ☎ 22272.
0900-1830 Mon-Sat. Grills,
fish & chips, Ulster fry.

Roe Valley Country Park
Spinning Wheel Café.
☎ 22074. 1030-1700 Mon-Fri,
until 2000 Sat & Sun. 1000-
1800 Sun in winter. Snacks.

Roe View Inn
160 Ballyquin Rd. ☎ 62550.
1230-1430 Mon-Sat,
1900-2100 Sun. Snacks.

Roebuck Inn
25 Main St. ☎ 68558.
1200-1430 Mon-Sat. Fish,
chicken, salads.

Shanvey
109 Aghanloo Rd. ☎ 50229.
1200-1400 & 1700-2300
Fri-Sat. Salmon steak, trout.
A la carte.

Shenandoah
88 Main St. ☎ 64366.
1700-1930 Mon-Fri, 1700-
2100 Sat. Pub grub.

**Sunflower Chinese
Restaurant**
4 Catherine St. ☎ 63151.
1200-1400 Thur-Fri, 1700-
2330 Mon-Thur, until 2400
Fri-Sat, 1700-2300 Sun.
Chinese.

Thatch Bar
10 Catherine St. ☎ 64876.
1200-2200 Mon-Sat,
1230-1430 & 1900-2100
Sun. Pub grub. A la carte.

LONDONDERRY
(STD 01504)

Abrakebabra
Strand Rd. ☎ 264407.
2400-0200 Mon-Wed & Sun,
until 0300 Thur & Fri, until
0400 Sat. Turkish kebabs,
burgers.

Acorn
3 Pump St. ☎ 262539.
1000-1730 Mon-Sat. Soup,
stew, home-made savouries,
salads, pastries.

Londonderry   **Co. LONDONDERRY**

Andy Cole's Bar ♀
125 Strand Rd. ☎ 265308.
1230-1430, 1730-2130 Mon-Sat. Pub grub.

★ **BADGERS** ♀

16-18 Orchard St. ☎ 360763.
1200-1430 & 1800-2200
Mon-Sat.

★ **BEECH HILL COUNTRY HOUSE HOTEL** ♀

32 Ardmore Rd. ☎ 49279.
Last orders 2145. M££. E£££.

Beechtree Bar ♀
106 Beechwood Avenue.
☎ 268568. 2000-2200
Mon-Sat. Pub grub.

Beehive
101 Richmond Centre.
☎ 264661. 0900-1730
Mon-Sat, until 2100 Thur & Fri. Soup, stew, salads.

Bogside Inn ♀
21 Westland St. ☎ 269300.
1200-1430 Mon-Sat. Pub grub.

Boston Tea Party
42 Shipquay St. ☎ 263326.
0900-1730 Mon-Sat.
Sandwiches, pies.

Bound for Boston
29 Waterloo St. ☎ 266351.
1200-1430 & 1800-2100
Mon-Sat. Black Velvet pie.
Vegetarian dishes.

Brendan's Diner ♀
164 Spencer Rd. ☎ 44875.
1200-2400 Mon-Sat,
1600-2230 Sun. Hamburgers, fish & chips, duck, salmon.

Brewster's Bistro ♀
13 Little James St. ☎ 264768.
1200-1500 & 1900-2200
Mon-Sat, 1200-1500 Sun. A la carte.

Broomhill House Hotel ♀
Limavady Rd. ☎ 47995.
Last orders 2130. ££.

★ **BROWN'S** ♀

1 Victoria Rd. ☎ 45180.
1230-1430 Tues-Fri,
1730-2330 Tues-Sat,
1230-1430 & 1730-2130 Sun.
Modern European. Irish lamb, Kilkeel fish, vegetarian. E££.

Carraig Bar ♀
121 Strand Rd. ☎ 267529.
1200-1430 & 1900-2300
Mon-Sat. Soup, grills, sandwiches.

Caspers Bar & Lounge ♀
Waterloo St. ☎ 263278.
1200-1500 Mon-Sat.
Pies, burgers, stews.

Castle Bar ♀
26 Waterloo St. ☎ 263118.
1230-1500 Mon-Sat. Lunch, grills. Live traditional music Fri & Sat.

Co. LONDONDERRY — Londonderry

Chat & Chew
23 William St. ☎ 269376.
0900-1700 Mon-Sat, until
1400 Thur. Soup, stew, rolls.

Churn
37 Great James St.
☎ 268001. 0900-1600
Mon-Fri, until 1500 Sat.
Soup, stew, scones. Café in
home bakery.

City Restaurant ♀
27 Shipquay St. ☎ 271011.
1200-2230 Mon-Thur, until
2400 Fri-Sun. Chinese &
European.

Claddagh Bar ♀
5 Chamberlain St. ☎ 265877.
1200-1500 Mon-Sat. Fish,
chicken.

Clarendon Bar ♀
44 Strand Rd. ☎ 263705.
1230-1400 & 1800-2200
Thur-Sun. Pub grub.

Clarendon Café
3 Lower Clarendon St.
☎ 267165. 0900-1600
Mon-Sat. Breakfast, lunch,
grills.

The Coffee Shop
32 Waterloo St. ☎ 266612.
0900-1700 Mon-Sat. Ulster
fry, sandwiches, home-made
pastries.

Coffee Stop
Drumahoe Shopping Centre.
☎ 301068. 0900-1700
Mon-Sat. Lasagne, quiche.

Crusty Kitchen ☺
304 Richmond Centre.
☎ 260637. 0900-1730
Mon-Sat, until 2100 Thur &
Fri. Coffee, cakes.

Curry King
8 Campsie Rd. ☎ 46502.
1200-2400 Mon-Sun. Burgers,
pizza, American chicken.

Da Vinci's ♀
Culmore Rd. ☎ 264507.
1730-2200 Mon-Sat, 1230-
1430 & 1900-2100 Sun.
Pub grub.

Da Vinci's Restaurant ♀
Culmore Rd. ☎ 372074.
1730-2230 Mon-Sun. A la
carte. Marinated mussels,
seafood chowder, Chicken
Leonardo (chicken fillet stuffed
with garlic and cream cheese).

Delacroix ♀
Buncrana Rd. ☎ 262990.
1200-1430 & 1800-2200
Mon-Sat, 1230-1430 Sun.
Toasties, soup. A la carte.

The Diamond
13 Ferryquay St. ☎ 263795.
1030-1800 Mon-Sat. Chicken,
burgers.

Doherty's Bar ♀
10 Magazine St. ☎ 360177.
1200-2200 Mon-Sat. Burgers,
salads, grills.

Londonderry   **Co. LONDONDERRY**

Duffy's No.17
17 Foyle St. ☎ 361362.
1200-1500 Mon-Fri. Set lunch.
Fish dishes, salads, pies.

Dungloe Bar
41 Waterloo St. ☎ 267716.
1230-1430 Mon-Sat.
Pub grub. Live traditional music.

Ebrington House
6 Ebrington Terrace.
☎ 44692. 1200-1500
Mon-Sat, 2100-2400
Fri-Sat. Pub grub.

Emerald Palace
26 William St. ☎ 267706.
1630-0200 Mon-Sat, until 2400 Sun. Chicken, pizza, chips.

★ **EVERGLADES HOTEL**
Prehen Rd. ☎ 46722.
Last orders 2145, Sun 2115.
Set meals, à la carte. £££.

Fat Freddy's
Castle St. ☎ 373222.
1100-2200 Mon-Sat & 1100-2000 Sun. Italian & European.

★ **FIORENTINI'S**
47 Strand Rd. 0900-2130
Mon-Fri, 0900-1730 Sat & Sun. Earlier closing in winter.
Snacks, ice cream.

Forum
24 Foyle St. ☎ 360066.
1200-1430 Mon-Sat.
Sandwiches, burgers, salads.

Gallery & Gilhooly's
14 Dungiven Rd. ☎ 43698.
1230-1430 Mon-Fri & 1730-2200 Mon-Sat. Steak, salmon.

The Galley
12a Shipquay St. ☎ 370260.
0900-1730 Mon-Sat. Baked potatoes, roasts, lasagne. £.

Glendermott House Bar
Glendermott Rd. 1200-1500
Mon-Sat. Home-made soups and pies.

Glue Pot
34 Shipquay St. ☎ 267463.
1130-1500 Mon-Sat. Soup, sandwiches, toasties, sweets.

Grand Central
27 Strand Rd. ☎ 267826.
1200-2300 Mon-Sat,
1230-1430 Sun. Soup, hamburgers, salad, pies.

Gweedore Bar
59 Waterloo St. ☎ 263513.
1200-1500 Mon-Sat. A la carte, high tea. Live traditional music.

Hennessey's
64 Strand Rd. ☎ 371833.
1200-1500 Mon-Sat. Grills, set lunch.

T & E Howie
23 The Diamond. ☎ 262168.
0900-1730 Mon-Sat, until 1900 Fri. Baked potatoes, quiche, salads.

Co. LONDONDERRY — Londonderry

India House
51 Carlisle Rd. ☎ 260532.
1800-2330 Mon-Thur,
until 2400 Fri & Sat, 2230
Sun. Indian.

Inn at the Cross
171 Glenshane Rd. ☎ 301480.
1730-2115 Mon-Sun. 1230-1430 Sun. Pub grub. A la carte. E£.

Iona House
17 Spencer Rd. ☎ 43529.
1230-1430 Mon-Sat. Pub grub.

Kam House
14 William St. ☎ 372166.
1200-0200 Mon-Sat, 1630-0030 Sun. Chinese, European.

Kentucky Fried Chicken
2 Strand Rd. ☎ 372016.
1100-2400 Mon-Wed, until 0200 Thur, 0230 Fri & Sat, 1600-2300 Sun. Chicken, burgers, coleslaw.

Leprechaun
23 Strand Rd. ☎ 363606.
0930-1730 Mon-Sat. Set lunch. Scones, hamburgers, salads.

Linenhall Bar
Market St. ☎ 371665.
1230-1500 & 1800-2100 Mon-Sat. Pub grub.

Lisnagelvin Leisure Centre
☎ 47695. Open Mon-Sun.
Snacks. Café in leisure centre.

McCourt's Bar
91 Ardmore Rd. ☎ 49492.
1900-2300 Fri-Sat. Pub grub.

Magnet Bar
161 Culmore Rd. ☎ 354497.
1200-1430 & 1700-2200 Mon-Sat. Pub grub.

Malibu
6 Bishop St. ☎ 371784.
0930-1730 Mon-Sat, until 2030 Fri. Set lunch, Ulster fry.

Mandarin Palace
134 Strand Rd. ☎ 264613.
1630-0100 Mon-Thur, until 0200 Fri & Sat, 0030 Sun. Chinese & European.

Mario's
Foyle St. ☎ 262626. 1700-2400 Mon-Thur, 1100-2400 Fri-Sun. Grills, burgers, fish.

Marlene's
33 Shipquay St. ☎ 370145.
1100-1800 & 2030-0300 Mon-Wed, until 0400 Thur, 0430 Fri & Sat, 2030-0230 Sun. Grills, salads.

Martha's Vineyard
Brunswick Superbowl.
☎ 371999. 1200-1430 & 1800-2230 Mon-Sun. Chicken, fish.

★ **METRO**
3 Bank Place. ☎ 267401.
1200-1430 Mon-Sun. Soup, beef stew.

Londonderry — Co. LONDONDERRY

Morton & Simpson
Lisnagelvin Shopping Centre.
☎ 45446. 0930-1700 Mon, Tues & Sat, until 2100 Wed-Fri. Lunch, salads, sandwiches, sweets.

New Monico ♀
4 Customs House St.
☎ 263121. 1200-1445 Mon-Sat. Stew, soup.

New Tower Coffee Shop
Austin's department store, The Diamond. ☎ 261817. 0900-1700 Mon-Sat, until 2030 Fri. Soup, Irish stew, daily specials, salads, pastries. Panoramic view.

Oak Grove Bar ♀
86 Bishop St. ☎ 260856. 1230-1430 Mon-Sat. Pub grub.

Oval Bar ♀
94 Duke St. ☎ 244364. 1130-2300 Mon-Fri. Pub grub.

Paolo's Pizzeria ♀
5 Rockmills, Strand Rd.
☎ 268484. 1200-1500 & 1700-0100 Mon-Thur & Sun, until 0200 Fri-Sat. Pizza, pasta, steaks. £.

Peadar O'Donnell ♀
63 Waterloo St. ☎ 372318. 1230-1430 Mon-Sat. Pub grub. Live traditional music.

Peking Pagoda ♀
33 Foyle St. ☎ 267271. 1200-2400 Mon-Sat, 1700-2400 Sun. Chinese & European. E£.

Piemonte Pizzeria
Clarendon St. ☎ 266828. 1130-0100 Mon-Sun. Pizzas.

Pilot's Row Leisure Centre
Rossville St. ☎ 269418. 1200-1430 & 1900-2200 Mon-Sat. Coffee, hamburgers.

Pizza Hut ♀
Quayside Centre, Strand Rd.
☎ 269696. 1200-2400 Mon-Sat. 1200-2300 Sun. Pizzas, pastas.

Pizza Prima
22 Shipquay St. ☎ 264627. 1200-1400 & 1700-2330 Mon-Sun. Pizza, pasta, kebabs. £.

Rafters ♀ ☺
Northland Rd. ☎ 266080. 1130-2300 Mon-Sat, 1230-1430 & 1900-2200 Sun. Lasagne, quiche, daily special.

Reggies Seafood Restaurant ♀
165 Strand Rd. ☎ 262050. 1000-2200 Mon-Sat. Fillets of John Dory panfried served with a warm lemon butter vinaigrette.

Co. LONDONDERRY

Londonderry

Rosie's Kitchen
8 Sackville St. ☎ 370066.
0900-0200 Tues, Thur & Sat,
until 1600 Wed, 1700-0200
Sun. Steaks, roasts.

The Sandwich Company
61 Strand Rd. ☎ 266771.
0800-1700 Mon-Fri,
1000-1700 Sat. Sandwiches,
rolls. Live music Sat.

The Sandwich Company
The Diamond. ☎ 372500.
0830-1630 Mon-Sat.
Sandwiches, sausage rolls,
scones.

★ **SCHOONERS** ♀
59 Victoria Rd. ☎ 311500.
1200-2200 Mon-Sat & 1700-
2100 Sun. Chillied vegetable
taco, marinated seafood on a
fish paella, trio of oriental
chicken. A la carte, carvery.
E£.

Shantallow House ♀
64 Racecourse Rd. ☎ 353344.
1200-1430 Mon-Sat,
1230-1430 & 1900-2200
Sun. Salads, sandwiches.

Spencers ♀
42 Spencer Rd. ☎ 42900.
1730-2200 Mon-Sun. Grills, à
la carte.

The Storyteller ♀
45a Carlisle Rd. ☎ 263512.
1200-1430 Mon-Fri, 1730-
2200 Tues-Sun. Steaks,
vegetarian. A la carte. E££.

Superbites
44a Waterloo St. 1100-0230
Mon-Sat, 1800-0030 Sun.
Chicken, fish, burgers.

Terminus Rest
Foyle St. ☎ 268042.
0800-1700 Mon-Sat, 1130-
1600 Sun in winter, until
1800 in summer. Fish & chips.

Thran Maggie's ♀
Craft Village, Shipquay St.
☎ 264267. 1130-2200 Mon-
Sat, 1230-1430 & 1900-2200
Sun. Steaks, roasts,
à la carte. E£.

Three Mile House ♀
21 Drumahoe Rd. ☎ 311638.
1200-1430 & 1800-2130
Mon-Sat, 1230-1430 & 1900-
2200 Sun. Barbecued
ribs, peppered steak. ££.

Townsman ♀
33 Shipquay St. ☎ 260820.
1130-1700 Mon-Sat. Soup,
sandwiches, hamburgers,
salads.

Tracy's Bar ♀
1 William St. ☎ 269700.
1200-1500 Mon-Sat, 1230-
1430 Sun. Home-made soups,
pies, fresh vegetables.

Venue ♀
Northland Rd. ☎ 266080.
1230-1430 & 1700-2200
Mon-Sat, 1230-1430 &
1900-2130 Sun. Steak,
chicken, grills, fish. E£.

Londonderry-Magherafelt — **Co. LONDONDERRY**

Villa's Inn
77 Victoria Rd. ☎ 311589.
1200-2300 Mon-Sat.
Grills, steaks. £.

★ **WATERFOOT HOTEL**
Caw Roundabout,
14 Clooney Rd. ☎ 45500.
1230-2230 Mon-Sat, 1215-1415 & 1700-2115 Sun. Hot & cold buffet. E££.

Waterloo Bar & Nite Club
3 Strand Rd. ☎ 266067.
1200-1500 Mon-Sat.
A la carte.

Wheeler's
Springtown Shopping Centre,
Northland Rd. 0930-1730
Mon-Sat, until 2100 Wed-Fri.
Snacks.

Wheeler's
30 Shipquay St. ☎ 363337.
1100-0200 Mon-Wed, until
0230 Thur, 0300 Fri & Sat,
1645-2400 Sun. Fish,
sausages, sandwiches.

White Horse Inn
68 Clooney Rd, Campsie.
☎ 860606. Gee Gees 0700-2215 Mon-Sat & 2115 Sun.
Last orders 2215, Sun 2100.
Carvery. Salmon, steaks. A la carte. E££.

Woodburn
Blackburn Crescent, Waterside.
☎ 41438. 0930-1745 Mon-Sat,
until 1945 Fri. Self-service
snacks. Set lunch. Grills.
A la carte evening only.

MAGHERA
(STD 01648)

Classic Coffee Shop
6 Hall St. ☎ 45004. Home-baked bread, pies, pastries.
Café in home bakery.

Crawford's Coffee Lounge
Main St. ☎ 43877.
0900-1730 Mon-Sat.
Sandwiches, pies, pastries.

Hideout
Main St. ☎ 42315.
1130-1700 Mon-Sat. Pub grub.

Maggie's Bar
94 Upper Main St. ☎ 43682.
1200-1700 Mon-Sat.
Pub grub, grills.

Rab's Bistro
6 Coleraine Rd. ☎ 44180.
0900-1800 Mon-Sat, 1130-1830 Sun. Chicken, quiche,
rolls, cakes.

MAGHERAFELT
(STD 01648)

The Bay Leaf
Meadowlane Shopping Centre.
☎ 34299. 0900-1730
Mon-Wed & Sat, 0900-2000
Thur & Fri. Soup, rolls,
sandwiches.

Co. LONDONDERRY — Magherafelt

BT's Hot Food
Market Square. ☎ 31422.
1200-2400 Mon-Sat, 1700-2400 Sun. Ulster fry, southern fried chicken, fish.

★ CLOISTERS ♀
23 Church St. ☎ 32257.
1230-1500 & 1700-2200 Wed-Sat. 1700-2200 Tues. 1230-1430 & 1700-2130 Sun. Smoked eel, fillet of beef with oysters, lamb.

Coachman ♀
58 Rainey St. ☎ 33527.
1200-1400 Mon-Sat.
Pub grub.

Coffee Pot
7 Meeting St. ☎ 31293.
0900-1730 Mon-Sat. Homemade soup, cakes, rolls. Set lunch, roasts, chicken.

Coffee Time
9 Broad St. ☎ 33347.
0900-1730 Mon-Sat.
Afternoon tea, set lunch.

The Depot ♀
2 Union Rd. ☎ 31244. 1200-1430 Mon-Sat. Club sandwiches, casseroles.

★ DITTY'S BAKERY ☺
33 Rainey St. ☎ 33944.
0830-1730 Mon-Sat. Home baking, sandwiches.

★ FIOLTA'S BISTRO ♀ ☺
4 Union Arcade. ☎ 33522.
1030-2130 Mon-Sat, 1200-1430 & 1700-2100 Sun. Garlic mushrooms, lasagne, steak Bushmills. ££.

Greenvale Leisure Centre
Greenvale. ☎ 33410.
0930-2145 Mon-Fri, 1100-1730 Sat, 1400-1800 Sun. Rolls, pizzas, salads, hamburgers, pastries.

Imperial Palace ♀
15 Queen St. ☎ 31709.
1200-1400 & 1700-2400 Mon-Thur, until 2430 Fri & Sat, 1700-2400 Sun. Chinese & European. £.

Karaoke ♀
7 Market St. ☎ 34136.
1230-1430 Mon-Wed & Fri.
Set lunch.

Korner Kafe
51 Rainey St. 1100-2330 Mon-Sat. Ulster fry, burgers, chicken.

McErlains
26 Church St. ☎ 32465.
0800-1730 Mon-Sat.
Sandwiches, home baking.

★ MARY'S BAR & LOUNGE ♀ ☺
10 Market St. ☎ 31997.
1200-1430 Mon-Sat. Pub grub.

Magherafelt-Portstewart — **Co. LONDONDERRY**

Nito's ♀
28 Queen St. ☎ 33859.
1200-1430 Mon-Sat. Pub grub.

Snack Box
76 Rainet St. ☎ 33710.
1200-2300 Mon-Sun. Burgers, fish, lunchtime special.

Taste Buds
18 Rainey St. ☎ 32484.
0900-1730 Mon-Sat. Soup, sandwiches, set lunches.

Town & Country Inn ♀
28 Union Rd. ☎ 32473.
1200-1500 Mon-Sat.
Chicken, curries.

MAGILLIGAN

Angler's Rest ♀
Seacoast Rd.
☎ (015047) 50265.
1200-2200 Mon-Sat, 1230-1500 & 1900-2200 Sun. Pub grub.

Ballymaclary House ♀
573 Seacoast Rd.
☎ (015047) 50283.
1030-2130 Mon-Sat. Home-made pie of the day (savoury). Lobster, sole, steak specialities. High tea. A la carte. E£££. 18th-century country house.

Mallard Bar ♀
401 Seacoast Rd.
☎ (015047) 50288.
1200-1430 & 1800-2100 Mon-Sat. Pub grub. A la carte. E£.

Point Bar ♀
107 Point Rd.
☎ (015047) 50440.
1230-1430 & 1700-2130 Mon-Sat. Pub grub.

MONEYMORE
(STD 016487)

Bier Keller ♀
18 Stonard St. ☎ 48282.
1230-1430 & 1700-2100 Mon-Sat. Pub grub.

Drapers Arms ♀
2 High St. ☎ 48647.
1130-2230 Mon-Sat. Pub grub.

Springhill House
☎ 748210. 1400-1900 Mon-Sun July-Aug, closed Tues. Reduced hours rest of year. Coffee shop in National Trust house.

PORTSTEWART
(STD 01265)

Anchor Bar ♀
87 The Promenade. ☎ 832003.
1230-2130 Mon-Sat. Pub grub.

Co. LONDONDERRY — Portstewart

Cassonis ♆
Church St. ☎ 834777/832150.
1700-2300 Mon-Sun. Italian.
Steaks, chicken, £.

The Chocolate Strawberry
68 The Promenade.
☎ 833377. 1000-2300 March-
October. Soups, stews,
toasties.

Cookery Nook
18 The Promenade. ☎ 834103.
0900-1730 Oct-June,
until 2230 summer. Set lunch.
Soup, Irish stew, apple pie.

Edgewater Hotel ♆
88 Strand Rd. ☎ 833314.
Last orders 2130, Sun 2000.
A la carte. E££.

Galvey Lodge ♆
158 Station Rd. ☎ 832218.
1130-1430 Mon-Sun, 1700-
2330 Mon-Thur, 0100 Fri &
Sat, 2200 Sun. Lunch, grills.
A la carte.

Good Food & Company ☉
44 The Promenade. ☎ 836386.
0900-2200 Mon-Sat July &
Aug, 0900-1730 rest of year.
Closed Sun. Home baking.

Heathron Diner
29 The Promenade.
☎ 834569. 0900-2300
Mon-Sat, 1200-2300 Sun in
summer, reduced hours rest
of year. Steaks, salads.

Lis-na-rhin
6 Victoria Terrace. ☎ 833522.
Last orders 1800. Wild
salmon, turbot, brill.
Booking essential. £.

Montagu Arms ♆
68 The Promenade.
☎ 834146. 1200-2300
Mon-Sun. Grills. ££.

★ **MORELLI'S/NINO'S**

57 The Promenade. ☎ 832150.
1000-2300 Mon-Sun summer
& Easter, 1000-1800 winter.
Baked potatoes, pasta, pizza,
ice cream.

Mulroy
8 Atlantic Circle. ☎ 832293.
Set meals. A la carte.
Booking essential.

Nelly's ♆
170 Coleraine Rd. ☎ 834238.
1200-1400, 1700-2030 &
2130-2400. Mon-Sat. Pub
grub. Evening à la carte, oak-
smoked salmon, entrecôte
frenzo, gateau. E££.

Peppercorn
67b The Promenade.
☎ 834691. 1700-2400 Mon-
Thur & Sun, until 0200 Fri &
Sat. Indian & European. E£.

Portmore Bay ♆
3 Kinora Terrace. ☎ 832688.
Last orders 2030. A la carte.
E£.

Portstewart-Swatragh **Co. LONDONDERRY**

Prom Fast Food
The Promenade. ☎ 832586.
1200-1400 & 1700-0200
Mon-Sun. Pizza, vegetarian burgers, fish.

Shenanigans ♀
78 The Promenade.
☎ 836000.
1230-1430 Mon-Sun,
1730-2100 Mon-Sat, 1900-2100 Sun. Chargrilled steaks, lasagne, curry, tagliatelli.

Sundae Garden
53 The Promenade. ☎ 832150.
0930-2230 Mon-Sun
Easter-Sept, 0930-1800
Mon-Sat, until 2030 Sun winter. Ice cream, coffee, cakes, fish & chips.

Windsor Hotel ♀
8 The Promenade. ☎ 832523.
Last orders 2000. Set meals.
Local salmon. £.

York Bar ♀
2 Station Rd. ☎ 833594.
1230-1430 & 1730-2030
Mon-Sat, 1230-1415 Sun.
Seafood, steaks, chicken, pasta.

SWATRAGH
(STD 01648)

Rafters Bar ♀
2 Kilrea Rd. ☎ 401206.
1130-2300 Mon-Sat,
1230-1430 & 1900-2200 Sun.
Pies, curries, hamburgers.

McGIRR'S of GORTNAGARN

LOUNGE BAR & RESTAURANT

* Daily lunches * evening meals

Private functions * weddings * exhibitions

Meals available from 12 noon till 10 pm

Entertainment • Dancing

☎ *Omagh 242462/245841*

COACH INN

OMAGH

☎ **243330**

Special Lunches Daily
12 noon to 3 pm
(Chef's special daily)
Full à la carte menu
3 pm to 10 pm
**Special table d'hote
dinner menu..........for two
SUNDAY LUNCH
12 noon to 2 pm
A la carte ... 7 pm to 10 pm**
*Please note: Meals served
to 10 pm*
Sunday lunch - booking advisable

* Large selection of wines available *

SCALLON'S

**Wine Bar
& Restaurant**

BALLYMAGORRY,
STRABANE, Co TYRONE.

OPEN DAILY

12 noon - 2.30 pm
5.30 pm - 10 pm

Lunchtime specials
Extensive wine bar and
à la carte menu each
evening.

*FUNCTION ROOM AVAILABLE
FOR THAT SPECIAL OCCASION*

☎ **(01504) 382905**

Escape to...

OTTER LODGE

RESTAURANT AND WINE BAR

26 Dungannon Road, Cookstown • Telephone: (016487) 65427

Situated on an idyllic River Bank setting, we serve
good food at unbeatable value, seven days a week
Private Functions, Weddings and Family Events a Speciality

COUNTY TYRONE

AUGHER

Queen Anya Steak House
42 Main St. ☎ (016625) 48615.
0900-1930 Mon-Sat. Steaks,
set lunch.

★ **ROSAMUND'S COFFEE SHOP**

Station House. ☎ (016625)
48601. 0900-1700 Mon-Sat.
Set lunch. Wheaten bread,
bacon baps, Clogher Valley
cheese. Selection of Irish
crafts in restored former
railway station.

AUGHNACLOY

Lynn's
158 Moore St.
☎ (016625) 57546.
1700-2400 Mon-Sat, 1700-
2330 Sun. Chinese &
European.

Peking Garden ♀
69 Moore St.
☎ (016625) 57269.
1200-1400 Mon-Sat,
1700-2300 Mon-Sun, closed
Tues. Chinese & European.

Silver Star ♀
86 Moore St.
☎ (016625) 57420. 1230-1430
& 1700-2200 Mon-Sat, 1900-
2200 Sun. Pub grub.

BALLYGAWLEY
(STD 016625)

Kelly's Inn ♀
Garvaghey House,
232 Omagh Rd. ☎ 568218.
1130-2200 Mon-Sat,
1230-1430 & 1900-2200
Sun. Pub grub. A la carte ££.

Martray House Interiors
19 Martray Rd. ☎ 568517.
1000-1730 Mon-Sat. Scones,
pies, cakes, home baking.
Speciality teas. Tea shop in
store.

★ **SUITOR GALLERY**

17 Grange Rd. ☎ 68653.
1000-1730 Mon-Sat & bank
hols. Soup, scones, tray bakes.

BENBURB
(STD 01861)

Benburb Valley Heritage Centre
Cornmill Tea Room,
89 Milltown Rd. ☎ 549752.
1000-1700 Tues-Sun Easter-
Sept & 1000-1700 Mon-Fri
Oct-Easter. Teashop in heritage
centre.

Co. TYRONE — Beragh-Castlederg

BERAGH
(STD 016627)

Corner House ♀
29 Main St. ☎ 58155.
1130-2130 Mon-Sat. Pub grub.

CALEDON
(STD 01861)

Arctic Star ♀
1 Castle Park. ☎ 568688.
1230-1430 Mon-Fri.
Hamburgers, pub grub.

Caledon Arms ♀
44 Main St. ☎ 568161.
1730-2300 Mon-Sun. Set lunch, grills. A la carte. E£.

Deer Park Lounge & Bar ♀
18 Main St. ☎ 568255.
1130-2300 Mon-Sat. Steaks, salads, chicken.

CASTLECAULFIELD

Parkanaur House
57 Parkanaur Rd.
☎ (01868) 761272. Booking essential.

Quinn's Corner
Edencrannon. ☎ (01868) 767529. 1230-2200 Mon-Sat, 1230-1430 & 1900-2200 Sun. Burgers, salads, pies.

CASTLEDERG
(STD 016626)

Allstar Café
13 Ferguson Crescent.
☎ 70488. 1600-2400 Mon-Thur, until 0200 Fri & Sat. Grills.

Castle Inn ♀
48 Main St. ☎ 71501.
1200-2100 Mon-Sat. Bar snacks.

Crescent Inn ♀
1 Ferguson Crescent.
☎ 71161. 1230-1430 & 1900-2200 Mon-Sun. Pub grub.
Live music.

Derg Arms ♀
43 Main St. ☎ 71644.
1200-1430 & 1900-0030 Mon-Sat. Lunch, afternoon tea. A la carte. E£.

Derg Valley ♀
34 William St. ☎ 70860.
1030-2300 Mon-Sat. Set lunch. A la carte. E£.

Forge Inn ♀
13 Ferguson Crescent.
☎ 70488. 1100-2300 Mon-Sat, 1100-2200 Sun. Last orders 2100. Set lunch, à la carte.

Market Bar ♀
59 Main St. ☎ 71247.
1230-1430 Mon-Sun pub grub. 1900-2200 Fri-Sun steaks, fish, salads E£.

Punter's Inn ♆
38 Main St. ☎ 71339.
1200-2400 Mon-Sat. Pub grub.

Vienna Coffee Shop
75 Main St. ☎ 71379.
1000-1730 Mon-Sat, closed Wed. Soup, stew, salads, breads, cakes.

Village Inn ♆
☎ 71490. 1700-2300 Mon-Sat. Pub grub.

CLOGHER
(STD 016625)

The Coffee Shop
31 Main St. ☎ 48605.
0900-1700 Mon-Sat. Soup, quiche, sandwiches.

Kelly's Café
5 Main St. ☎ 48183.
1130-2300 Mon-Sat, 1500-2330 Sun. Pies, grills, chicken.

McSorley's Tavern ♆
39 Main St. ☎ 48673.
1130-2300 Mon-Sat, 1230-1430 & 1900-2200 Sun. Soup, toasties, pies.

Rathmore Bar ♆
127 Main St. ☎ 48240.
1130-2300 Mon-Sat, 1230-1430 & 1900-2200 Sun. Lunch, toasties.

Trident Inn ♆
97 Main St. ☎ 48924.
1130-2100 Mon-Sat. Pub grub. A la carte from 1900. £.

COAGH
(STD 016487)

Water's Edge Boat Inn ♆
201 Battery Rd. ☎ 36367.
1800-2300 Fri-Sun. Pub grub.

Hanover House ♆
24 Hanover Square.
☎ 37530. 1200-2200 Tues-Sat, 1200-1500 & 1700-2100 Sun. Set lunch, high tea. Duckling in orange sauce. A la carte £.

COALISLAND
(STD 01868)

Golden Grill
Main St. ☎ 740533.
1030-2300 Mon-Sat, 1030-1330 Wed. Soup, chicken, fish, chips.

Gervin Bar
Barrack Square. ☎ 747536.
1200-1500 Mon-Sat, 1800-2200 Thur-Sat, 1800-2100 Sun. Grills, burgers, salad.

Landi's Café
The Square, 3 Dungannon Rd.
☎ 740211. 1030-0030 Mon-Sat, closed Thur. Grills, sandwiches, sweets.

Co. TYRONE — Coalisland-Cookstown

Pyramid Centre
11 Mountjoy Rd. ☎ 748881.
1230-1430 & 1730-2200
Mon-Sat, 1900-2200 Sun.
Steak, fish, chicken.

The Venue
26b The Square. ☎ 740633.
1230-1500 Mon-Sat, 1700-2000 Thur-Sat & 1900-2000 Sun. Set lunch. A la carte.

COOKSTOWN
(STD 016487)

Al Capone's
58 James St. ☎ 64356.
1100-2400 Mon-Thur, until 0300 Fri & Sat, 1600-0230 Sun. Baked potatoes, burgers.

Braeside Bar
221 Orritor Rd. ☎ 62664.
1400-2300 Mon-Thur,
1130-2300 Fri-Sat. Pub grub.

Brewery Grill Bar
58 William St. ☎ 65934.
1100-2400 Mon-Sat,
1600-2400 Sun.
Soup, burgers, stew.

The Café
4 Burn Rd. ☎ 64456.
1100-1800 Mon-Sat. Snacks.

Cartwheel
25 James St. ☎ 63672.
1230-1430 Mon-Sat, 1900-2200 Fri & Sat. Pies, burgers.

Chequers
12 Oldtown St. ☎ 65122.
1200-1500 & 1700-2200
Mon-Sat. Chicken kiev, set lunch. A la carte. £££.

Clubland & Black Horse
21 Molesworth St. ☎ 64946.
1230-1430 Mon-Sat. Carvery.

Coffee Room
40 William St. ☎ 63438.
0900-1730 Mon-Sat. Set lunch. Sandwiches, salads. Self service.

Conway Inn
86 Chapel St. ☎ 65028.
1230-1430 Mon-Sat. Pub grub.

Cookstown Leisure Centre
Fountain Rd. ☎ 63853.
1000-2200 Mon-Fri,
1100-1800 Sat. Pizzas, hamburgers, scones.

★ COURTYARD

56 William St. ☎ 65070.
0900-1800 Mon-Sat,
0900-1500 Wed. Set lunch, savoury pies, home-made sweets.

Dempsey's Food Depot
Central Arcade, James St.
☎ 63035. 0900-1730 Mon, until 2130 Tues-Thur, 2230 Fri & Sat. 1500-2200 Sun. Pizzas, grills, salads. £££.

Cookstown   Co. TYRONE

Dragon Palace ♀
44 Loy St. ☎ 63311.
1200-1400 & 1700-2400
Mon-Thur, until 0100 Fri,
1600-0100 Sat, 1600-0030
Sun. Cantonese & European. E£.

Dunleath Bar ♀
58 Church St. ☎ 62644.
1130-2300 Mon-Sat,
1230-1430 & 1900-2200
Sun. Pub grub.

Farmhouse Restaurant
95 Cookstown Rd. ☎ 47125.
0900-1900 Mon-Wed, until
2300 Thur-Sat. Grills, snacks.

Gables ♀
40 Cookstown Rd. ☎ 61580.
1230-1430 Mon-Sat, 1900-
2130 Sun. Set lunches.
A la carte ££.

Gaslight ♀
40 Loy St. ☎ 65640.
1130-2300 Mon-Sat,
1230-1430 & 1900-2200
Sun. Pub grub.

Glenavon House Hotel ♀
52 Drum Rd. ☎ 64949. Last
orders 2130, Sun 2100. A la
carte. Hot & cold carvery. E£.

★ **GREENVALE HOTEL** ♀ ☉
57 Drum Rd. ☎ 62243. Last
orders 2130. Set lunch.
A la carte. E££.

Halfway House ♀
81 Pomeroy Rd. ☎ 66372.
1600-2300 Mon-Thur. 1230-
1430 & 1900-2200 Sun.
Pub grub. A la carte. £.

Joe Mac's
32 Molesworth St. ☎ 63371.
1130-2330 Mon, Tues & Thur,
until 0100 Fri, 0230 Sat,
1700-2330 Sun. Grills, pizzas,
Ulster fry.

McGlaughlin's
10 James St. ☎ 63493.
0900-1730 Mon-Sat, closed
Wed. Set lunch, salads.

Mill Wheel Bar ♀
60 Dunamore Rd. ☎ 51280.
1200-1700 Mon-Sat. 1230-
1400 Sun. Set meals, grills.

Mistletoe
13 Old Town St. ☎ 63476.
0900-1730 Mon-Sat, until
1430 Wed. Café behind
confectionery shop. Set lunch.

Otter Lodge ♀
26 Dungannon Rd.
☎ 65427. 1200-1400 & 1730-
2200 Mon-Sat. 1200-1400 &
1700-2130 Sun. Carvery, à la
carte. E££.

Penny Farthing
54 William St. ☎ 64922.
1030-1630 Mon-Sun, closed
Wed. Pastries, scones.

Co. TYRONE — Cookstown-Dungannon

Prairie ♀
9 Corvanaghan Rd.
☎ 51226. 1800-2200 Fri-Mon, 1900-2200 & 1230-1430 Sun. Grills, salads. A la carte. E£.

Railway Bar ♀
63 Union St. ☎ 63278.
1130-2300 Mon-Sat, 1900-2200 Sun. Hamburgers, pies.

Rossiter's
19 William St. ☎ 63388.
0900-1700 Mon-Sat.
Pizzas, lasagne.

Royal Hotel ♀
64 Coagh St. ☎ 62224. Last orders 2145. Steaks, chicken. A la carte. ££.

Sinley ♀
92 Church St. ☎ 64572.
1700-2400 Mon-Thur, 1700-0030 Fri-Sun. Chinese, European. £.

Sperrin Room (Menary's)
39 William St. ☎ 63364.
0900-1730 Mon-Sun.
Chicken pie, lasagne.

Taj-Mahal
8 Orritor St. ☎ 65922. 1700-2400 Tues-Sun. Closed Mon. Indian & European. ££.

Thatch Lounge ♀
19 Molesworth St. ☎ 63787.
1200-1400 & 1900-2100
Mon-Sat. Pub grub.

White Pheasant
3a Burn Rd. ☎ 64249.
0900-1700 Mon-Thur & Sat, until 1830 Fri.
Grills, snacks, chips.

DROMORE

Salt & Pepper
30 Main St.
1200-2400 Mon-Thur,
1130-0130 Fri & Sat,
1730-0130 Sun.
Chicken & chips, curry.

DRUMQUIN
(STD 01662)

Eddie O'Kane's ♀
22 Main St. ☎ 831233.
2000-0010 Thur-Sun.
Pub grub.

Post Inn ♀
2 Main St. ☎ 831329.
1900-2100 Thur-Sat.
Pub grub.

DUNGANNON
(STD 01868)

The Carleton
3 Thomas St. ☎ 753577. 0930-1730 Mon-Sat. Quiche, stew, soup. Coffee shop in home bakery.

Dungannon — **Co. TYRONE**

The Square ♀
35 Market Square. ☎ 753315.
1200-1500 Mon-Sat. Pub grub.

American Pie Pizza Company
Thomas St. ☎ 723999.
0800-2400 Mon-Sat & 1700-2400 Sun. Steak, pizzas, pies, scones.

Cohannon Inn Autolodge ♀
212 Ballynakelly Rd, Tamnamore. ☎ 724488.
Last orders 2130. A la carte. E£.

Country Kitchen ♦
88 Granville Rd. ☎ 724254.
0900-1700 Mon-Fri.
Home baking.

Dee's
5 Thomas St. ☎ 752202.
0900-1730 Mon-Sat.
Sandwiches, salads, scones.

Dunowen Inn ♀ ☺
Market Square. ☎ 723144.
1200-1500 & 1800-2200 Mon-Sat. Set lunch, pub grub. A la carte. E££.

Edwin's Place ♀ ☺
20 Coash Rd. ☎ 740430.
1230-1430 Wed-Fri, 1800-2130 Fri-Sun. Smoked salmon, steak, baked potatoes.

Fort ♀
33 Scotch St. ☎ 722620.
1200-1430 Mon-Sat.
Pub grub.

Gables ♀
40 Cookstown Rd. ☎ 761580.
1230-1430 & 1900-2130 Sun.
A la carte. E£.

★ **GRANGE LODGE** ♦

7 Grange Rd. ☎ 784212.
Fri & Sat evenings, booking essential. Home cooking in country house. E£££.

Hedley's Coffee House ☺
The Arcade, Scotch St.
☎ 724605. 0900-1700 Mon-Sat. Home-baked pies, cakes, vegetarian meals.

★ **INN ON THE PARK HOTEL** ♀ ☺

Moy Rd. ☎ 725151. Last orders 2130, Fri & Sat 2200. Steak, lobster bisque, rainbow trout, lemon pancakes. ££.

Killymaddy Tourist Centre ♦
Ballygawley Rd. ☎ 767323.
0830-2100 Mon-Sun in summer, 0900-1800 Mon-Thur, until 2000 Fri-Sun in winter. Grills, snacks. Sat evening, dinner only.

Landis Café
7 Irish St. ☎ 740211. 0930-1900 mon-Sat & until 1400 Wed. Fish & chips, grills, sandwiches.

Lough Neagh Lodge ♀
Maghery. ☎ (01762) 851901.
1200-2100 Mon-Sat.
A la carte. ££.

Co. TYRONE — *Dungannon*

Lorna's Grill
64 Church St. ☎ 753222.
0915-1800 Mon-Sat.
Sandwiches, quiche.

No. 15 ◔
Murray Richardson's.
15 Church St. ☎ 753048.
0830-1730 Mon-Sat. Pies,
pastries, vegetarian. Café in
bookshop.

Normandy
40 Main St. ☎ 722397.
0800-2200 Mon-Fri,
1200-1900 Sat. Fish & chips.

Northland Arms ♀
Georges St. ☎ 723693.
1200-2100 Mon-Sat. Hot &
cold carvery. Soup,
sandwiches, basket meals.

Oaks Bistro
Oaks Centre. ☎ 753022.
0900-1700 Mon-Wed. 0900-
2030 Thur-Fri & 0900-1700
Sat. Breakfast, home-made
pies, sweets. Café in shopping
centre.

Pagni's
7 Irish St. 1000-1900
Mon-Sat, until 1430 Wed.
Fish, chicken.

Por Do Sol Bistro ♀
2 Perry St. ☎ 753753.
1700-2300 Wed-Sun. ££.
Portuguese, fish.

Rainbow Chinese Restaurant
59 Scotch St. ☎ 726556.
1700-0030 Sun-Thur, until
0100 Fri & Sat. Chinese &
English. A la carte.

Rialto
21 Irish St. ☎ 727317.
0930-2030 Mon-Sat. Italian.

Tally's Bar ♀
Galbally. ☎ 758231.
1230-1430 all week. 1900-
2200 Thur-Sun. Pub grub.
A la carte. E£.

★ **TOP BAR** ♀

73 Castlecaulfield Rd.
☎ 761349. 1800-2230 Tues-
Sun, 1800-2200 Thur & Fri,
1230-1430 & 1900-2200 Sun.
Bistro, à la carte, set meals.

Tree Tops
15 Northland Place.
☎ 723508. 0900-1830 Mon-
Sat & until 2230 Fri. Lunches,
high tea. £.

Tyrone Crystal Tea Shop ◔
Killybrackey, Coalisland Rd.
☎ 725335.
0900-1700 Mon-Sat.
Snacks, lasagne, pies.

White Horse Inn ♀
70 Scotch St. ☎ 724130.
1230-1430 Mon-Sat.
Set lunch, salads, grills.

Fintona-Moy **Co. TYRONE**

FINTONA
(STD 01662)

Charlie's Grill
53 Main St. ☎ 841266.
1130-1500 Mon-Sat & 1730-2400. Grills.

Eccles Arms ♀
128 Main St. ☎ 841220.
1130-2200 Mon-Sat, 1230-1430 Sun. Hamburgers, pies, grills.

Kitty's Kitchen
☎ 841746. 0900-1800 Mon-Fri, until 1930 Sat. Home baking, lunches, lasagne.

FIVEMILETOWN
(STD 013655)

Chestnut Bar ♀
113 Main St. ☎ 21398.
1200-2300 Mon-Sat.
Pub grub.

Fourways Hotel ♀
41 Main St. ☎ 21260. Last orders 2300. Mixed grill, omelettes. E£.

Top Note ♀
100 Main St. ☎ 21830.
1700-2130 Wed-Sun. French & Italian. A la carte. ££.

Valley Hotel ♀
60 Main St. ☎ 21505.
Last orders 2200, Sun 2130. Avocado with prawns, pork fillet & apple sauce. A la carte. E££.

GORTIN
(STD 016626)

Glenelly Kitchen
Sperrin Heritage Centre.
☎ 48142. 1100-1800 Mon-Sat, 1400-1900 Sun. Snacks.

McCullagh's ♀
16 Main St. ☎ 48157.
1800-2100 Mon-Sat. Pub grub.

Picador ♀
62 Main St. ☎ 48315.
1130-2300 Mon-Sat,
1230-1430 & 1900-2200 Sun. Pub grub.

MOY
(STD 018687)

Argory Tea Rooms
The Argory. ☎ 84753.
1400-1800 Sat & Sun April, May, June & Sept. 1400-1800 Fri-Mon June. 1400-1800 Mon-Sun July & Aug. Garden tea rooms opened by arrangement (National Trust).

Ascot
Charlemont St. ☎ 84552.
0900-1730 Mon-Sat. Set lunch, hamburgers, salads.

Bridge Bar ♀
149 Portadown Rd, Charlemont. ☎ 84271.
1130-2330 Mon-Sat,
1230-1430 & 1900-2200 Sun. Sausage rolls, pies, hamburgers.

Co. TYRONE — Moy-Newtownstewart

Grand Bar ♀
24 The Square. ☎ 84840.
1130-2300 Mon-Sat,
1230-1430 & 1900-2200
Sun. Pub grub.

Old Fort Bar ♀
33 Main St, Charlemont.
☎ 84808. 1130-2300 Mon-Sat,
1230-1430 & 1900-2200 Sun.
Grills, salads, stews.

Stables ♀
The Square. ☎ 84629.
1200-1500 & 1800-2200
Mon-Sun. Set lunch. A la
carte. E£.

Traynor's Inn ♀
86 Armagh Rd. ☎ 891753.
1130-2300 Mon-Sat,
1230-1430 & 1900-2200
Sun. Pub grub.

Welcome Inn ♀
Dungannon St. ☎ 84223.
1800-2200 Mon-Sat. Pub
grub.

MOYGASHEL

Normandy
40 Main St.
☎ (01868) 722397.
0800-2200 Mon-Fri,
1200-1900 Sat. Fish & chips.

NEWTOWNSTEWART
(STD 016626)

Castle Bar ♀
1 Castle Brae. ☎ 61039.
1300-1400 Mon-Sat. Pub
grub.

Coffee Pot
24a Main St. ☎ 61565.
0900-1800 Mon-Sat.
Pies, soup, stew, scones.

County Inn ♀
43 Main St. ☎ 62105.
1230-1700 Mon-Sat. Pub
grub.

Corner Bar ♀
2 Carnkenny Rd, Ardstraw.
☎ 61257. 1800-2130 Wed-
Sun. Pub grub.

Harry Avery Lounge ♀
19 Dublin St. ☎ 61431.
1230-1430 Mon-Sun,
1900-2200 Thur-Sun. Pub
grub.

McGuigan's Bar ♀
43 Main St. ☎ 62105.
1230-1430 Mon-Sun,
1900-2100 Wed, Fri & Sat.
Set meals, grills.

Milltown Café
Newtownstewart Rd,
Milltown. ☎ 61609.
0900-2400 Mon-Sat,
1100-2400 Sun. Soup, grills,
salads.

Newtownstewart-Omagh — **Co. TYRONE**

Olde Mill ♀
7 Millbrook Rd, Milltown.
☎ 62048. 1030-2130 Mon-Sun. Steaks, chicken chasseur, vegetarian. A la carte. E££.

Wel Cum Inn ♀
36 Main St. ☎ 61276.
1130-2300 Mon-Sat,
1230-1430 & 1900-2200 Sun. Pies, pub grub.

OMAGH
(STD 01662)

Bridge Restaurant
32 Bridge St. ☎ 0830-1800 Mon-Sat, until 1400 Wed. Salads, soup, sandwiches.

Bridge Tavern ♀
Eskra. ☎ 841521.
1230-1430 Mon-Sun. Pub grub, basket meals in evening.

Caesar's ♀
26 Bridge St. ☎ 251133.
1200-1400 Mon-Sat,
1700-2400 Mon-Sun.
Pizzas, lasagne, salads.

The Cake Shop
38 Market St. ☎ 251012.
0900-1730 Mon-Sat.
Salads, pastries

Campsie Bake Shop
80 Market St. ☎ 244038.
0830-1730 Mon-Sat.
Lasagne, quiche, Ulster fry.

Carlton Coffee Lounge
31 High St. ☎ 247046.
0900-1730 Mon-Sat. Home baked scones. Lasagne, quiche, Ulster fry.

Cellar Bar ♀
Bridge St. ☎ 247577.
1130-1400 Mon-Fri.
Pub grub.

The Clock ♀
Old Market Place.
☎ 247355. 1200-1430 Mon-Sat. Pub grub. River view.

Coach Inn ♀
Dromore Tamlaght Rd.
☎ 243330. 1200-1500 Mon-Sat. Set lunch.

Dragon Castle ♀
2 High St. ☎ 245208.
1200-1400 & 1700-2400 Mon-Thur, 1600-2400 Sun. Chinese & European. £.

Eddie's Crossroads Bar ♀
Greencastle. ☎ (016626) 48266. 1230-1430 & 1800-2030 Mon-Sat. Grills, salads.

El Paso ♀
62 Market St. ☎ 243125.
1230-1430 Mon-Sat.
Pub grub.

Expressway Restaurant
1 Mountjoy Rd. ☎ 243637.
0900-2400 Mon-Thur, until 0300 Fri & Sat. Salads, scones coffee.

Co. TYRONE — Omagh

Giovanni's
9 John St. ☎ 252025. 1200-1400 Mon-Thur, 1700-2400 Sun, 1700-0300 Fri & Sat. Italian.

★ GREENMOUNT LODGE
58 Greenmount Rd, Gortaclare. ☎ 841325. 1900-2130 Fri & Sat. Dinner. Booking essential. E£.

Halfway House ♕
Tattyreagh. ☎ 243720. 1130-2300 Mon-Sat, 1900-2200 Sun.
Soup, sandwiches.

Omagh Leisure Centre ☉
Old Mountfield Rd.
☎ 246711. 1000-1430 & 1530-2100 Mon-Fri, 1000-1700 Sat & 1400-1700 Sun. Snacks.

Libbi
52 Market St. ☎ 242969. 0900-1730 Mon, Tues & Thur-Sat, until 1400 Wed. Coffee, cakes.

Old McDonald's
6 Bridge St. ☎ 247666. 0800-1900 Mon-Sat.
Breakfasts, salads, sandwiches.

McElroy's ♕
30 Castle St. ☎ 244441. 1200-1430 Mon-Fri & 1200-1800 Sat.

McGirr's of Gortnagarn ♕
Mountjoy East. ☎ 242462. 1230-1430 & 1830-2130 Mon-Sat. Grills. A la carte Fri & Sat.

★ MELLON COUNTRY INN ♕ ☉
134 Beltany Rd. ☎ 661224. 1030-2330 Mon-Sat, 1200-2030 Tues. Set lunch.
A la carte evenings. E££££.

Mill ♕
212 Gorticashel Rd.
☎ 248451. 1200-1500 Mon-Sat. Pub grub.

Mr G's
2 Old Market Place.
0930-1730 Mon-Sat, until 1400 Wed. Lunches, snacks, lasagne, quiche.

Nichol & Shiels
41a Market St. ☎ 249663. 0900-1730 Mon-Sat.
Home-made pies, tray bakes, coffee.

Nite Bite
55 Derry Rd. ☎ 252770. 1000-2400 Mon-Sat, 1700-2400 Sun. Breakfast, Irish stew, stuffed sausage and bacon.

Number Seven ♕
7 John St. ☎ 246587. 1230-1430 Mon-Sat.
Savoury lunches, sweets.

Omagh — **Co. TYRONE**

Omanni
2 Derry Rd. ☎ 247500.
1700-2400 Tues-Thur,
1600-0100 Fri & Sat, until
2330 Sun. Chinese, Asian &
European. £.

Pink Elephant
19 High St. ☎ 249805.
0900-1800 Mon-Sat,
1200-1500 Sun. Snacks,
lunches.

Pizzarama
78 Market St. ☎ 244799.
1200-1400 Mon-Sat,
1700-2400 Mon-Sun.
Pizzas, salads, garlic bread,
baked potatoes.

★ **ROYAL ARMS HOTEL**
51 High St. ☎ 243262.
Last orders 2130, Sun 2030.
A la carte. ££.

Sally O'Brien's
35 John St. ☎ 242521.
1200-1430 & 1900-2100
Thur-Sat. Grills.

Shoppers Rest
38 High St. ☎ 243545.
0730-1800 Mon-Sat.
Toasties, lunches, salads,
sandwiches.

Silverbirch Hotel
5 Gortin Rd. ☎ 242520.
Last orders 2100. £.

Sperrin Restaurant
86-88 Beltany Rd. ☎ 243775.
0900-2100 Mon-Sat, 1230-
2100 Sun. Home-made soups,
steaks, stuffed turkey.

Taste of India
8 Campsie Rd. ☎ 248342.
1630-2430 Mon-Sun.
Indian. ££.

Ulster-American Folk Park
Mellon Rd, Castletown.
☎ 243292. 1030-1830 Easter-
September & 1030-1700 Oct-
Easter. Sandwiches, scones,
grills.

Ulster History Park
Cullion, Lislap. ☎ 48188.
1030-1815 Mon-Sat & 1130-
1845 Sun April-Sept, 1030-
1645 Mon-Fri Oct-March, Sat
& Sun Oct-March. Salads &
snacks. Café in visitor centre.
B48 north of Omagh.

Village Inn
Killyclogher. ☎ 243865.
1200-1500 Mon-Sat, 1200-
1700 snacks. Pub grub.

★ **WOODLANDER**
28 Gortin Rd. ☎ 251038.
1200-1430 & 1800-2200
Mon-Sat. Sole, red snapper,
beef Robert, home-made
desserts. M£. £££. A la carte.

Co. TYRONE — Plumbridge-Strabane

PLUMBRIDGE

Pinkertons Café
25 Main St.
☎ (016626) 48327.
1100-2200 Mon-Sat,
1400-2100 Sun.
Steak, chicken, curries.

Sperrin Heritage Centre
Cranagh. ☎ (016626) 48142.
1100-1800 Mon-Fri,
1130-1800 Sat, 1400-1900
Sun. Sandwiches, scones,
pastries. 8 miles east of
Plumbridge, on B47.

POMEROY
(STD 01868)

Corner Bar ♆
81 Main St. ☎ 758709.
1130-2300 Mon-Sat,
1230-1430 & 1900-2200
Sun. Pub grub.

SION MILLS
(STD 016626)

Marshall's ♆
☎ 58638. 1200-1900 Mon-Sat.
Pub grub.

SIXMILECROSS

Tavern ♆
12 Main St. ☎ (016627)
58461. 1230-1430 Mon-Sa.
Pub grub.

Whistler's Inn ♆
26 Main St. ☎ (016627)
58349. 1100-1900 Mon-Thur,
until 2230 Fri & Sat. Set lunch.
Steak, chicken.

STEWARTSTOWN
(STD 01868)

Drumcairn Inn ♆
32 The Square. ☎ 738216.
1200-1430 Mon-Sat & 1800-
2230 Fri-Sat. Pub grub, grills.

Duffy's ♆
32 The Square. ☎ 738216.
2000-2400 Thur-Sat. Pub grub.

Hoff's ♆
The Square. ☎ 738402.
2000-2400 Thur-Sun.
A la carte E£.

Lakeview Inn ♆
15 The Square. ☎ 738106.
1130-2300 Mon-Sat.
Pies, burgers.

STRABANE
(STD 01504)

Butlers
19 Abercorn Square.
0900-1800 Mon-Thur, until
0200 Fri & Sat. Fish & chips,
pies.

Ballymagorry Arms ♆
421 Victoria Rd, Ballymagorry.
☎ 382905. 1230-1430 &
1730-2145 Mon-Sat. Pub
grub.

Strabane   **Co. TYRONE**

Blue Parrot
19 Castle St. ☎ 382687.
1200-1500 Mon-Sat.
Snacks. A la carte. Evenings as required.

Bonne Tasse
Abercorn Square. ☎ 383422.
0900-1730 Mon-Sat. Hot & cold snacks, sandwiches, drinks.

Buttery Tavern
30 Market St. ☎ 884466.
1200-1430 Mon-Sat. Set meals. Pub grub. A la carte. E£.

Coach Inn
366 Victoria Rd. ☎ 384362.
1130-2300 Mon-Sat, 1230-1430 & 1900-2200 Sun. Pub grub.

Country Kitchen
Lower Main St. ☎ 382621.
0900-1730 Mon-Sat.
Breakfast, afternoon tea, home baking.

Fir Trees Lodge Hotel
Melmount Rd. ☎ 382382.
Last orders 2130.
A la carte. E££.

Flann O'Brien
3 Derry Rd. ☎ 884427.
1230-1430 Mon-Sat.
Set lunch, grills.

Floyd's
421 Victoria Rd. ☎ 382905.
1230-1430 & 1730-2200 Mon-Sat, until 2130 Sun.
A la carte, carvery. E£.

Home Cuisine
55 Main St. ☎ 382002.
0930-1715 Mon-Sat.
Snacks, grills.

Kelly's Bar
Abercorn Square. ☎ 883551.
1130-0100 6 days. Pub grub.

Kurly Wurly's
9 Bowling Green. ☎ 383353.
1100-2300 Mon-Sat, 1200-1500 & 1700-2200 Sun. Soup, sandwiches, pies.

Mill House Inn
37 Patrick St. ☎ 382690.
1130-2300 Mon-Sat. 1230-1430 & 1900-2200 Sun.
A la carte. E££.

Piccolo
Abercorn Square. ☎ 382784.
0900-1800 Mon-Sat.
Grills, sandwiches.

Railway Bar
64 Railway Rd. ☎ 882366.
1130-2300 Mon-Sat,
1230-1430 & 1900-2200 Sun. Pub grub.

Teashop
29 Abercorn Square.
0800-1730 Mon-Sat.
Salads, lasagne, chips.

Town Hall Bar
Market Centre, Market St.
☎ 382424. 1200-1500 Mon-Sat. Fish, quiche.

Co. TYRONE — Strabane-Trillick

Welcome Inn
38 Patrick St. ☎ 382528.
1130-2300 Mon-Sat,
1230-1430 & 1900-2200 Sun.
Sandwiches, pies.

Wembley
10 Castle Place. ☎ 382307.
0900-1900 Mon-Sat.
Fish & chips.

TRILLICK
(STD 01365)

Bridge Inn
2 Kilskeery Rd. ☎ 61201.
1230-1430 & 1800-2200.
Pub grub.

McAloon's
19 Main St. ☎ 61208.
1200-1400 & 1700-2000
Mon-Sat. Pub grub.

Dunowen Inn

Function rooms available for weddings, functions, business conferences, meetings etc., anything up to 200 catered for.

Table d'hôte 12-30 pm
A la carte 6-10 pm
Bar food 12 noon-10.30 pm

We will be happy to oblige if you wish to plan your menu for that special occasion.

Private car park at rear of premises

Market Square, Dungannon
☎ *722030 or 723144*

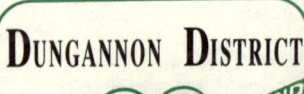

DUNGANNON DISTRICT

ULSTER'S HEARTLAND

CAMPING + CARAVANNING · FISHING ·
GOLF · PONY TREKKING · WALKING ·
CLAY PIGEON SHOOTING · CAKE
ARTISTRY · ART SCHOOL · LANGUAGE
SCHOOL · GENEALOGY · INDUSTRIAL +
CULTURAL HERITAGE · U.S. GRANTS
ANCESTRAL HOME · TYRONE CRYSTAL ·
CRAFTS

You'll Love It!

further information from
**Dungannon District Council,
Leisure Services Dept.,
Circular Road, Dungannon.**
☎ 01868 725311

Ireland
GIANT'S CAUSEWAY
Ballintoy
Ferry
Portrush
Portballintrae
Bushmills
Ballycastle
MAGILLIGAN POINT
Portstewart
Downhill
Castlerock
LOUGH FOYLE
Bellarena
Coleraine
Benvarden
Cushendun
Eglinton
Limavady
Ballymoney
Cushendall
Ballykelly
Aghadowey
LONDONDERRY
Waterfoot
Cloughmills
GLENS OF ANTRIM
Garvagh
Carnlough
Ferry from Cairnryan
Dungiven
Kilrea
Claudy
LONDONDERRY
Glenarm
Ferry from Stranraer
Ferry from Stranraer
DONEGAL
Broughshane
Ballygalley
SPERRIN MOUNTAINS
Maghera
Portglenone
Ballymena
Larne
REPUBLIC OF IRELAND
Strabane
ANTRIM
IRISH SEA
Sion Mills
ISLAND MAGEE
Draperstown
Kells
Plumbridge
Castledawson
Newtownstewart
Toomebridge
Gortin
Magherafelt
Ballyclare
Whitehead
Castlederg
Antrim
Carrickfergus
Moneymore
Templepatrick
Helen's Bay
Groomsport
Cookstown
Belfast International
Newtownabbey
Ferry from Isle of Man (summer)
Omagh
TYRONE
LOUGH NEAGH
Crawfordsburn
Bangor
Holywood
Donaghadee
Crumlin
Kesh
Sixmilecross
BELFAST
Millisle
Dromore
Belfast Harbour
L. LOUGH ERNE
Fintona
Newtownards
Belleek
Dungannon
Lisburn
Comber
Garrison
Irvinestown
Ballywalter
Ballygawley
THE BIRCHES
Greyabbey
LOUGH MELVIN
Derrygonnelly
Augher
Moy
Lurgan
Moira
Ferry from Liverpool
Monea
Ballinamallard
Clogher
Aughnacloy
Craigavon
Hillsborough
Ballyhalbert
Enniskillen
Benburb
Portadown
Dromore
Saintfield
Lisbellaw
Fivemiletown
Bellanaleck
Brookeborough
Richhill
Cloughey
Belcoo
FERMANAGH
Caledon
Gilford
Ballynahinch
Killyleagh
LOUGH MACNEAN
ARMAGH
DOWN
Ferry
Portaferry
MARBLE ARCH CAVES
Tandragee
Banbridge
Florencecourt
Strangford
Lisnaskea
Downpatrick
U. LOUGH ERNE
Markethill
LEITRIM
Keady
ARMAGH
Dundrum
Rathfriland
Ardglass
Castlewellan
Derrylin
Bessbrook
Killough
Hilltown
Newtownhamilton
Newry
Newcastle
MONAGHAN
MOURNE MOUNTAINS
Warrenpoint
Forkhill
Rostrevor
Annalong
CAVAN
LOUTH
Kilkeel
©N.I.T.B

Index to towns and villages

Aghadowey 171
Aghalee 105
Ahoghill 71
Aldergrove 71
Annalong 119
Antrim 71
Ardglass 119
Armagh 105
Augher 191
Aughnacloy 191

Ballinamallard 159
Ballintoy 73
Ballycastle 73
Ballyclare 74
Ballygalley 75
Ballygawley 191
Ballygowan 119
Ballykelly 171
Ballymena 76
Ballymoney 81
Ballynahinch 120
Ballywalter 121
Banbridge 121
Bangor 122
Belcoo 159
Belfast 33
Bellanaleck 159
Belleek 159
Belleeks 108

Benburb 191
Beragh 192
Bessbrook 108
Blackwatertown 108
Brookeborough 159
Broughshane 82
Bushmills 82

Caledon 192
Camlough 108
Carnlough 83
Carrickfergus 83
Carrowdore 127
Carryduff 128
Castlecaulfield 192
Castledawson 171
Castlederg 192
Castlereagh (see Belfast)
Castlerock 172
Castlewellan 128
Claudy 172
Clough 129
Clogher 193
Cloughmills 85
Coagh 193
Coalisland 193
Coleraine 172
Comber 129
  (for La Mon see Belfast)
Conlig 130
Cookstown 194

Index to towns and villages

Craigavon 108
Crawfordsburn 130
Crossgar 130
Crossmaglen 109
Crumlin 85
Cullybackey 86
Cultra 130
Cushendall 86
Cushendun 86

Derry (see Londonderry)
Derrygonnelly 160
Derrylin 160
Dervock 86
Doagh 87
Donaghadee 131
Downpatrick 132
Draperstown 175
Dromara 133
Dromore (Co. Down) 133
Dromore (Co. Tyrone) 196
Drumquin 196
Dunadry 87
Dundonald (see Belfast)
Dundrum 133
Dungannon 196
Dungiven 175
Dunmurry 87

Ederney 160
Eglinton 176
Enniskillen 160

Fintona 199
Fivemiletown 199
Florencecourt 164
Forkhill 110

Garrison 164
Garvagh 176
Giant's Causeway 89
Gilford 135
Glarryford 89
Glenariff 89
Glenarm 90
Glengormley 90
  (see also Newtownabbey)
Gortin 199
Greyabbey 135
Greysteel 176
Groomsport 136

Hamiltonsbawn 110
Helen's Bay 136
Hillsborough 136
Hilltown 137
Holywood 137

Irvinestown 165
Islandmagee 91

Katesbridge 139
Keady 110
Kells 91
Kesh 167

209

Index to towns and villages

Kilkeel 139
Killinchy 141
Killough 141
Killylea 111
Killyleagh 141
Kilrea 176
Kinawley 167
Kircubbin 142
Knockcloghrim 177

Larne 91
Letterbreen 167
Limavady 177
Lisbellaw 167
Lisburn 94
Lisnarick 168
Lisnaskea 168
Londonderry 178
Loughbrickland 142
Loughgall 111
Lurgan 111
  (see also Craigavon)

Maghera 185
Magherafelt 185
Magilligan 187
Mallusk 97
Markethill 113
Middletown 114
Millisle 142
Moira 142
Moneymore 187

Mountnorris 114
Moy 199
Moygashel 200

Newcastle 143
Newry 146
Newtownabbey 97
Newtownards 149
Newtownbutler 168
Newtownhamilton 114
Newtownstewart 200

Omagh 201

Plumbridge 204
Pomeroy 204
Portadown 114
Portaferry 152
Portballintrae 99
Portglenone 99
Portrush 100
Portstewart 187

Randalstown 102
Rathfriland 153
Rathlin Island 103
Richhill 117
Roslea 169
Rostrevor 154

Index to towns and villages

Saintfield 154
Scarva 155
Seaforde 155
Sion Mills 204
Sixmilecross 204
Stewartstown 204
Stoneyford 103
Strabane 204
Strangford 155
Swatragh 189

Tandragee 117
Temple 156
Templepatrick 103
Tempo 169
Toomebridge 103
Trillick 206

Waringstown 156
Warrenpoint 156
Waterfoot
 (see Glenariff)
Whiteabbey 104
Whitecross 117
Whitehead 104

Please note

This book is intended only as a convenient reference guide to eating out in Northern Ireland. Care has been taken to ensure entries are up to date. However, information has been gathered from a wide range of sources and the Northern Ireland Tourist Board does not accept responsibility for errors and omissions. In addition, changes will inevitably occur after the book goes to press, so it is advisable to make your own enquiries.